Crowd Violence in
American Modernist Fiction

Crowd Violence in American Modernist Fiction

Lynchings, Riots and the Individual Under Assault

BENJAMIN S. WEST

McFarland & Company, Inc., Publishers
Jefferson, North Carolina, and London

LIBRARY OF CONGRESS CATALOGUING-IN-PUBLICATION DATA

West, Benjamin S., 1979–
 Crowd violence in American modernist fiction : lynchings, riots and the individual under assault / Benjamin S. West.
      p.   cm.
 Includes bibliographical references and index.

ISBN 978-0-7864-7108-9
softcover : acid free paper ∞

 1. American fiction—20th century—History and criticism.
 2. Violence in literature.   3. Lynchings in literature.
 4. Group identity in literature.   I. Title.
PS374.V58W47 2013
813'.5093552—dc23   2013004399

BRITISH LIBRARY CATALOGUING DATA ARE AVAILABLE

© 2013 Benjamin S. West. All rights reserved

No part of this book may be reproduced or transmitted in any form or by any means, electronic or mechanical, including photocopying or recording, or by any information storage and retrieval system, without permission in writing from the publisher.

On the cover: *The Murder of Powell*, 1872 (Library of Congress); background texture © 2013 Shutterstock

Manufactured in the United States of America

McFarland & Company, Inc., Publishers
  Box 611, Jefferson, North Carolina 28640
    www.mcfarlandpub.com

For the crowd that has so gently fashioned my identity.

Table of Contents

Prologue: Captivity, Mob Violence and Early American Identity in Mary Rowlandson's Narrative   1

Introduction: Crowd Violence and Punishing Identities in American Modernist Fiction   23

Chapter I
Lynch Mobs and Racial Identity in Modernist Fiction   41

Chapter II
Joe Christmas, Bigger Thomas and Legalized Lynching   58

Chapter III
Female Identity, Southern Womanhood and Crowd Narration in Faulkner's Fiction   80

Chapter IV
The Crowd at War and at Home in Hemingway's and Fitzgerald's Fiction   103

Chapter V
The Great Depression and Migrating Crowds in Steinbeck's and Faulkner's Fiction   128

The Road to a Conclusion   157
Chapter Notes   175
Works Cited   179
Index   187

Prologue: Captivity, Mob Violence and Early American Identity in Mary Rowlandson's Narrative

The captivity narrative, it has been argued, is the only literary genre native to the North American continent. As the English colonies in North America began to fashion their own identity as separate from French, Spanish, and Native American groups, the captivity narrative served a specific and localized purpose that helped define the identity of the individuals residing in these early American colonies. For the Puritan colonists especially, this identity is often formed through direct contact with American Indians, and through narratives of mob violence and captivity involving American Indians. English settlers in the North American colonies began to define themselves as a separate and distinct culture, self-fashioning the identity of a new chosen people fleeing persecution and hoping to settle in a new but dangerous land. In this way, portrayals of mob violence and captivity were used to analyze matters of identity long before the Modernist era of American literature, and in fact, from the captivity narrative onward, American authors have consistently used scenes of mob violence to interrogate various aspects of the self-fashioning of American identity.

Captivity narratives produced by North American writers during the seventeenth and eighteenth centuries can be considered a unique literary genre because of their common characteristics, and this genre has proven to be significant in relation to subsequent literary portrayals of American identity formation and enforcement. Richard Slotkin famously defines captivity narratives as literary works wherein

> a single individual, usually a woman, stands passively under the strokes of evil, awaiting rescue by the grace of God. The sufferer represents the whole, chastened body of Puritan society.... In the Indian's devilish clutches, the captive

had to meet and reject the temptation of Indian marriage and/or the Indian's "cannibal" Eucharist. To partake of the Indian's love or of his equivalent of bread and wine was to debase, to un-English the very soul. The captive's ultimate redemption by the grace of Christ and the efforts of the Puritan magistrates is likened to the regeneration of the soul in conversion. The ordeal is at once threatful of pain and evil and promising of ultimate salvation. Through the captive's proxy, the promise of a similar salvation could be offered to the faithful among the reading public, while the captive's torments remained to harrow the hearts of those not yet awakened to their fallen nature [94–95].

Slotkin's influential definition displays some of the key archetypes of the captivity narrative genre, and Slotkin's main focus is clearly on the religious purposes such narratives served. Puritan culture surely valued the overt religious messages that are prevalent in most captivity narratives, but captivity narratives served other purposes that proved to be equally valuable to Puritan colonists looking to form a homogenous identity in a new and diverse land.

Certainly, English Puritans were not the only European settlers who came to the New World looking to practice their religion, yet as Gordon M. Sayre notes, "the genre's importance is unique to the English literature of America, however. It is not central to colonial New Spain, New France, or Portuguese Brazil, even though Native Americans certainly did take many colonials captive in those regions" (4). Captivity narratives were a favorite genre of English American colonists in the region that came to be known as New England because of the Puritan religious messages such narratives invoke, and this influential group established many of the cultural norms that early American literature would reinforce. Numerous captivity narratives were produced by New England authors during the first century of New World colonization, and typically these narratives were written by Puritan authors, as was the case with the most famous and original of all captivity narratives, Mary White Rowlandson's *The Sovereignty and Goodness of God, Together, With the Faithfulness of His Promises Displayed; Being a Narrative Of the Captivity and Restauration of Mrs. Mary Rowlandson*. Such narratives were wildly popular in Puritan society, making them, along with the Bible, the most common reading in Puritan households.

Like the Bible, these captivity narratives served a clear religious purpose in Puritan society, depicting the dangers of sin and evil that Puritans saw as pervading the new lands they were settling. In addition, these narratives, through the captive's faith and ultimate restoration, served as literary examples of Puritan faith at work, as individuals suffered through trials and tribulations to reach ultimate redemption, realizing during their captivity the weakness of their faith and character prior to captivity. Aside from this purely religious purpose that captivity narratives served as secondary religious texts that supplemented scripture, the American captivity narrative served three other key roles in defining early American identity for English colonists. For the English Puritans, captivity narratives, as Slotkin and many others have observed, first served a vital function in defining Puritan identity by contrasting their predominantly Christian, orderly, and businesslike culture with the American Indian culture of perceived pagan and savage disorder. Captivity narratives thus provided a key nation-building tool, contrasting the homogenous identity of the colonists with a clear racial Other. Secondly, captivity narratives served an equally vital role in the Puritan understanding of womanhood. In rather overt ways, captivity narratives defined women as physically and morally weak subjects in need of protection and even strict control, especially in dealings with any racial Other. Subversively, the captivity narrative also provided a platform for women to express their own identity within this strictly patriarchal social order. Thirdly, captivity narratives constructed and imposed a stereotypically savage American Indian identity, portraying a devilish racial Other and thereby justifying the oppression of American Indians and the ultimate removal of American Indians from their long-inhabited lands.

Interestingly, each of these purposes relies upon rhetoric of mob violence and identity formation. One of the most popular literary genres of early America—indeed, the only literary genre initially introduced on what would become United States soil—is deeply fraught with images of the struggle between individuals and collective forces, more specifically, persecuted individual Puritans and violent mobs of American Indians. This focus on mob violence and identity mirrors a focus that can be seen in the proceeding literature of American authors, especially American authors writing in the first half of the twentieth century. It is this persistent trope of American literature that is the ultimate focus of this study.

Rowlandson's narrative, commonly shortened to *The Narrative of the Captivity of Mary Rowlandson*, has proved to be a useful document for scholars seeking to understand Puritan religion, as well as Puritan social views related to gender and race. The captivity narrative's specific use of mob violence to understand such identity issues has not been discussed, however, nor has the captivity narrative's position as an early precursor to later focuses on mob violence and identity in American literature been recognized. Using Rowlandson's narrative as the most comprehensive example of the captivity narrative genre, I will outline the ways in which Rowlandson's narrative, and indeed most captivity narratives, rely on depictions of mob violence in order to formulate matters of individual identity. Many of the same tactics Rowlandson and others use in these narratives can be seen in later American literature, showing that images of mobs persecuting individuals are a common representation of the process of identity self-fashioning in United States literary culture.

My approach to Rowlandson's narrative is greatly influenced by Stephen Greenblatt's ideas regarding self-fashioning and identity formation, and Margaret H. Davis has taken a similar approach to Rowlandson, arguing that "Mary White Rowlandson's self-fashioning occurs in the manner suggested by

Greenblatt, at the point of encounter between an authority and an alien, and results in the production of an identity in which some amount of individuality is exchanged for participation in the social and religious covenant" (58). In Greenblatt's *Renaissance Self-Fashioning: From More to Shakespeare*, he defines self-fashioning as "the power to impose a shape upon oneself" (1). Greenblatt goes on to add that self-fashioning "is linked to manners or demeanor, particularly that of the elite; it may suggest hypocrisy or deception, an adherence to mere outward ceremony; it suggests representation of one's nature or intention in speech or actions" (3). When applied to Rowlandson, or other writers of early American captivity narratives, Greenblatt's notions of self-fashioning allow us to see the ways in which these authors, usually women, fashion themselves in accordance to their society's prevailing notions concerning religion, gender, and race. Yet Greenblatt explicitly references "deception," showing that self-fashioning is not necessarily synchronous with cultural conformity. Rowlandson's attempts at self-fashioning show her both conforming to and subversively undermining Puritan notions of identity, especially gender and racial identity.

For Rowlandson, as well as for other captivity narrative authors, the presence of the American Indian Other is necessary for this self-fashioning to take place. As Greenblatt argues, "Self-fashioning is achieved in relation to something perceived as alien, strange, or hostile. This threatening Other—heretic, savage, witch, adulteress, traitor, Antichrist—must be discovered or invented in order to be attacked and destroyed" (*Renaissance Self-Fashioning* 9). As Davis adds, American Indians served as this alien, strange, and threatening Other. The point of cultural contact between the Puritan and the American Indian thus becomes the place where self-fashioning occurs, "at the point of encounter between an authority and an alien" (*Renaissance Self-Fashioning* 9). This point of encounter for early American writers is portrayed through the popular captivity narrative genre.

As this study presumes, and as Greenblatt has already argued in *Renaissance Self-Fashioning*,

> self-fashioning derives its interest precisely from the fact that it functions without regard for a sharp distinction between literature and social life. It invariably crosses the boundaries between literature and social life. It invariably crosses the boundaries between the creation of literary characters, the shaping of one's own identity, the experience of being modeled by forces outside one's control, the attempt to fashion other selves [3].

Rowlandson's narrative and other similar captivity narratives create a place where several early American identities are fashioned. Hostile cultural contact between Puritans and American Indians gives Puritan writers such as Rowlandson the opportunity to self-fashion a shared religious identity that unifies the Puritan community against outside influences. In captivity narratives, this cultural contact is much more than mere contact—the captive must live amongst, and ultimately reject, the pagan culture of the American Indian, strengthening the captive's own religious values, and symbolically, Puritan culture's religious values, in the process. Since captivity narratives usually focused on female subjects, captivity narratives served as a textual space wherein Puritan women could conform to and simultaneously react against Puritan gender expectations, self-fashioning an empowered female voice that challenged Puritan concepts of gender. Finally, the captivity narrative allowed captives, as representatives of Puritan culture, to self-fashion their whiteness, both in skin color and in perceived religious purity, in opposition to the redness and/or blackness of their captives.

The most obvious identity that Rowlandson fashions in her own narrative is that of the Puritan suffering in an evil, trying world. Puritans often interpreted the world around them symbolically, and therefore, Puritans believed that battles between good and evil, God and Satan, manifested themselves throughout their daily lives. Through the events typically portrayed in captivity narratives, writers like Rowlandson could provide accounts of these dramas, and use these accounts to teach religious lessons like those mentioned by Slotkin. In addition to these religious lessons, these narratives also reinforced the normative values of the Puritan community. By representing a chosen people in a new and hostile land, captivity narratives reflected the Puritan belief that the saved must be tempted by a Satanic force, and by displaying subjects overcoming this Satanic force, Puritan religious, cultural, and even economic values were reinforced and reinvigorated within the community. Constantly fearful of dissent, Puritans used captivity narratives to ultimately unify the Puritan community against the dangerous mobs of American Indians and other non–Puritan groups that threatened the desired normativity of their community. In these ways, captivity narratives served important community-building functions, and later, nation-building functions.

From the beginning of her narrative, Rowlandson depicts these images of a godly Puritan community under attack from a devilish mob. Rowlandson's narrative is completely de-historicized, even though she begins the narrative with a specific date, writing that "on the tenth of February 1675, came the Indians with great numbers upon Lancaster" (137). Rowlandson's opening, and indeed her entire narrative, ignores the ongoing conflict that leads to the bloody attack at Lancaster, specifically, the fact that King Philip's War is raging and that atrocities on both sides have led to the storming of her village. King Philip's War would eventually end the lives of nearly one-third of the American Indians living in Southern New England, and as Sayre notes, "because most captives were taken in wars between colonists and Indians or between rival European countries, it makes sense to think of them as prisoners of war, rather than as victims of some instinctual 'savage' aggression" (7). The dual-sided violence that has led to the destruction of Lancaster is ignored, however, as Rowlandson instead emphasizes religious rhetoric that depicts her solitary and innocent village being overrun by a mob of un-instigated savages. The historical contexts of King Philip's War do not seem to matter to Rowlandson in her narrative, and indeed, such contexts are rarely mentioned in any 17th- or 18th-century captivity narrative. For a genre that seems to claim historical authenticity through its narrative voices, historical analysis is typically lacking in such narratives. Rowlandson's narrative is instead meant to display the Puritan settlers as being tested by an evil force, carrying on a religious motif that can be traced to the Biblical account of Adam and Eve. Thus, the actual conflict of King Philip's War is unimportant to her Biblical, non-historical narrative, and her purpose is to self-fashion Puritan identity rather than to provide a historical account of a conflict with a specific group of American Indians.

In order to self-fashion this Puritan identity, Rowlandson must contrast herself and her fellow Puritans with the savage mob of American Indians that attack her village and take her prisoner. As Maureen L. Woodard argues, "By using racial difference to indicate the moral or cultural inferiority of people other than themselves, these primarily Puritan settlers were able to reinforce their own sense of self, safety, and superiority" (118). Throughout the narrative, Rowlandson depicts her American Indian captors as devilish figures, reinforcing her own superiority. To Rowlandson, the natives are "murderous wretches" (137), "infidels" (138), "black creatures" (140), and "wild beasts of the forest" (146), while those living at Lancaster are innocent, Christian, white, and civilized. As Rebecca Blevins Faery puts it, "The indigenous peoples served as a convenient 'other' against whom the Puritans could construct, and 'prove' through difference, their colonial identities" (25). Rowlandson's people view themselves as God's chosen, representative of John Winthrop's notion of the "city upon a hill," and this identity is fashioned through direct contrasts with the American Indians. As God's chosen, the Puritans must face trials and tribulations inspired by the Devil himself in order to test their faith. Rowlandson's narrative builds upon these tropes as she suffers and ultimately overcomes her suffering through faith and reliance on Biblical messages. As Gordon M. Sayre argues, "The text operates on both literal and theological planes, as both a personal narrative of conversion and an allegory for the larger war, according to a figural logic common in Puritan New England writing" (128), a figural logic that posits King Philip's War as a war not between colonizers and natives, but between Puritan good and Satanic evil.

Rowlandson somehow survives the initial attack and is taken captive, and it is in her captivity, not in the bloody attack the opening of her narrative so gruesomely narrates, that Rowlandson, surrounded by the savage mob, faces her ultimate test. As a representative of God's chosen people, Rowlandson manages to survive the ordeal and even strengthen her Puritan faith in the process, making the narrative as much about her own personal conversion as it is about violent conflict with a racial Other. As she leaves her razed hometown for the first time, she notes, "God was with me, in a wonderful manner, carrying me along, and bearing up my spirit, that it did not quite fail" (141). Whenever she feels defeated she notes, "The Lord renewed my strength still, and carried me along, that I might see more of his power" (141). Such statements drive home Rowlandson's message that Puritan faith is necessary in overcoming the adversity her people face. As the first Sabbath since her captivity arrives, Rowlandson "then remembered how careless I had been of God's holy time, how many Sabbaths I had lost and misspent, and how evilly I had walked in God's sight" (142). Her recognition of her own sinful lapses prior to her captivity allows her to recognize God's plan in permitting her to survive the savage attack and captivity, as "it was easy for me to see how righteous it was with God to cut off the thread of my life, and cast me out of his presence forever" (142). Rowlandson, in her suffering and captivity at the hands of the violent mob of savages, becomes identified with all Puritans who must constantly be aware of the temptations of evil to avoid lapses in faith.

Rowlandson, nursing a Christ-like injury in her side, continually uses her faith as an explanation for her survival. Much has been made of the Bible verses Rowlandson cites continually in her account, an infusion of quotations that clearly takes place in retrospect to her captivity and in fact may explain why Rowlandson's account was allowed to be published in her strict Puritan culture. These Biblical quotations allow the entire account to read much like a New England sermon, and according to Rowlandson, the Bible played an integral role in helping her cope with her captivity. Before the Fourth Remove (Rowlandson's account is broken up into "removes," periods when her captors move from one place to the next to avoid English armies, as a method for keeping track of time and place), Rowlandson, through "the wonderful mercy of God" (144), receives a Bible, and from that point on, she uses Bible passages throughout her captivity in order to soothe herself and to interpret the events that she witnesses and suffers through. When her heart aches for her "poor children," whose whereabouts are unknown to her, she states that she "opened my Bible to read, and the Lord brought that scripture to me" that ends up being "a sweet cordial" (146). As Faery has noted, "Citation of biblical passages is a primary interpretive strategy in the narrative as well as one of the structuring motifs of Rowlandson's text; it represents the conventional Puritan self to which she tries to cling as a way of explaining her captivity as well as a means of surviving and eventually escaping it" (30). Like all Puritans, Rowlandson is expected to turn to the Bible for answers to the real-world conflicts that she faces, and her narrative serves the didactic role in Puritan society of emphasizing this aspect of Puritan identity.

Perhaps because of this reliance on the Bible as a key to interpreting experience, it becomes clear that Rowlandson's faith is often misplaced. Several kind acts by her captors allow her to survive and even thrive within the confines of her captivity, yet she always credits her God for these actions, not the individual American Indians who act kindly towards her. Rowlandson is quick to blame the violent acts of the original attack and her capture on devilish savagery, but never gives the natives credit for the kindnesses they show her, such as providing her with a Bible that was part of their "plunder" (144). There are numerous other moments in her narrative when her captors treat her humanely. As Rowlandson notes during the Fifth Remove, "I was somewhat favored in my load; I carried only my knitting work and two quarts of parched meal" (146). Her captors seem to pity Rowlandson as they travel, and it is noted that on several occasions she is asked to a carry a lighter burden than the natives themselves. When one of her captors gives her shelter, "some ground nuts," and a place by a "good fire," she does not thank her captors, but "the good providence of God" for providing her with "comfortable lodging that night" (154).

Perhaps the most important act of compassion shown by her captors was her overall relative safety, both from physical and sexual abuse. Again, Rowlandson thanks God for these mercies, not her often benevolent captors. Early in her narrative, she states, "And I cannot but admire at the wonderful power and goodness of God to me, in that, though I was gone from home, and met with all sorts of Indians, and those I had no knowledge of, and there being no Christian soul near me; yet not one of them offered the least imaginable miscarriage to me" (152). While Rowlandson suffers occasional violence for disobedience, such as when she is slapped in the face for refusing to carry her share of the load during the Twelfth Remove, her captors never seriously harm her. Most importantly, considering that Rowlandson was the wife of a Puritan minister and a woman who had to reintegrate into society after her captivity, Rowlandson claims that she was never threatened with or forced to suffer any sexual abuse. Again, she credits God, not a native sense of sexual decorum, for preserving her in this way:

> O the wonderful power of God that I have seen, and the experience that I have had: I have been in the midst of those roaring lions, and savage bears, that feared neither God, nor man, nor the devil, by night and day, alone and in company: sleeping all sorts together, and yet not one of them offered me the least abuse of unchastity to me, in word or action. Though some are ready to say, I speak it for my own credit; but I speak it in the presence of God, and to His glory [171–2].

This interesting point in the narrative shows Rowlandson's desire to give all credit to God, and to clear her own name of any accusations of sexual transgressions with her native captors. In doing so, she self-fashions herself as a religious devout, sexually pure and ready to be re-assimilated into Puritan society. As Davis asserts, such "self-fashioning always takes place in the context of community and social goals of the congregational group, and, because Puritans uphold communally-held conventions, self-fashioning must conform the self to approved status" (56).

Rowlandson's survival, credited to her own reawakened faith, the wisdom of the Bible, and ultimately God's all-powerful grace, enables her to author a narrative that reinforces these same Puritan values, while also reinforcing Puritan social attitudes towards work, trade, and money, important aspects of peacetime Puritan society. Rowlandson's overtly stated purpose is "to declare the works of the Lord, and His wonderful power in carrying us along, preserving us in the wilderness, while under the enemy's hand, and returning us to safety again, and His goodness in bringing to my hand so many comfortable and suitable scriptures in my distress" (149). Using "us" as her personal pronoun to represent the Puritan community, Rowlandson claims that her narrative is meant as an allegory for all Puritan suffering in the New World, leading Woodard to argue that "Rowlandson's text reflects the anxieties of an entire community" (115). Ultimately, the Puritan way of life, Rowlandson believes, will be preserved and restored as she was.

This Puritan way of life was not only based on religious concepts, but economic concepts as well. During her captivity, Rowlandson makes herself valuable to her captors through her skills of sewing and trade. Her work and the bartering of her work allow her to enjoy freedoms much like Cabeza de Vaca relates in his own narrative penned over 100 years prior to Rowlandson's, and she claims a merchant role in her captive state that would have been denied her as a Puritan woman. This economic role is a clear expansion of Rowlandson's domestic duties. Such issues of gender are explored later in this chapter, but the fact that Rowlandson becomes a valued member of the American Indian community through trade, and that her abilities allow her to come and go as she pleases and to trade for items like food that were typically rationed, show the usefulness of production and exchange in the burgeoning New World economy. In this way, Rowlandson fuses the economic necessities of life in the New World to the presumably religious narrative of captivity. In order to survive the devilish trials and temptations of life in the New World wilderness, Rowlandson shows that production and trade can be used to overcome suffering and allow prosperity in the colonies, emphasizing the importance of these activities to the Puritan identity. From the start, American values joined religion and trade.

In these ways, captivity narratives such as Rowlandson's performed important nation-building purposes in the New England colonies. Always fearful of religious dissent, New England Puritans used captivity narratives to unite the colonies in a common battle against the American Indians who inhabited New

World lands. These narratives reinforced religious myths central to Puritan society, showing that the challenges faced by early settlers could only be overcome by faith and devotion to Puritan concepts of God and the Bible. Through such portrayals, Puritan writers reinforced notions of a homogenous society centered on conformity, faith, and the desire for economic prosperity.

This kind of rhetoric, steeped in Puritan religious belief, provided important unifying principles in the New England colonies. While Roy Harvey Pearce has argued that "the first, and greatest, of the captivity narratives are simple, direct religious documents" (2), Rowlandson's narrative is as much about communal, gendered, and racial constructs as it is about religious principles, and these configurations of gender and race are also intended to reinforce the precepts of Puritan society. Thus, captivity narratives like Rowlandson's, full of Biblical allusions, were meant as sermons that taught not only religious lessons, but socially acceptable configurations of community, gender, and race as well.

The issue of gender in Rowlandson's narrative and in other captivity narratives written by women has been an especially important area of study, allowing scholars to understand the normative social constructs Puritan society assigned to women, as well as allowing scholars to identify points in early American literature where women rebelled, in both writing and action, however covertly, against these constructs. Rowlandson's text, as Sayre asserts, is considered "the classic of the captivity narrative" (127) in part because of its depictions of both these normative roles assigned to women and it's depictions of the subversive ways in which women like Rowlandson re-imagined or resisted these roles. In Rowlandson's narrative, we witness traditional Puritan rhetoric regarding the need to protect the home (the place of Puritan women), as well as traditional Puritan rhetoric (and I would argue, traditional *American* rhetoric) regarding the need to protect women, the presumptive weaker sex, from the dangers of racial interbreeding. At the same time, Rowlandson's narrative defines women as property with the potential to be bought, sold, and traded, as Rowlandson is bartered for throughout the text as colonists attempt to exchange goods with her captors for her life. Finally, captivity narratives such as Rowlandson's gave women the opportunity to proclaim a voice in early American literature, and through this political voice that cannot be silenced, women are able to imagine and portray communal roles outside of the confines of the home. In many ways, Puritan society used the threat of mob violence to fashion female gender identity, and women writers such as Rowlandson used the occasions of mob violence commonly represented in captivity narratives to rebelliously self-fashion their own identity.

In several ways, Rowlandson's narrative appears to reaffirm normative constructs of Puritan society. The Puritan colonists lived in fear and terror of American Indian attack, and much religious rhetoric was aimed at representing these colonies as the New Israel, a promised land in need of protection from violent, savage, and devilish forces. Within these colonies were the individual homes of Puritans, the domestic spaces assigned to women like Rowlandson. Thus, as Nancy Armstrong notes, "The American captivity narrative took advantage of the inherently conservative fantasy that each man's home is his castle and put that fantasy to work on British America, where it allowed readers to imagine a new land transformed into an English nation household by household of an apparently limitless whole" (389). At the center of this fantasy is the Puritan female or goodwife, and as Lisa Logan has argued, the socially assigned "place" of the Puritan woman was in the household. This sense of place was important to Puritan women's identity. Logan argues that Rowlandson's "removal from home poses a loss of identity" since her identity "is dependent on her place: minister's wife, mother, sister, friend, housekeeper" (266). If the Puritan woman's place is in the household, then much of the Puritan rhetoric regarding the need to protect the household from Indian attack centers on the notion that women must be protected, implying feminine weakness and necessitating violent masculine protection. Female identity in the Puritan colonies thus becomes dependent on male safeguarding. In all social relations, as Davis has shown, "Puritan society defined a woman's identity by the relationships that prevailed in her sphere; in the church, she was bride to Christ; in the home she was wife to husband, mother to child, goodwife to servant—designations altogether gender-based and hierarchical" (52).

In her narrative, Rowlandson exaggerates her role as a helpless goodwife in order to show the failings of these social constructs. When the bloody attack on Lancaster takes place, Rowlandson's husband is not home to defend his wife from attack. Other men are home, but even so, these men are unable to defend their women and children. Rowlandson writes, "There were five persons taken in one house, the father, and the mother and a suckling child, they knocked on the head; the other two they took and carried away alive" (137), showing the perilous position of all women and children in the village, regardless of the availability of male protection. Puritans defined the household as synonymous with womanhood, as a sacred place in need of protection from a violent mob, but Rowlandson shows that women are endangered even when their protective husbands are present. As the attackers close in on Rowlandson's home, Rowlandson's "brother-in-law (before being wounded, in defending the house, in or near the throat) fell down dead whereat the Indians scornfully shouted, and holloed, and were presently upon him, stripping off his clothes" (138). Rowlandson and other Puritan women were taught that men like her brother-in-law were the heads of, and the protectors of, the household and village, but in these scenes of mob violence, Rowlandson shows that such men are really no protection at all.

Of course, the Lancaster settlement is in a region of New England where

King Philip's War had been prominently raging for months, meaning that ultimately, the English army was responsible for protecting such settlements. Throughout her narrative, Rowlandson pointedly blames the English army for failing to protect Lancaster and subsequently, for failing to properly rescue her from her captors. She notes "the strange providence of God in preserving the heathen," stating that many of them were "sick," "lame," carried children, and were women, and yet, "on that very day came the English army after them to this river, and saw the smoke of their wigwams, and yet this river put a stop to them. God did not give them the courage or activity to go over after us" (147). While Rowlandson always suggests God's agency in reference to these military failures, her disappointment with the ineffective protection of the English army is obvious. Later in her narrative, when Rowlandson provides an account of the "few remarkable passages of providence, which I took special notice of in my afflicted time," she first notes "the fair opportunity lost" by "our English army" that was "in pursuit of the enemy," an enemy in "distress for food" (169). Then, Rowlandson notes that she "cannot but remember how the Indians derided the slowness, and dullness of the English army, in its setting out" (169). Rowlandson is clearly dissatisfied with the cultural myth of male protection, and in these moments, she shockingly seems to side with her captors in their mocking of the British forces. Rowlandson's criticisms of the military and the concept of male protection are very unique for her time.

Ironically, given Rowlandson's agreement with her captors and their mockery of the English army in these passages, captivity narratives were a popular way Puritan society preached the dangers of racial mixing, especially between white women and dark-skinned male Others. Much like the rhetoric used later in the American South to justify slavery and lynching, Puritan society justified American Indian oppression and removal in part by arguing that such actions were necessary to protect Puritan women sexually. "Although Puritan doctrine insisted on the equality of all humans in the eyes of God," Woodard remarks, "the belief that women had a closer affinity to nature than men also implied that women were perhaps closer to the wilderness or heathen culture of the Indians" (122). Southern white males in the post–Civil War South often justified the violence of lynching by arguing that lynching would deter black lust for white women and discourage white women from sexual relationships with black men. Likewise, Puritan society depicted women as weak and vulnerable in terms of potential sexual acts with native men. Woodard explains that Puritan society viewed women as being dangerously close to nature, noting in relation to Rowlandson's narrative the fear that

> a woman may easily cross over and literally become a part of the forest. She thus reinforces these assumptions about feminine nature, which ironically serve to undermine her assumed role or identity as the virtuous wife of a Puritan minister. The narrative seems to suggest that if even orthodox women like

Rowlandson are able to enter into and become a part of the world of the other, the strict racial distinctions asserted by the Puritan community are permeable and perhaps illusory [123].

The real apprehension at work here is the notion that Puritan women, feared to be linked to nature, might be tempted to assimilate into native cultures, and that Indian marriage and sexual intercourse might be part of this assimilation.

Indeed, there are several moments in Rowlandson's narrative where Rowlandson is seen adopting the habits of her captor's culture. Rowlandson states, "The first week of my being among them, I hardly ate anything," noting that she considered their foods to be "filthy trash." However, she adds that by "the third week," these foods were "sweet and savory to my taste" (147). At one point, Rowlandson devours a piece of bear meat while noting that previously, the "thought" that it was bear would have made her "tremble" (152). In one of the more grotesque moments in the narrative, Rowlandson relates that her captors "killed a deer, with a young one in her" and that they "gave me a piece of the fawn, and it was so young and tender, that one might eat the bones as well as the flesh, and yet I thought it very good" (159). Near the end of her captivity, Rowlandson even goes so far as to steal food from one of the English children being held captive along with her. After eating her own portion of boiled horse meat, she notes that the child eating the same "could not bite it, it was so tough and sinewy, but lay sucking, gnawing, and slobbering of it in the mouth and hand" (162). Even this saliva-covered piece of horse meat is not "filthy trash" to Rowlandson at this point, and she admits that she "took it of the child, and ate it myself, and savory it was to my taste" (162). While Logan argues that Rowlandson's "text seeks to reestablish the superiority of the Puritan world view and, in effect, reenact on the Native Americans the silencing which she experienced as a captive" (269), as Woodard argues, perhaps the strongest and most dangerous challenge to her Puritan roots and community is the

> transformation Rowlandson undergoes while with the Indians. This transformation proves so subversive because it challenges the very notion of identity promoted by the Puritan community by blurring the line between self and other. While Rowlandson may attempt to emphasize the difference between her own reliance on the Bible and Puritan beliefs and the Indians' heathen ways and assumed association with the devil, as she moves away from her community and into the world of the Indian, these differences begin to disappear [121].

Rowlandson's dangerous transformation is most evident in regards to the foods she devours, showing the ways in which her immersion into native culture causes her to simultaneously devour native cultural norms and digest the cultural values that are supposed to differentiate her from her captives. Imagining herself as standing in contrast to the mob that represents her captives, Rowlandson's own sense of personal identity is at times consumed by the circumstances of her captivity.

Rowlandson's most drastic immersion into native culture is hinted at, even though she ultimately attempts to refute it. On numerous occasions throughout the narrative, Rowlandson is offered shelter and comfort from American Indian men, and scorn and even violence from American Indian women, especially as the narrative progresses and her time as a captive lengthens. For example, during the Twelfth Remove, Rowlandson notes that she is slapped by her mistress for complaining that her load "was too heavy" (153). Rowlandson adds that at this point in the narrative, her "master" is gone, and she calls him "the best friend that I had of an Indian" (154). Left alone without protection, Rowlandson faces threats from both men and women as she searches for a place to stay before "at last an old Indian bade me come to him" and allowed her to stay with him and his wife (154). Later, her master becomes drunk after bartering for some liquor and calls for her. She writes, "I trembled to hear him, yet I was fain to go to him" (169). The sexual tension is obvious in such scenes, yet Rowlandson is quick to note that he showed no "incivility," even though his wife ends up running from him, forcing him to chase her (169). Faery observes, "The behavior required of a woman if she was to survive captivity, then, often required transgressing gender expectations in ways that would arouse suspicion of her once she returned to her home culture. Most often that suspicion located itself primarily in the question of her sexual integrity during captivity" (33). Rowlandson, enjoying the relative autonomy of authoring her own account, could easily have left out such sexual tensions, tensions that at times serve to destabilize the religious message of her narrative. However, she chooses to include such passages in the narrative, and even emphasizes them at times, much the way Harriet Jacobs would later in accounting for her experiences as a slave in *Incidents in the Life of a Slave Girl*. Like many accounts of enslaved females, Rowlandson's narrative shows persistent conflicts with her female masters and persistent sexual tensions with her male captors and her female rivals.

Of course, Rowlandson provides a disclaimer in her narrative, one that could be interpreted as a preemptive strike against the assumed accusations of sexual impropriety she would likely face, or, as a coded admission of guilt and a defense of American Indian sexual behavior. As Michelle Burnham has noted, "Since the first seventeenth-century colonial American captivity narratives, female captives, whether authentic or fictional, were predominantly mothers who endured physical and psychological hardship but who also consistently defended their captors against accusations of seduction or rape" (73). While Burnham goes on to note that "not until the Revolutionary War do fictionalized narratives begin to portray the captivity of young girls who are tortured and threatened with rape" (73), Rowlandson does not offer this disclaimer until near the end of her narrative, when her freedom and her subsequent return home begin to become narrative realities. Rowlandson's sexual disclaimer cited previously comes *after* the events she has narrated where she and the natives have slept "all sorts together." Thus, Rowlandson saw fit to make this kind of sexual tension prevalent in her narrative until its conclusion, a conclusion that portrays her re-assimilation into Puritan society. As Faery argues, "The sexual history of a woman who survived captivity, therefore, because of all it symbolically represented, was a matter of considerable concern to the whole Puritan community upon her return" (41). As Sayre has also noted, "Perhaps the most salient critical debate over the text concerns the degree to which Rowlandson's writing may have been influenced, coerced, or edited by the powerful Puritan ministers who managed and interpreted the war effort" (130). Most assume, for example, that "The Preface to the Reader" that appears at the beginning of the first publication of Rowlandson's narrative was penned by Cotton Mather as a form of literary sponsorship, since women of the period were not encouraged to write or allowed to publish without such sponsorship. Perhaps, Mather or one of the other "powerful Puritan ministers" mentioned by Sayre forced Rowlandson to add her sexual disclaimer so that the text might serve its intended religious purpose without fears of such impropriety. Without this disclaimer, the sexual tensions evident in Rowlandson's narrative would be inexplicable within Puritan culture.

Whatever the case, gender, and especially sexual norms, are clearly at stake in Rowlandson's narrative. Faery argues that captivity narratives involving women "helped in significant ways to produce the difference, at first cultural but eventually racial, in which stories of contending 'red' men and 'white' men were grounded and which became the rationale for European conquest and the emergence of a nation founded on white male supremacy" (10). Such themes, first introduced in North America by Rowlandson's narrative, would continue throughout American literature, and as will be shown later in this study, such themes played a significant part in the justification of lynching in the American South. As Faery puts it, captivity narratives "initiated what would become a persistent trope in articulations of racial difference in the United States: white women, their bodies and their sexuality, positioned as guardians of the boundaries of race to serve the territorial and political purposes of white men and their claim to dominance" (10). This trope, consequently, is persistently realized through literary portrayals of mob violence and identity formation.

Even setting aside the question of Rowlandson's assimilation into American Indian culture as seen in her narrative, by simply penning the narrative of her captivity, Rowlandson is stepping out of the normative gender confines forced upon her by Puritan culture. As William J. Scheick notes, prior to the eighteenth-century, "colonial female authors simply had no authority whatsoever to venture into the male preserve of scriptural interpretation" (12). Replete with Biblical passages that Rowlandson uses to interpret the events of her captivity, her captivity narrative asserts her authority as a scriptural interpreter. Rowlandson, because her text could be used by her contemporaries to enforce normative religious, racial, and gender identities, is given a voice in her patriarchal society, allowing her to not only narrate the story, but allowing her to also incorporate Bible passages into the text. These passages serve the dual purposes of interpreting her own experience and shedding new light on the ways in which these Bible passages might be shown as manifesting themselves in the lives of Puritans. Thus, as Davis notes, the publication of Rowlandson's narrative "suggests that under certain conditions Puritan women's writing was approved" (49). Even though Rowlandson's writing is likely to have been strictly edited to conform to Puritan social conditions, as Christopher Castiglia has shown, by "writing against the discursive grain of race and gender in order to experiment with other articulations of identity, captive white women position themselves as subjects speaking to other captives, other women, and hence as agents, not objects, of cultural exchange" (9). Even though the patriarchs of her society allow her to publish her work in order to enforce normative social positions, these same patriarchs, with a worldview that relies heavily on a singular interpretive position, underestimate the inherent value of any written text's ability to adhere to multiple interpretations, both normative and otherwise. In doing so, they ignore the potential for women like Rowlandson to re-imagine their own personal identity when empowered with a narrative voice.

As previously mentioned, Rowlandson crosses Puritan boundaries for women in both word and action. Castiglia adds that "in entering the Indian economy, Rowlandson transforms herself from an object of exchange in a trade conducted between men (the Indians and the British haggle over Rowlandson's 'worth' in terms of tobacco and firearms) to an agent of exchange. Her new economic role seems to allow Rowlandson more physical agency" (47). Rowlandson's ability to produce goods and trade these goods during her captivity provides her with an opportunity she did not have in her home Puritan society. Although Davis argues that Rowlandson's narrative "imposed no blasphemous competition to the patriarchal hegemony because she maintained the stance of bride-like submission required of women, subjecting herself first to God as ultimate authority and then to males as his earthly representatives" (50), Castiglia aptly notes that "yet Rowlandson's acceptance of Indian life seems to begin precisely at the moment when she assumes an economic position in the community. That position gives her an agency among the Indians that she would not necessarily have had in her own culture" (51). Rowlandson is surely encouraged to publish her narrative because of the religious message it provides, and because of the message it provides that enforces normative gender and racial roles within her culture. However, since she is empowered with the opportunity to proclaim a voice within Puritan culture, Rowlandson invites interpretations of her narrative that subversively counter these socially ascribed roles. As Faery argues, "Paradoxically, Indian captivity represented for Puritan women of New England an expansion of experience rather than what we might ordinarily think would be a contraction or restriction of experience" (31).

In spite of some of the subversive tendencies shown in Rowlandson's narrative, her narrative still defines her captors' identity as an animalistic, pagan, and violent mob that should be annihilated or otherwise removed. Commentators like Castiglia have rightly noted that "while our culture still teaches young women that their greatest enemies are men of color and that they have nothing in common with women of color, the captivity narratives stress the urgent need for cooperation between culturally separated people" (12), but Rowlandson only stresses this cooperation for her own benefit. Her experience as a captive does empower her with some opportunities that she did not have before, but these acts do not amount to cooperation with her captors. In fact, her narrative reinforces racial stereotypes regarding American Indians that attempt to justify the further eradication of native peoples in the region.

The stereotypes Rowlandson reinforces in her depictions of American Indians are most obvious in the scenes of mob violence she portrays. Narrating the attack on Lancaster, Rowlandson describes one individual who begs for his life, only to have the mob of attackers react with violence; they "knocked him in the head, and stripped him naked, and split open his bowels" (137). In her own house, some "were fighting for their lives, others wallowing in their blood, the house on fire over our heads, and the bloody heathen ready to knock us on the head, if we stirred out" (138). Images of fire play an important role in this early scene of mob violence, and nearly 300 years later, Elias Canetti would link fire with crowds and mob violence. Rowlandson opens her narrative by noting that the colonists at Lancaster first heard "the noise of some guns," only to look outside and notice that "several houses were burning" (137). Fire, like the spread of mob violence, swells through Lancaster, implying that the town is being consumed by a hellish, destructive force. These early images set the stage for Rowlandson's narrative and its persistent portrayals of her captors as bloodthirsty devils.

Often, Rowlandson's images of mob violence are very similar to the images of lynchings that would be commonly portrayed in later African American literature, and these portrayals, as I argue throughout this book, are important throughout American literary history. Rowlandson relates a story that she hears, rather than witnesses, concerning a "poor woman" who later "came to a sad end" (145). Apparently, the woman had begun to trouble her captors, "having much grief upon her spirit, about her miserable condition" (145). According to the story passed on to Rowlandson, the "poor woman ... would often be asking the Indians to let her go home" (145). Rather than obliging the woman's request, Rowlandson states that the captors

> gathered a great company together about her, and stripped her naked, and set her in the midst of them; and when they had sung and danced about her (in their hellish manner) as long as they pleased, they knocked her on head, and the child in her arms with her: when they had done that, they made a fire and put them both into it, and told the other children that were with them, that if they attempted to go home, they would serve them in like manner [145].

Rowlandson's description of this incident is inconsistent with the rest of her narrative, a narrative that promises to narrate *her own* captivity and restoration. This aside is clearly added for its rhetorical value. As is commonly the case in narratives that describe lynchings, Rowlandson's brief aside about the "poor woman" provides images of a mob who are celebrating their violent act. The violent act involves stripping the victim naked, heightening the sexual nature of the scene while also providing an example of the type of violence women were supposed to be protected from—sexualized violence enacted by a dark Other. Rowlandson describes the "hellish manner" of the mob, inciting images of hell, fire, and deviltry. The victims are placed into the fire, eradicating their identity by transforming their physical bodies. Finally, the mob proclaims the scene to be a warning to others who might consider such behavior, in this case forming and enforcing specific identities for passive, adopted captives who are expected to stop worrying about home and to quickly adopt their new identity in their new culture, however foreign.

By narrating such ritualized brutality, and in this particular case, ritualized brutality that Rowlandson did not even witness, captivity narratives enabled Puritan society to further demonize and dehumanize American Indian peoples. In this way, as Frances Roe Kestler has argued, "Puritan accounts reinforced the belief that Indians were too far removed from civilization to be redeemed, and this alienation justified killing them and seizing their land" (xxv). Such justifications are commonly provided through images of ritualized mob violence. Kestler also notes, "At first the Puritans looked upon the heathen native as being redeemable from the power of Satan; later they felt these devils should be exterminated at any cost" (4). This change in objective from conversion to extermination can best be explained by the prolific scenes of mob violence evident in captivity narratives such as Rowlandson's. Religious conversion of native peoples would not stabilize the Puritan community—the dark Other would still be present, and religious conversion might even imply an acceptance of American Indian humanity, even interracial sexual relationships. Scenes of ritualized violence, such as Rowlandson's secondhand account of the "poor woman," play a prominent role in captivity narratives, defining the American Indians as violent devils opposed to God's chosen people.

Images of conversion instead become images of consumption. Richard Vanderbeets has argued that captivity narratives "derive their essential integrity" from "the core of ritual acts and patterns" that such narratives often depict (549). Fear of ritualized cannibalism, for example, was considerable in early America, and Rowlandson references this fear early in her own narrative, writing "out we must go, the fire increasing, and coming along behind us, roaring, and the Indians gaping before us with their guns, spears, and hatchets to devour us" (138). Rowlandson's narrative makes little mention of overtly cannibalistic acts, but Vanderbeets explains that "in most tribes, eating of human flesh was acceptable only as ritual" (551). Rowlandson apparently never witnesses such a ritual, but the fear of cannibalism in early America is important in connection with literary depictions of lynchings. As has been shown in numerous accounts, lynchings often involved the removal of the black victim's phallus, an act symbolic of the lynch mob's desire to transfer mythical black sexual prowess from the victim to those conducting the ritualized lynching. In the same way, white colonists like Rowlandson fear, as Vanderbeets notes, "the practice of eating flesh," a practice "derived from the belief that the eater could acquire the courage and strength of his victim, a belief that is part of a primitive system of sympathetic or homeopathic logic" (550). The Puritans would have to consume, by eradicating native peoples and occupying native lands, the threat they were facing in order to keep their homogenous community safe while still obtaining the power the American Indians represented.

Rowlandson tries to define the race of the natives she encounters by depicting them as a mob, a mob that might devour and consume her identity if she allows it. In several places in her narrative, she describes her captors as a devilish crowd threatening to envelop her. During the Sixth Remove, Rowlandson describes "a great Indian town" where "the Indians were as thick as the trees" (148). Here, she seems to be on the brink of being consumed into the crowd, writing that "if one looked before one, there was nothing but Indians, and behind one, nothing but Indians, and so on either hand, I myself in the midst, and no Christian soul near me" (148). This scene only strengthens her own self-fashioned identity as a Christian, a woman somehow fundamentally different from her captors, as she ponders "how hath the Lord preserved me in safety! Oh the experience that I have had of the goodness of God, to me and mine?" (148). One of the miracles Rowlandson cites is her ability to maintain an identity apart from her captors, a self-fashioned identity that defines her as different from, and superior to, these captors. Given the predicament she is relating, it would be easy to question God's "goodness" towards her in this situation, but Rowlandson attempts to strengthen her own sense of identity through these encounters, writing as a restored captive and as a restored Christian who, looking back on her ordeal, feels grateful for her perceived ability to keep her own sense of personal identity intact.

Such scenes, like the scene of wild dress and dancing that Rowlandson narrates in the Twentieth Remove, only further contrast Rowlandson with her captors, allowing her to continually fashion and refashion her own identity. It is this process, the process of defining one's own identity in confrontation with a mob or other collective group, which is repeated continually throughout captivity narratives and in later American literature. Such narratives of self-fashioning, written, as Rowlandson's narrative is, from the perspective of a member of the dominant homogenous group, likewise fashion predominant, Othering identities for individuals such as American Indians who do not fit into a culture striving for racial homogeneity. As Woodard posits,

> The uncivilized chaos and brutality the Indians seemed to embody for Rowlandson and her readers continued to be attributed to any figure of dark otherness that remained (most notably African slaves, and all those who did not fit the white European Protestant norm). However, the ambiguous and often contradictory messages found in the later texts also begin to imply that these threats to social order are inherent in the dominant white culture as it attempts to define itself against the various marginalized or "othered" groups in its midst [116–117].

Rowlandson does not seem to realize it, but in order for her to self-fashion her own identity, an identity of a white, Puritan female, Rowlandson *needs* this American Indian presence. By extension, Puritan society, and indeed a great part of all of the early American colonies, seemed to use this native presence in order to fashion a national identity built on racial and spiritual whiteness. For Faery, "Racial difference as we know it in the United States today, then, as a discursive practice—and as a social and political reality—arose as a product of colonialism, especially in the encounters between English colonizers and their racialized 'others' in the New World" (10). As Faery adds, "The captivity story was a crucial vehicle for Anglo-Americans to become white, as well as for the construction of 'dark' and supposedly inferior category that finally included both Indians and Africans, an 'other' whom whites had to displace, discipline, and control in order to achieve their colonial aims" (12).

Clearly, there has been great critical recognition of these currents running through captivity narratives and continually informing subsequent American culture, especially American literary culture. For example, Faery argues that Rowlandson's "narrative and the history of its reproductions offer compelling evidence that the figure of the white woman captive has been a primary site for the construction of race, gender, and national identity in U.S. culture" (25). Faery thus recognizes the common themes of the captivity narrative focused on in later works by American authors. Likewise, Castiglia has noted that "while many critics have assumed that the captivity narrative vanished with the Puritans or passed from Rowlandson to such literary sons as Charles Brockden Brown and James Fenimore Cooper, there extends between Rowlandson and Hearst a long and complex line of white women who wrote captivity narratives in America" (2). Castiglia adds, "Even today, romance novels mass marketed for women frequently feature captivity plots, while the dynamics of the captivity story, especially its exploration of the relationships between race and gender, confinement and community, inscription and collective action, continue to animate American feminist discourse" (2).

Literary critics have been correct in noticing these fruitful literary relationships and patterns of influence, but literary connections between crowd violence and identity formation, from Mary Rowlandson to contemporary American fiction writers such as Cormac McCarthy, are likewise hugely important in deciphering these cultural phenomena. These connections, however, have not received a great deal of critical analysis. Scenes of crowd violence have been used throughout American literature as a way to understand identity, to self-fashion identity, to create and enforce normative identities, and to show the ways in which identities that are objectionable to dominant normative society are prescribed and punished. Therefore, one of the predominant tropes of the captivity narrative, the struggle between individual identity and crowd forces, has been, and continues to be, alive and well in American literature. As this entire study will assert, the struggle between the individual and the community, the inherent conflict between founding notions of rugged individualism and idealism regarding a government *by the people*, is constantly played out in American literature.

American Modernism, one of the most studied eras in American literature and thus a central period for understanding canonical American literature, proves to be an important era in terms of understanding American identity and the continual influence such tropes have had on American literature. Modernist-era American writers, influenced by Ezra Pound's mantra to "make it new," often portrayed themselves and their work as free from the dominant literary influences that came before them. Studying manifestations of crowd violence and identity formation within American Modernist texts is one way that the captivity narrative's influence in the American literary canon can be understood. More importantly, studying these manifestations of crowd violence in Modernist-era texts helps to redefine both the American Modernist period and canonical American literature, from Rowlandson to McCarthy.

Introduction: Crowd Violence and Punishing Identities in American Modernist Fiction

Throughout this book, I will argue that the struggle depicted by Mary Rowlandson in her captivity narrative, a struggle that takes place between an individual struggling to self-fashion an identity and a violent crowd, is similarly prominent in a variety of works of American literature, from the texts that emerge from the first European exploration of the American continents to the present. This focus, I will simultaneously argue, is especially foundational in the literature produced by American Modernist writers, a highly canonized group of writers that helped inspire the hyperactive field now recognized as the field of American Literature. The canonization of these authors, and their often implicit focus on struggles between individual identity and crowd forces, seems to imply that this topic would already have received a great deal of critical attention over the years. However, that has not always been the case, and in fact, a primary motivation in my producing this study is aimed at inspiring, through my own critical insight or my own lack thereof, further exploration of the literary, but also the sociological, political, and historical ramifications, of the American infatuation with crowd violence and individual identity.

While I find myself shocked by the lack of critical discussion alluding to this topic, especially considering the great wealth of literary criticism focused on the authors that are the subjects of this book, I must admit that I read a great deal of American literature, especially texts considered to be American Modernist texts, before I began to recognize this struggle that now seems to me so fundamental to any understanding of what I might loosely call the "American experience." It was not until the spring of 2007, when I was enrolled in Dr. Veronica Watson's graduate English course "Black Writers, White Lives" as a doctoral student at Indiana University of Pennsylvania, that I first began exploring the effects of crowds on individual identity, especially the effects of crowd violence. Dr. Watson, the director of the Frederick Douglass Institute for Intercultural Exchange, showed my small graduate seminar a video found on the website withoutsanctuary.org. The website, through a narrated Flash movie and a gallery of images, displays photographs and postcards of lynchings that took place throughout the United States during the height of American lynch violence, roughly 1900–1940. Collected by James Allen and, as I later learned, published as a book also entitled *Without Sanctuary*, these graphic photographs illustrate the United States' unique and disturbing history of racially motivated mob violence and lynching. These graphic images include close-up shots of African American men with nooses around their necks, and these are some of the least shocking images found on the website. Other images show badly burned and mutilated bodies with smoke rolling off of them, victims of lynchings hanging from street lamps and displayed prominently in downtown areas, and tortured faces showing their heartbreaking pain.

The images are still disturbing to me, even though I have been studying the subject of crowd violence, especially lynching, since that night. When Dr. Watson showed these images to my class, I observed one class participant leaving the room looking sick and distraught, and I noticed tears in the eyes of a couple of my classmates. We had all read about lynching and mob violence in the course—for example, earlier in the class we had read James Weldon Johnson's *Autobiography of an Ex-Colored Man*—but the actual visual images were an entirely new experience for most of us. Most shocking to me, on that night, were not the bodies of the tortured and lynched, but the images portrayed in the background of many of these photos. These photographs were not images captured randomly by a passing citizen camera, such as the familiar images of the Rodney King beating in Los Angeles on March 3, 1991, that were used to expose police brutality and led to the Los Angeles Riots of 1992 after the acquittal of the white police officers charged in the case. Rather, these lynching photographs were purposefully staged and produced in order to record and celebrate this kind of brutality, not to expose it in order that it might be corrected, as is surely the purpose of the website they appear on today. As the slideshow continued and the horrific images of mutilated bodies became overwhelming, my gaze shifted to the faces of the individuals that made up the crowds, the spectators as they engaged in the pictured lynchings or stood by passively, yet voyeuristically. I saw numerous faces staring directly at the camera or the body of the victim, many smiling, others looking almost as if they were in a state of rapture. I had always thought, rather naively I will admit, that lynching was a kind of underground, unpublicized activity, but here were crowds gathered in public places, in front of both courthouses and centers of business. No Ku Klux Klan hoods or other attempts at disguise were present in these images. Actual faces stared back at me—undisguised faces of well-dressed businessmen, housewives, and even young children. These crowds, taken as a whole, seemed impressed and pleased with their violent work.

This book originated in my mind that evening as I became intently interested in the crowd mindset that enabled these lynchings to occur, the obvious struggle taking place in these lynching images between isolated individuals and crowd forces, and the way in which struggles between crowds and individuals might be portrayed in the literature produced during the height of lynching violence in America. This period, as I quickly realized, is typically identified as the heyday of American Modernism, and this period is full of other types of crowd violence. In addition to the racially motivated violence of lynching, American Modernism has always been connected with other forms of collective violence; the circumstances of World War I, the changes in traditional gender roles that followed World War I, and widespread labor battles all involved crowd forces and systematic violence.

Of course, the American Modernist era is not the only period of American literature that is inseparable from issues of crowd violence, especially the persecution of individuals through crowd violence. When I turned my attention to American literature and manifestations of crowd violence in this literature, I was surprised by what I saw. Crowd violence is so prevalent in American history and the literature it has produced that I came to the conclusion that I outline throughout this book, that American literature and the theme of crowd violence cannot be separated in *any* historical or literary period. To understand the literature of the United States, we must understand the stream of crowd violence that runs through it, sometimes clearly over the surface of the literature and oftentimes, as is the case with many American Modernist literary works, deep beneath it. Furthermore, we must identify the diverse ways that different American writers in different periods of American history have portrayed this persistent theme.

Certain periods of American literature involve crowd violence in overt and obvious ways, and a general pattern emerges from this persistent treatment of crowd violence. Early exploration narratives are rife with fears of mutiny, the fear of a crowd turning against its leader, both in the narratives concerned with the events aboard explorative vessels and the narratives of the first settlements on land. Thus, from its very beginning, American literature has been shaped by this theme. As discussed in this book's prologue, early American colonial literature is obsessed with the captivity narrative, a genre solely focused on the struggle between an individual and a hostile crowd. The captivity narrative thus becomes the predominant genre of the period and arguably the only literary genre specifically invented by American writers. Mary Rowlandson, like many other captivity narrative authors, is also quick to suggest that she personally belongs to a chosen few, elected by God but surrounded by the

Godless masses. Puritan individualism and John Winthrop's famous "city upon a hill" metaphor couple with a fear of the savage, misunderstood, mob "other" to inform a national identity.

This version of rugged individuality greatly served in uniting the colonies against the oppressive English empire, an empire often rhetorically described as a crowd of "Redcoats" imposing unjust policies on the individuals inhabiting the growing colonies. English attempts at employing American Indians during the Revolutionary War only heightened the fear of mobs and savage crowds in a growing national consciousness, leading to a newfound nation most popularly personified by individuals such as Benjamin Franklin, self-professed self-made men, models of what Ralph Waldo Emerson would later term, while writing in his Puritan-influenced New England, "Self-Reliance." Later, writers from the American Renaissance would further define American individuality, with authors such as Nathaniel Hawthorne consistently depicting individuals as the victims of cruel and oppressive society in *The Scarlett Letter*, "Young Goodman Brown," and other works, while Herman Melville resuscitated the captivity narrative in his novels *Typee* and *Omoo*.

The vast system of American slavery was often threatened by the peril of mob violence, real or imagined, as individual plantation owners grew increasingly fearful of mutiny and insurrection. The importation and impregnation of slave laborers rightfully caused fears of insurrection as the black population exceeded, eventually exponentially, the white population in numerous American slaveholding communities. Meanwhile, abolitionists rightfully argued in favor of the rights of individual citizens, including those used as slaves, fighting against the collective force of a Southern political economy thriving on slave labor and advocating for the rights of the state. A great deal of the effectiveness that can be attributed to abolitionist works such as Harriet Beecher Stowe's *Uncle Tom's Cabin* is based on the violent inequalities Stowe and other writers portray individuals suffering at the hands of the American slave system.

The violence and inequality of slavery, a system held precariously in place by mutual fears of the consequences of uncontrollable mob violence and aggression, inevitably led to a violent Civil War. Depending on who is asked, the Civil War was fought to end slavery and liberate African Americans abused by this system, or the Civil War was fought as an issue of states' rights. Mob violence is a necessary precondition of any system of inequality as brutal as slavery, in any system where collective bodies are held in place by powerful individuals. Individual slaves were threatened by crowd violence, and this threat played an important role in discouraging African American slaves from fleeing their masters or rising up violently against the system that enslaved them. Mob rhetoric, as it was in the case of the Revolutionary War, was also used by Southerners in justifying the Civil War, as political arguments coming from the region referenced individual state governments being essentially mobbed by a collective, centralized, overreaching national government. Once Southern defeat was imminent, images of an invading crowd of Yankees became commonplace, and the Reconstruction era following the Civil War is replete with crowd violence, as evidenced by the rise of the Ku Klux Klan. Indeed, as this brief and very general glimpse of crowd violence and rhetoric in United States history attests, many of the nation's main political issues have hinged upon a perceived struggle between individuals and mob forces, real or perceived, metaphorical or literal.

In the period following the Reconstruction era, a period when Modernist aesthetic values greatly influenced American literary sensibilities, lynching violence became more and more frequent. Simultaneously, World War I broke out in Europe, and the years after the war led to a period of excess and financial irresponsibility that would eventually instigate great labor unrest and crowd violence during, and in the wake of, the Great Depression. The preponderance of crowd violence during the American Modernist era makes American Modernist-era literature an important field of study for examinations of crowd violence in American history and culture. Likewise, canonical Modernist American literature is an ideal period for the study of crowd violence, given the great emphasis placed on this period in general formulations of the American literary canon, showing the literature's profound influence on American cultural values. The celebration and elevation of American Modernist works by the New Critics would make the literature produced in this period seminal in a growing effort at creating an American literary canon, and this literature's place in the American consciousness reflects a continuing trend regarding crowd violence's central importance in American culture.

Still, there is a third reason for studying manifestations of crowd violence specifically in literature written by American authors during the first half of the twentieth century. The importance of crowds, mobs, and communal bodies has been overlooked in the Western world and especially in the United States because of a general championing of individuality over community and collectivity, and attempts to philosophize, historicize, and theorize crowd entities are often lacking. Gustave Le Bon's *The Crowd* (1896) and Elias Canetti's *Crowds and Power* (1960) are not only the most often cited treatments of crowd and mob behavior; in many cases, they are the *only* cited works that attempt to theorize crowd behavior. These theorists alone represent the importance of the study of crowd behavior and crowd violence as Le Bon, a social psychologist and sociologist, and Canetti, a multifaceted writer, demonstrate the important intersections between the fields of inquiry they worked in. Fittingly, the span between their crowd-related works covers both the Modernist era and a period of U.S. history full of lynchings and other forms of mob violence. Fiction written between these publications, especially in the United States, seems especially concerned, albeit often covertly or subconsciously, with the dynamics between individuals and crowds, and this writing, while often following a general pattern that shows the individual as subjected to oppression from crowd entities, also offers attempts to theorize crowd psychology and behavior in ways that have not been done, even in Le Bon's and Canetti's works.

Of course, any examination of Modernist literature should start with an attempt to define Modernism.[1] When I refer to Modernism and American Modernist works in this study, I am referencing the general artistic climate of the early 20th century, mainly in Europe and the United States, a time when a range of experimental trends, often inspired by Ezra Pound's dictate to "make it new," heavily influenced Western literature. Writers and thinkers from this period predominantly rejected Enlightenment thinking and instead championed the production of art through aesthetic values that likewise directly challenged Enlightenment notions of reason and certainty. In order to represent an unreasonable and uncertain world, Modernist writers, unlike the Romantics who rebelled against the same Enlightenment ideals the century before, tend to challenge their readers with experimental forms and the use of fragmentation, dislocation, indirection, juxtaposition, and multiple perspectives. Modernist-era U.S. fiction, typically fiction published between 1900 and 1950 when Modernist aesthetics received the most critical attention, unsurprisingly seems obsessed with literary portrayals of the interplay between crowd dynamics and individual identity, and literature, as many have theorized, is perhaps the best place to examine such cultural manifestations, providing a mix of historical and psychological analysis.

The Modernist focus on issues of identity has been discussed rather thoroughly by scholars in a variety of fields. Rather than rehashing these arguments, I will only add here that, given the already postulated connections between Modernist aesthetics and representations of individual identity, the Modernist period's explicit concerns with new formulations of subjectivity, Freudian psychological approaches, and the ever-increasing industrialization of the modern world all reflect a new focus on various concepts concerning individuality. This increased focus on identity and individuality makes the period's concurrent treatment of crowd dynamics and crowd violence especially fruitful. While a variety of definitions of identity exist in social science fields and especially in psychology, this study is greatly informed by Stephen Greenblatt's notion of identity self-fashioning, a concept referred to in the prologue to this book as part of my analysis of Mary Rowlandson's captivity narrative. For Greenblatt, self-fashioning represents an important process individuals undertake in order to fashion their identity in relation to others, and Greenblatt argues that this self-fashioning is an important aspect of personal freedom and autonomy. As Greenblatt asserts in no uncertain terms, "To abandon self-fashioning is to abandon the craving for freedom, and to let go of one's stubborn hold upon selfhood, even selfhood conceived as a fiction, is to die" (*Renaissance Self-*

Fashioning 257). Although Greenblatt clearly refers here to a kind of spiritual death, as we often see in American literature and especially American literature produced during the Modernist era, crowd forces, in an attempt to control and define an individual's identity, often physically maim and even kill individuals who insist on self-fashioning an identity independent from the group and the socially constructed normative behaviors that crowds and groups often impose. In reference to the English Renaissance, Greenblatt argues that "fashioning oneself and being fashioned by cultural institutions—family, religion, state—were inseparably intertwined" (*Renaissance Self-Fashioning* 256); during the American Modernist era, attempts to self-fashion identity and crowd attempts to fashion the identities of individuals often lead to crowd violence and an unraveling, rather than an intertwining, of individual identity. As Greenblatt describes this conflict, "Self-fashioning occurs at the point of encounter between an authority and an alien, that what is produced in this encounter partakes of both the authority and the alien that is marked for attack, and hence that any achieved identity always contains within itself the signs of its own subversion or loss" (*Renaissance Self-Fashioning* 9). In Modernist American literature, this authority is often a crowd whose authority comes solely from sheer physical dominance.

Greenblatt's historicist ideas have also had an important influence on this study. The struggle to self-fashion an identity separate from crowd forces is a conflict that holds specific historical and cultural significance, and literary texts serve as important areas of study in attempts to understand this conflict. This is especially true in the case of crowd violence, a topic that has received little theoretical treatment outside of Le Bon and Canetti. Perhaps it is no coincidence that the two most thorough and commonly cited works attempting to theorize crowd behavior are Le Bon's 1896 work *The Crowd: A Study of the Popular Mind*, and Canetti's influential 1960 work *Crowds and Power*. The period between these publications covers the span of American Modernism, as well as a period of U.S. history that is full of various forms of crowd violence. Le Bon, a French psychologist and sociologist, focuses on crowd psychology, starting with the premise that when a number of "individuals are gathered together in a crowd for purposes of action, observation proves that, from the mere fact of their being assembled, there result certain new psychological characteristics" (*Crowd* 5). Le Bon's depiction of the crowd mind as separate from the individual mind is groundbreaking, offering a new way to theorize crowd behavior. His assertions that "the substitution of the unconscious action of crowds for the conscious activity of individuals is one of the principal characteristics of the present age" (*Crowd* 5) and that "the age we are about to enter will in truth be the era of crowds" (15) seem prophetic given the events that would occur in the years that followed his study. The fifty years after the initial publication of *The Crowd* would see two world wars, worldwide labor unrest, rampant industrial expansion, and, in the United States especially, an explosion of racially motivated mob violence.

Le Bon does not mention lynching or racially motivated crowd violence specifically, a fact that emphasizes lynching's place as an especially American aspect of the Modernist era. His explanations of the crowd mindset, however, can be helpful in understanding collective violent behavior, behavior that seems entirely inhumane and irrational. Le Bon argues that crowds "are always unconscious," and adds that "this very unconsciousness is perhaps one of the secrets of their strength" (*Crowd* 9). Because crowds, according to Le Bon, are "little adapted to reasoning," they are "quick to act" (*Crowd* 17) and likewise "only powerful for destruction" (*Crowd* 19). According to Le Bon, then, crowds act upon impulse, without conscious thought, and this fact alone makes them prone to violence.

Like several of the writers I discuss, especially John Steinbeck, Le Bon clearly sees the psychological processes of the crowd as completely distinct from the psychological processes of the individual, as individual responsibilities, beliefs, and sympathies are temporarily forgotten within the confines and contexts of the crowd. For Le Bon, any sense of individuality is lost within the crowd as individual notions transform into group actions:

> The sentiments and ideas of all the persons in the gathering take one and the same direction, and their conscious personality vanishes. A collective mind is formed, doubtless transitory, but presenting very clearly defined characteristics. The gathering has thus become what, in the absence of a better expression, I will call an organized crowd, or, if the term is considered preferable, a psychological crowd. It forms a single being, and is subjected to the *law of the mental unity of crowds* [*Crowd* 26].

Le Bon seems to absolve any action taken by individuals within a crowd, arguing that "the individual forming part of a psychological crowd ... is no longer conscious of his acts" (*Crowd* 35), becoming instead "an automaton who has ceased to be guided by his will" (*Crowd* 36). For Le Bon, the automatons assimilated into a crowd are unable to judge their own actions by normal standards, and are therefore absent "of all sense of responsibility" (*Crowd* 56). Le Bon theorizes that when freed from these normal responsibilities, "dictatorialness and intolerance are common to all categories of crowds" (*Crowd* 60), and thus "a crowd is always ready to revolt against a feeble, and to bow down servilely before a strong authority" (*Crowd* 61). This "revolt against a feeble" is seen throughout American Modernist fiction as crowds continually offer violence against any individual, even individuals whose only weakness is their difference. Importantly, especially when related to later arguments concerning crowds such as those posited by Canetti, Le Bon states that "the figurative imagination of crowds is very powerful, very active, and very susceptible of being keenly impressed" (*Crowd* 75), adding, "The usual motive of the crimes of crowds is a powerful suggestion, and the individuals who take part in such crimes are afterwards convinced that they have acted in obedience to duty, which is far from being the case with the ordinary criminal" (*Crowd* 183). In sum, Le Bon sees crowds as inherently unreasonable and irrational, subject to strong swings of emotion and behavior often based on figurative suggestion, and prone to acts of violence motivated by intolerance. It is, then, not surprising that Le Bon's notion of crowd psychology has been noted as having influenced Freud's notion of the instinctive individual unconscious, the id. Crowds, according to Le Bon, seem to operate on an unconscious level, often controlled by figurative suggestion. For Le Bon, an individual's assimilation into a crowd causes a transformation of identity, and likewise, individuals not a part of the crowd face challenges to their ability to self-fashion an identity independent from the pressures of the crowd.

Although Le Bon typically depicts crowds as violent or potentially violent, in Modernist-era fiction, some crowds are discussed as potentially positive social forces. Likewise, Le Bon states, "Without a doubt criminal crowds exist, but virtuous and heroic crowds, and crowds of many other kinds, are also to be met with" (*Crowd* 20). However, it is important to note that Le Bon's study of crowds, while certainly influential, is also greatly flawed. Written after the French Revolution, one of Le Bon's unstated goals is to show powerful individuals how the crowd mind works so that these powerful individuals might better control and manipulate crowds, and this intention becomes clearer in his 1913 work *The Psychology of Revolution*. Le Bon states in *The Crowd*, "A crowd is a servile flock that is incapable of ever doing without a master" (134), and adds, "The arousing of faith—whether religious, political, or social, whether in a work, in a person, or an idea—has always been the function of the great leaders of crowds" (135–36). *The Crowd* is both an examination of crowd psychology and a guidebook for political figures who might manipulate crowds to achieve or to maintain power. These features are more clearly seen in *The Psychology of Revolution*, wherein Le Bon argues that "the crowd represents an amorphous being which can do nothing, and will nothing, without a head to lead it. It will quickly exceed the impulse once received, but it never creates it" (24). When he states that "the laws of the psychology of crowds show us that the people never act without leaders, and that although it plays a considerable part in revolutions by following and exaggerating the impulses received, it never directs its own movements" (*Psychology of Revolution* 66), it becomes clear that Le Bon is interested in helping political leaders to better understand crowds in order to more easily manipulate them.

Le Bon's ultimate goal is thus political rather than scientific. Michael Tratner asserts, "Le Bon was clearly ambivalent about the crowd: it is violent, ferocious, primitive, but also spontaneous, heroic, and enthusiastic. The crowd becomes the ideal mobilizer of revolution, the vehicle of social change" (26).

Le Bon sees crowds as potential dangers, but also as political capital that can be used to carry out political objectives. J.S. McClelland adds that "the secret of Le Bon's success was to use science to frighten the public, and then to claim that what science could understand it could also control" (196). Hence, as McClelland, Tratner, and other observers have since noted, Le Bon's work, while highly influential and one of the few of its kind, is suspect, if not seriously flawed, given the author's apparent political motives. As McClelland surmises,

> Le Bon sets out to make the crowd as frightening as possible in order to peddle a particular kind of elitist ideology.... Crowd theory in Le Bon is used to offer a theory of history and an analysis of present troubles; crowd theory points to a group which is the cause of those troubles, identifies an elite which is threatened by them, and crowd theory makes predictions about the future by urging the elite to learn the lessons of crowd theory so that the devil does not have all the good tunes; the elite can use crowd theory to outwit the crowd by using the techniques of the crowd's own leaders in order to slip elite leaders into the crowd from the outside. The crowd can then be manipulated in the service of values and aspirations which, if left to itself, the crowd would undermine and eventually destroy [201].

The purpose of Le Bon's crowd theory seems to be to describe a powerful weapon to political leaders and inform these leaders how best to use the weapon.

Canetti's *Crowds and Power* is generally regarded as the most authoritative work on the topic of crowds and crowd psychology, and it lacks the flaws inherent in Le Bon's approach. Many of Canetti's conclusions are likewise present in the Modernist-era literature written years before. Canetti, the 1981 Nobel Prize winner for literature, identifies four basic traits of all crowds; he argues that the crowd always desires growth, that there is equality within the crowd, that crowds desire density, and that crowds need direction (29). Like Le Bon, Canetti defines crowds as collections of individuals usually formed quickly and spontaneously. Canetti asserts, "One important reason for the rapid growth of the baiting crowd is that there is no risk involved. There is no risk because the crowd have immense superiority on their side. The victim can do nothing to them" (49). Both Canetti and Le Bon see crowds as powerful and potentially dangerous entities, often formed to punish an individual or victim, and Canetti outlines two ways crowds inflict these punishments: "expulsion," wherein an "individual is marooned," made apart from the crowd, and "collective killing," where "the condemned man is taken out to a field and stoned. Everyone has a share in his death" (50). Canetti adds, "Once a baiting crowd has attained its victim it disintegrates rapidly" (52). Canetti realizes that crowds often behave violently because, as Le Bon has noted, a sense of personal responsibility has been lost within the structure of the group. Then, once a crowd achieves its purpose, the crowd breaks apart, its individual pieces again becoming individuals.

Collectively, Modernist-era fiction writers depict several different types of crowds, and Canetti also identifies different categories of crowds. Important within the economic and political climate of the Modernist era, Canetti discusses what he calls "prohibition crowds," a label he derives for crowds that work collectively by refusing, or prohibiting, certain actions, and Canetti adds, "In our time the best example of a negative, or prohibition, crowd is the *strike*" (56) Canetti also discusses "reversal crowds," noting that these crowds are formed in response to inequalities, as those who are treated unfairly seek reversal against those who have denied them certain rights or opportunities (58). Like Le Bon, Canetti argues that his contemporary era is an era of crowds, and like many Modernist-era writers such as Ernest Hemingway, Canetti refers to modern warfare, arguing that soldiers involved in warfare often act with a crowd mentality (68). As is the case with Modernist-era writers such as John Steinbeck, Canetti is also clearly interested in modern capitalism, industrialization, consumerism, and the effect of these forces on the formation of crowds, discussing strikes as prohibition crowds and arguing that "the psychology of seizing and incorporating, like that of eating in general, is still completely unexplored" (203). Canetti sees his contemporary world as an era of crowds due to economic forces, noting, "If there is now one faith, it is faith in production, the modern frenzy of increase; and all the peoples of the world are succumbing to it one after the other" (465). Coincidentally, such faith leads to the formation of masses since "the more goods we produce, the more consumers we need" (466).

Crowds are an especially important phenomenon to understand when considering conceptions of American democracy, and like Le Bon, Canetti discusses crowds as both creating equality within those who form the crowd, and creating oppression by rejecting and othering those who do not become, or are not allowed to become, part of the crowd. As J.S. McClelland observes, "Canetti wishes us to see the relationship between crowds and power as always being problematic, and his way of doing that is by making the crowd's first 'attribute' its equality. A crowd does not make a crowd until its members lose their 'burdens of distance,' differences of rank, status, and property" (296). Those who are not members of the crowd become outsiders, and the crowd's exclusion of these outsiders defines and enforces normative identities, usually through the crowd's exclusion of certain individuals based on categories such as race or social status.

Neil Smelser is an often overlooked crowd theorist whose conception of the crowd builds on the notions posited by Le Bon and Canetti. Two years after Canetti's *Crowds and Power* was published, Smelser, an American sociologist, published the *Theory of Collective Behavior*. Here, Smelser adds to Le Bon's and Canetti's theories regarding crowd psychology. Smelser argues that crowd actions usually take place at specific times in history, noting, "Although wild rumors, crazes, panics, riots, and revolutions are surprising, they occur with regularity. They cluster in time; they cluster in certain cultural areas; they occur with greater frequency among certain social groupings—the unemployed, the recent migrant, the adolescent" (1). Thus, the prevalence of crowds in Modernist-era America is an example of one such "cluster." Like Canetti, Smelser attempts to develop categories of collective behavior, describing "the aggressive (lynching, rioting, terrorizing), the escape (panic), the acquisitive (looting) and the expressive" (5). Smelser notes, "Some form of strain must be present if an episode of collective behavior is to occur. The more severe the strain, moreover, the more likely is such an episode to appear" (48). Furthermore, Smelser discusses mob behavior as reflecting "norm-oriented movement," which he defines as an attempt to "restore, protect, modify, or create norms in the name of a generalized belief" (270). Smelser consistently unites crowd action with the oppression of individuals and the creation and enforcement of normative behaviors.

Although few have attempted to theorize the ways crowds act and react, the masses have been commonly studied in reference to twentieth century politics. As Tratner observes, "In the first two decades of the twentieth century, a new phenomenon swept across politics: the masses," and as a consequence, "politicians became intensely interested in understanding how to speak to and influence the masses" (1). According to McClelland, "The compulsion to treat the ruled as a crowd and a mob began very early in the political thought of the West" (1). Le Bon, Canetti, Smelser, and others view the twentieth century as an era of crowds, at least during the first half of the century, yet much of Western thought, especially in the United States, seems to reflect a belief in the cult of individuality. This dedication to individualism and the common depiction of individuals as victims of crowd action perhaps explains the negative connotations usually assigned to crowds and crowd activity.

As is the case with mob violence and lynching, the celebration of individualism has specific cultural meanings in the United States. It is not at all surprising that many Modernist-era writers depict conflicts between individuals and mobs in their work. Clifford Geertz observes that "individualism, or the belief in 'the person as a bounded, unique, more or less integrated motivational and cognitive universe ... organized into a distinctive whole' is 'a rather peculiar idea within the context of the world's cultures'" (126). According to Joseph Urgo, "Despite overwhelming evidence to the contrary, beliefs in the integral, autonomous self persist as vestiges of a defunct ideological system" (xiii). The idea of individual identity is often considered fluid and contingent by theorists, at the same time as United States culture has insisted on Emersonian "Self-Reliance" and rugged individualism. United States culture, and the literature it has produced, often reflects these notions of the independent self.

Perhaps this belief in the myth of individuality has led to the general lack of critical and theoretical attention to crowds and mob behavior, but it is important to note that, while crowds, mobs and collective bodies have received little attention as such, many thinkers have analyzed the effects of collective bodies on individuals. According to Michel de Certeau in *The Practice of Everyday Life*, individuals are subjected to vast systems of power, and Certeau focuses on the "status of the individual" as it "diminishes in proportion to the technocratic expansion of these systems" (xxiv). Certeau creates an oppositional relationship between individuals and the groups that construct these systems to impose limitations on individuals, arguing that as the individual becomes "increasingly constrained, yet less and less concerned with these vast frameworks, the individual detaches himself from them without being able to escape them and can henceforth only try to outwit them, to pull tricks on them, to rediscover, within an electronicized and computerized megalopolis, the 'art' of the hunters and rural folk of earlier days" (xxiv). Certeau sees the relationship between crowds and individuals as antagonistic, while recognizing the individual's dependence on these systems in fostering a notion of individual identity.

Certeau's influential work on the individual's relationship to a variety of often unnoticed social structures put into place by groups of power holders is helpful and explanatory, while continuing a theoretical tradition that consistently places the individual and the crowd in opposition to one another, positing the individual as the oppressed victim of group behavior. Nevertheless, as Greenblatt has argued, "The agents of exchange may appear to be individuals (most often, an isolated artist is imagined in relation to a faceless, amorphous entity designated society or culture), but individuals are themselves the products of collective exchange" (*Shakespearean Negotiations* 12). Greenblatt does not discount the notion that opposition exists between individuals and groups such as the community, but observes that "the concrete individual exists only in relation to forces that pull against spontaneous singularity and that draw any given life, however peculiarly formed, toward communal norms" (*Shakespearean Negotiations* 75). An exterior crowd, community, mob, or other collective body defines individual identity. Individuals cannot perceive of themselves as such without consciously recognizing an exterior crowd of others, while a crowd, mob, community, or any other collective body cannot form, as Le Bon and Canetti have shown, without being made of individuals who simultaneously undertake a single action. As Geertz argues, "The hallmark of modern consciousness ... is its enormous multiplicity" (*Local Knowledge* 161). This multiplicity is in direct confrontation with notions of individuality and static, individualized identity.

Modernist-era U.S. fiction not only provides rare theorization of mob violence; it also displays this "modern consciousness" referred to by Geertz, especially the integral part crowds and the potential for violent confrontations between individuals and crowds play in modern existence. Therefore, it is also literature's value as both historical artifact and cultural reflection that greatly informs this study. Such an examination of literature must of course follow Greenblatt's dictate "to look less at the presumed center of the literary domain than at its borders, to try to track what can only be glimpsed, as it were, at the margins of the text" (*Shakespearean Negotiations* 4). Mobs, crowds, and crowd violence are often found at the margins of the texts I discuss in this book. Dominick LaCapra notes "that all forms of historiography might benefit from modes of critical reading premised on the conviction that documents are texts that supplement or rework 'reality' and not mere sources that divulge facts about 'reality'" (11). Synthesizing Greenblatt and LaCapra's notions acknowledges that history and literature are indeed inseparable, and that both are best studied in relation to one another. The texts discussed here are literature and historiography, attempts to both create and reflect. Reading Modernist American fiction can provide an understanding of the consistent presence of crowd violence in the era. LaCapra argues that the novel, more than any other literary form, can be helpful in creating historical understanding, stating, "In this sense, there is something suspect about an approach to history—and particularly to intellectual history—that does not address the novel both as an object of study and self-reflexively as a way of coming to terms with problems in modern history itself" (116). Ignored in other fields, crowds and crowd violence are continually active forces in Modernist U.S. fiction. LaCapra adds that the novel's "value is in its referential functions—the way it serves as a window on life or developments of the past. The historian's focus is, accordingly, on the content of the novel—its representation of social life, its characters, its themes, and so forth" (125). The novels analyzed in this study are, in many ways, the best tools we have for understanding crowds and crowd violence during this era.

Such historicist arguments regarding the value of literature as historical documentation have become commonplace in literary criticism, yet it is important to note, as Certeau does, that "a social situation changes at once the mode of work and the type of discourse" (*Writing of History* 65). Certeau adds that the relationship between history and literature can be further problematized or legitimized since "what we initially call history is nothing more than a narrative.... A received meaning is imposed, in a tautological organization expressive only of the present time" (287). The narrative history that Modernist fiction passes on is a narrative about crowd violence and the struggle between individuals and crowd forces, and this struggle is often played out in canonical literary texts. Further study of the Modernist novel's form, and this form's relation to power struggles between individuals and crowd forces, would be useful in understanding both the genre and manifestations of crowd violence in the Modernist era. It is also important to note, as Catherine Gallagher and Greenblatt do, that "the study of literature, therefore, allows us to extrapolate the unthought, the unfelt, from the tensions in the constraining structures of feeling" (64). For Gallagher and Greenblatt, "Poetry, in this account, is not the path to a transhistorical truth, whether psychoanalytic or deconstructive or purely formal, but the key to particular historically embedded social and psychoanalytic formations" (7). U.S. fiction of the Modernist era seems a fitting place to examine the psychology of crowd action because references to the struggle between the individual and the group in these works are often subtle and "embedded," to borrow from Greenblatt and Gallagher, deep within the literary work. Furthermore, as John Brannigan posits, "For new historicism and cultural materialism the object of study is not the text and its context, not literature and its history, but rather literature in history. This is to see literature as a constitutive and inseparable part of history in the making, and therefore rife with the creative forces, disruptions and contradictions of history" (3–4). The Modernist era is certainly rife with these forces, especially the contradictions and conflicts between crowds and individuals.

These notions regarding history and literature greatly inform this study, as does the connection between these historicist approaches to literature and identity formation outlined by Brannigan, who notes, "One of the central assumptions and arguments of new historicist analyses is that identities are fictions which are formulated and adapted through narratives and performances, and that they are formulated and adapted in response to and as a way of interacting with the prevailing historical conditions" (61). Literary criticism analyzing American Modernist fiction has generally overlooked the prevalence of crowd violence and links between crowd violence and identity formation. Canonical Modernist fiction writers such as William Faulkner, Ernest Hemingway, and John Steinbeck actively explore these oppositions in their work. Ultimately, these writers use the prevalence of crowd violence in their culture, especially the mob violence associated with racially motivated lynchings, to examine crowd psychology and the effect of mobs on individual race, gender, national, and class identity.

In many of the texts produced by these writers, it becomes apparent that Modernist authors commonly engaged with identity issues through crowd imagery, if not outright depictions of mob violence. Maria Su Wang notes, "Mob is a shortened version of *mobile*, belonging to the epithet *mobile vulgus*, which literally translates as 'excitable, fickle crowd'" (186). Wang further posits that "as the eighteenth century progresses, *mob* acquires a variety of meanings, including an assemblage of the rabble or a tumultuous crowd, an aggregation of persons regarded as not individually important, or a heterogeneous collection" (189). As commonly used, according to Wang, "*Mob* now signifies the common mass of people, particularly the uncultured or illiterate class" (189), and while many Modernist writers are often seen as members of a bourgeois social class unconcerned with the "uncultured," according to Michael Tratner, "Modernism was an effort to escape the limitations of nineteenth-century individualist conventions and write about distinctively 'collectivist' phenomena" (3). Tratner cites the experimental characteristics of Modernist aesthetics as best "understood as efforts by authors to disrupt their own conscious personalities (and the conscious personalities of their readers) in order to reveal and perhaps alter the socially structured mentality hidden inside each person's unconscious" (3). Therefore, Tratner asserts that "Modernism was an effort to write from and to the id, the mass unconscious" (47).

For Tratner and for myself, "Modernism was not, then, a rejection of mass culture, but rather an effort to produce a mass culture, perhaps for the first time, to produce a culture distinctive to the twentieth century, which Le Bon called 'The Era of the Crowd'" (2). Perhaps because he is dealing mainly with British Modernism, however, Tratner does not explore the correlation between Modernist aesthetics and crowd violence, a correlation most obvious in the United States, given the nation's history of racially motivated mob violence. America's history of mob violence as it relates to lynching is one of the few areas of crowd psychology that has received ample attention, and recent works by Jacqueline Goldsby and Amy Louise Wood are evidence of ongoing interest in the subject. The types of mob violence associated with lynching and found in Allen's *Without Sanctuary* have not, however, been explored through theories of crowd psychology. Rather, both Goldsby and Wood attempt to ascertain the broad cultural systems that allowed, and even encouraged, extralegal violence such as lynching. Goldsby sees "anti-black mob murders as a networked, systemic phenomenon indicative of trends in national culture" (5), and believes that "the 'cultural logic' of lynching enabled it to emerge and persist throughout the modern era because its violence 'fit' within broader, national cultural developments" (6). According to Goldsby, "Lynching functioned as a tool of domination meant to coerce (and not rough-handedly correct), to deny (and not merely restrict), and to subjugate (not only banish or dispatch) black people, depriving them of the political, economic, social, and cultural opportunities promised by emancipation" (18).

As I often point out in the following study, American lynch violence is only one, albeit probably the most prominent, aspect of crowd violence in the U.S. Wood explores the systemic nature of lynch violence, noting that "lynching stood at the center of a long tradition of American vigilantism" (3). Wood also adds that "lynching assumed this tremendous symbolic power precisely because it was extraordinary and, by its very nature, public and visually sensational" (1). It is perhaps the symbolic power of lynching that provides Modernist writers with the drive to portray various identity conflicts with the imagery of mob violence. Wood adds that lynchings "were often deliberately performative and ritualized" (2), and it is this aspect of lynch mobs that seems to break with Le Bon's notions regarding individuals within crowds as being passively and mindlessly influenced only by what Freud would later term the id. Wood argues that individuals within lynch mobs are attempting to celebrate a version of their own individuality:

> Unlike the dominant image of the modern spectator, the crowds at lynchings were by no means passive or disembodied voyeurs. They cheered, hooted, clapped, grabbed souvenirs, and, at times, participated. Nor was the spectacle completely dominated by visual sensation; lynching included not only the sight of black desecration but also other senses. Spectators heard the speeches of the mob, the shouts of the crowd, the confessions of the victim, and, most of all, his dying shrieks and cries. In cases where the victim was burned, to witness a lynching was also to smell it. And, in all instances, the feel and push of the crowd created the sense of belonging and commonality that sustained the violence. In this respect, spectators did not watch or consume a lynching as much as they *witnessed* it—that is, they beheld or experienced it with active engagement [11].

The individualized experience here described by Wood takes into account the possibility that, although each mob is made up of a collection of individuals, these individuals do not entirely lose their sense of being individuals, as Le Bon suggests. Members of the crowd witness the action through their own senses; their experience, and their logic, is not merely collective, but also highly individualized.

The general failure to recognize Modernist American authors' engagement, albeit often indirectly, with America's racial past, including anti-black lynch violence, is partially explained by Toni Morrison's influential discussion of what she terms the "Africanist presence" in *Playing in the Dark: Whiteness and the Literary Imagination*. Morrison posits that "knowledge holds that traditional, canonical U.S. literature is free of, uninformed, and unshaped by the four-hundred-year-old presence of, first, Africans and then African Americans in the United States" (4–5), and certainly authors such as Hemingway, Fitzgerald, and Steinbeck have been read as such traditional and canonical figures whose work is essentially uninfluenced by America's racial history. But as Morrison rightly asserts, "The contemplation of this black presence is central to any understanding of our national literature and should not be permitted to hover at the margins of the literary imagination" (5). This study is in many ways influenced by Morrison's argument that "Americans choose to talk about themselves through and within a sometimes allegorical, sometimes metaphorical, but always choked representation of an Africanist presence" (17). The following chapters explore depictions, both literal and figurative, of crowd violence and lynching in several works that have not been discussed in this regard. Interestingly, Morrison's discussion of the Africanist presence deals specifically with issues relating to power dynamics between groups and individuals, as well as this dynamic's effect on American identity. Morrison suggests that

> these concerns—autonomy, authority, newness and difference, absolute power—not only become the major themes and presumptions of American literature, but that each one is made possible by, shaped by, activated by a complex awareness and employment of a constituted Africanism. It was this Africanism, developed as rawness and savagery, that provided the staging ground and arena for the elaboration of the quintessential American identity [44].

Like Morrison, I am therefore convinced "that the metaphorical and metaphysical uses of race occupy definitive places in United States literature, in the 'national' character, and ought to be a major concern of the literary scholarship that tries to know it" (63). While I argue, for example, that Hemingway and Fitzgerald are most concerned with issues of masculinity and that Steinbeck is most concerned with social class issues, it is clear that these writers, and others examined in this study, evoke the Africanist presence through interrogations of crowd violence, through analyses of the dynamics between crowds and racial, gender, class, and national identities.

This book, which began as an attempt to understand the brutal nature of crowds at the height of racially motivated lynching violence in early twentieth-century America, is a book that also attempts to understand crowd behavior in general through an analysis of various forms of crowd violence in Modernist America as it is depicted in the fiction produced in the period. Theories regarding crowd behavior, especially the penchant of crowds towards violence, may be lacking, but American literature, especially Modernist fiction, is rife with such theorization, and further exploration of this trope in all literature may be helpful in developing a more in-depth and coherent understanding of crowds. The analysis of crowds provided by some of the most celebrated Modernist American texts shows that there is still much to learn regarding crowd behavior; still, Modernist literature teaches us a great deal about the dynamics of crowds, especially the interaction between crowds and individual, non-normative concepts of identity. Conversely, these texts help us to understand American culture and history, and add to the ever-changing portraits we have of the American Modernist literary landscape.

CHAPTER I

Lynch Mobs and Racial Identity in Modernist Fiction

Racially motivated mob violence is the most prominent form of crowd violence found in the era of American Modernism, and the connections between this particular form of crowd violence and identity self-fashioning are undeniable. The persistent presence of lynchings, the rituals repeated at lynching events, the usage of these tactics to define and control black identity, and the ways in which such events undermined notions of American progress are all incorporated into the depictions of this specific form of mob violence that can be found in Modernist American literature. James Weldon Johnson's *Autobiography of an Ex-Colored Man* and Richard Wright's *Uncle Tom's Children* are examples of influential, canonical works of African American literature that focus on this relationship between crowd violence and identity self-fashioning, and these works provide important literary and historical documentation of these aspects of Modernist-era American society. Richard Kostelanetz has argued that "of all native writers, African American novelists in particular have frequently used fiction as an instrument for treating the historical experiences of their race" (3), and Johnson's and Wright's novels are examples of documents that portray not only the historical prevalence of crowd violence and the ever-present threat many African Americans faced, but the systematic and ritualized violence often performed at lynchings in an attempt to force African Americans to adopt certain identities.

Craig Werner has observed that "the central problem confronted by Afro-American culture closely resembles that confronted by mainstream modernism," adding that topics of Modernist concern such as "fragmentation, alienation, and sense-making" are often explored by African American authors (121). James Weldon Johnson explores these Modernist themes as they relate to crowd violence, identity self-fashioning, and the correlation between the two in his fictional *Autobiography of an Ex-Colored Man*. The novel can therefore be read not only as an important portrayal of racial passing, but also as a text that adheres to a Modernist focus on the relationship between crowd violence and identity self-fashioning. Likewise, in *Uncle Tom's Children*, especially in the first individual story entitled "Big Boy Leaves Home," Wright shows the unrelenting threat of crowd violence facing African Americans during the Modernist era, and his repeated accounts of such crowd violence are shown influencing the self-fashioning of identity by his characters.

The topic of lynching plays a central part in Johnson's intellectual career, perhaps more so than any other Modernist writer. Prior to writing *Autobiography of an Ex-Colored Man* (first published in 1912) and serving with the NAACP, which he began doing in 1916, Johnson had several personal experiences with racially motivated crowd violence. Yet even before these personal confrontations, Johnson and other African Americans of the period surely grew up hearing and reading stories of crowd violence like the following:

> I remembered that one morning in the boys' reading room at the university I had seen in the *Atlanta Constitution* that a party of Negro preachers going to a convention somewhere in Georgia, and traveling in the first-class car, had been met by a mob at one of the stations along the line and forcibly ejected. Out on the station platform one of the mob, it was reported, said, "Niggers, dance us a jig." When the preachers protested that that would not be in keeping with their Christian practices and their dignity, this member of the mob started firing into the floor close to the preachers' feet, and they, naturally, began picking their feet up. The whole mob followed this lead, and kept the party of preachers doing a sort of Hopi Indian dance until some of them were exhausted [85].

This account follows a pattern that can be seen in accounts of more violent and lethal racially motivated crowd violence, as black Americans are attacked and dehumanized by a racist mob intent on defining their identities as subhuman. Stories such as this, and other more violent accounts of crowd violence against blacks, were everyday occurrences in Johnson's America, and Johnson importantly uses the word "mob" here to call attention to a threatening confrontation between an individual and a violent group. Race riots, which often began with mob violence, were also common events during Johnson's life, and he personally witnessed a couple of these events. A race riot occurred in New York on August 15, 1900, while Johnson was there, and he relates in *Along This Way* that even though he had no involvement with the alleged crime that started the riot, or with the accused person at the center of the conflict, Johnson was warned by police that a "mob" was "attacking Negroes wherever they were found, and that it was not safe for any colored person to go through that section" (157). In such instances, Johnson's racial identity makes him, for no other reason, prey for a violent crowd. Robert E. Fleming notes that "Barry Carter, a friend of the Johnsons who was caught out on the street" during this same riot, "was beaten first by a white mob and later by the police officers to whom he fled for help" (100).

Johnson further relates in *Along This Way* that he was once captured by a violent mob after he had been seen meeting with a fellow writer, a white woman, in Jacksonville, Florida. Johnson is witnessed meeting with the woman and suspected of inappropriate behavior with her, and he describes the mob that apprehends him as they "rushed to the city with a maddening tale of a Negro and white woman meeting in the woods; there is no civil authority; the military have sent out a detachment of troops with guns and dogs to get me" (167). Johnson is lucky in this particular circumstance since, rather than being lynched immediately and without question (as was often the case in such matters), he is apprehended and brought before military leaders with whom he is previously acquainted and allowed to clear his name. However, the threat of lynching is still clear, and plays an important role in his understanding of identity.

Although Johnson biographer Eugene Levy argues that Johnson "grew up insulated from much of the racism, whether in the form of intolerance or outright discrimination," that other African Americans would be confronted with (19), it is clear in Johnson's writing, and in his work with the NAACP and the Dyer Anti-Lynching law, that the issue of lynching was of the utmost importance to him. It is also important to note that even if Johnson was more "insulated" from racism and racially motivated violence than some of his contemporaries, he still had several harrowing encounters with such violence, showing that no African American was immune from this prevalent threat during the era. As Jacqueline Goldsby observes, "When one considers the whole of Johnson's literary *oeuvre*, the most striking feature about those works is how frequently lynching occurs, almost as if Johnson could not write without depicting or at least mentioning this violence" (167). Johnson's fictional *Autobiography of an Ex-Colored Man* is centrally concerned with racial passing and identity, and as is so common in Modernist fiction, the ex-colored man's identity is forced upon him through a scene of mob violence, in this case an actual lynching. Johnson's novel is thus an instance of Modernist American writers' correlating crowd violence and identity fashioning.

My own reading of the novel focuses mainly on the lynching scene witnessed by the ex-colored man, a scene that forces him to self-fashion a white racial identity and simultaneously suppress his mixed-race lineage, and numerous critics have stressed the importance of identity in Johnson's novel. Martin Japtok has argued that "the question of identity" is "one of the central problems of the novel" (32), and Levy identifies "the development of a positive racial identity among blacks" as a "major theme" in *The Autobiography* (137), adding that "the traumatic discovery of his racial identity serves as the keystone of the narrative" (132). Kostelanetz seems to agree with Levy, noting that "the novel's theme is the many ambiguities of passing—moral, political, emotional; and its predominant action is the nameless narrator's shifting sympathies for white or black identity" (20). According to Fleming, the ex-colored man "never succeeds in his attempts to find his identity within the race to which the country's laws and customs consign him" (36). Valerie Smith, citing examples of the ex-colored man's silences, discusses the ways that the ex-colored man "avoids engaging with the meaning of his racial identity" (93). From these examples, it is clear that I am not the first to note the importance of identity in this novel. However, as I argue throughout this book, it is this coupling of issues of identity with depictions of crowd violence that is characteristic of Modernist American literature.

Along with matters of identity, the formal role of the narrator in *Autobiography of an Ex-Colored Man* is the most often discussed literary device of the novel, and close analysis of the role of this narrator further shows Johnson's explicit concern with identity in the novel. Johnson chooses to publish the novel with the appearance of a true-to-life autobiography, and this formal technique allows him to present the events as reality rather than fiction. His novel focuses on racial passing, while at the same time, his novel attempts to pass as a factual autobiography. The racial issues considered by the novel are not fiction, as Johnson stresses, but rather matters of everyday African American life. Johnson's invented first-person narrator further allows him to step out of the identity assigned to him as a black citizen by white normative society, and to speak out on racial matters, even depicting whites negatively in his critique of race relations. Johnson's narrator reports that blacks in the United States are forced to form their identities "not from the viewpoint of a citizen, or a man, nor even a human being, but from the viewpoint of a *colored* man" (9). Thus, identity *self*-fashioning, Johnson asserts, is often denied to African American citizens—white racists typically try to invent and force black Americans to adopt certain, often dehumanizing and stigmatizing racial identities. Because of this complication to black identity self-fashioning, Johnson's narrator notes, "It is a difficult thing for a white man to learn what a colored man really thinks" (9). This, Johnson seems to argue, is partly explained by the fact that some whites of the period were obsessed with defining what African Americans thought, without actually wanting to hear truthful explanations from African Americans themselves. Again, Johnson's narrator helps clear up this disconnect, speaking freely and directly for an audience both white and black. As Levy argues, "The effectiveness of the first-person narrative derives largely from the lack of personal communication between the races" (129). Johnson's choice of narrator in the *Autobiography* allows him, through his fictional narrator, to speak openly on matters of race without risking the real-life punishment awaiting blacks who offend whites. Johnson's choice of narration is therefore an authorial choice to transcend the identity white society might assign and enforce, and attempt to self-fashion a unique individual identity. However, Johnson shows that such attempts to self-fashion individual identity within the black community are often undermined by racially motivated crowd violence.

Johnson's narrator's mixed-race parentage further allows him to self-fashion a unique identity that can simultaneously operate within both black and white communities. As the son of a black mother and white father, the ex-colored man's skin color causes all facets of racial identity to be questioned. As John Sheehy argues, "The creation of such an identity, with all its ambiguity, is crucial in allowing the ex-colored man to work through the complexities of the dialogue of race in America" while also allowing "the recognition of what even the most fundamental received notions of identity design to repress" (408). This kind of narrator also satisfies white curiosity regarding black identity, as noted by Levy, who points out that "for whites, reading a black man's autobiography often served as a kind of vicarious substitute for personal contact with blacks" (130). Johnson's racially-mixed, well-educated, intelligent, musically talented, and physically attractive narrator represents a new kind of identity for individuals with black blood, while also questioning Jim Crow and *Plessy v. Ferguson* political policies regarding legally defined racial categories. Likewise, as Michaels asserts, the possibility of racial passing undermines categories of racial identity altogether:

> The very idea of passing—whether it takes the form of looking like you belong to a different race or of acting like you belong to a different race—requires an understanding of race as something separate from the way you look and the way you act. If race really were nothing but culture, that is, if race really were nothing but a distinctive array of beliefs and practices, then, of course, there could be no passing [133].

Johnson's ex-colored man is symbolic of these kinds of racial questions and the absurdity of early twentieth century conceptions of race and racial purity. Johnson's novel is most concerned with challenging common conceptions and perceptions of racial identity, asking fundamental questions about what it means to be white or black, and questioning notions of difference between the two.

Importantly, as Kathleen Pfeiffer has noted, the ex-colored man's lack of a proper name signals Johnson's focus on identity in the novel.[1] The narrator's lack of a proper name only adds to the novel's concern with identity—without this name, the narrator's identity must always be questioned. This namelessness also highlights the novel's claims to realism and authenticity. It is unlikely that any African American would make the statements that Johnson's narrator makes in the novel without the protection of anonymity, especially if he had been passing as a white man and were married to a white woman, as Johnson's ex-colored man is at the end of the novel. By using an anonymous narrator,

Johnson has added to the authenticity of his text. In other words, Johnson's choice of narrative style forces readers to consider the truth of his narrative, depicting the connection between crowd violence and identity self-fashioning, for example, as a real-life, not a merely symbolic, relationship.

Many critics agree that identity is a central theme of the novel, and many also identify the lynching scene witnessed by the ex-colored man late in the novel as the turning point in his quest to understand his own identity, essentially forcing the ex-colored man to forsake his black heritage and self-fashion the identity of a white man in order to avoid racially motivated mob violence. Indeed, the ex-colored man appears to be obsessed with classification, comparison, and identification, mirroring the white social tendencies his novel is in part satirizing. In the course of his narration, the narrator attempts to classify and identify different groups of black southerners; later, he outlines the different ways that gamblers behave when they lose, and during the narrator's travels in Europe, he provides lengthy comparisons between major European cities such as Paris and London. His narration is replete with comparisons between the white and black world, and his narrative constantly describes characters, such as the ex-colored man himself, who cross back and forth between white and black communities.

This obsession with these classifications and comparisons likely stems from the narrator's own struggle to understand his own racial identity. From an early age, the narrator's racial identity has been problematic for him. He considers himself white, for example, until his school principal comes to his class one day and asks "all of the white scholars to stand for a moment," and when the narrator stands, the teacher tells him to "sit down for the present, and rise with the others" (7). The narrator is shocked by this socially constructed racial revelation, and upon leaving school that day, the white kids call him "a nigger too" and the black children state that they "knew he was colored" (7). This revelation eventually causes the ex-colored man to self-fashion a black identity, allowing white normative social constructions to influence his understanding of his own identity. Likewise, he decides to work as a scholar and musician in order to contribute to a black community that he identifies as his own. However, the lynching scene near the end of the novel becomes the deciding factor in the ex-colored man's ultimate decision to self-fashion a white identity; my intent is not merely to claim the lynching scene's importance, which has been done aptly already by others, but to show how the specific events narrated in the lynching scene are examples of the ways that identity self-fashioning and crowd violence would become interconnected, not only in Johnson's narrative, but in numerous novels written by Modernist American writers.

Near the end of Johnson's novel, the ex-colored man, after attending a Negro spiritual in the South, returns to his room for the night, only to be awakened by "the gallop of a horse, then of another and another" as a crowd forms in reaction to "the rumor that some terrible crime had been committed, murder! rape!" by a black offender (87). As was often the case at this time, rumors of the crime travel by word of mouth, and whether or not the alleged crime actually involves a rape, the rape charge becomes part of the allegation, causing outrage in the white community that justifies the community's resorting to mob violence. As has been previously shown, claims of murder and rape as the reasons for lynching were often unfounded; more likely, a member of the African American community has merely offended a white person.

The ex-colored man feels safe rushing out to witness the lynching because of his ambiguous racial identity, knowing that his "identity as a colored man had not yet become known in the town" (87). Outside, the ex-colored man finds "a crowd of men, all white," "all of them armed," "fierce," and "determined" (87). These men break into bands to hunt for the suspected offender, and once the accused is found, a lynching scene occurs that hauntingly echoes the scenes described in numerous nonfictional accounts of lynchings:

> A space was quickly cleared in the crowd, and a rope placed about his neck; when from somewhere came the suggestion, "Burn him!" It ran like an electric current.... A railroad tie was sunk into the ground, the rope was removed and a chain brought and securely coiled around the victim and the stake.... Fuel was brought from everywhere, oil, the torch; the flame crouched for an instant as though to gather strength, then leaped up as high as the victim's head. He squirmed, he writhed, he strained at his chains, then gave out cries and groans that I shall always hear. The cries and groans were choked off by the fire and smoke; but his eyes were bulging from their sockets, rolled from side to side, appealing in vain for help. Some of the crowd yelled and cheered, others seemed appalled at what they had done, and there were those who turned away sickened at the sight.... Before I could make myself believe that what I saw was really happening, I was looking at a scorched post, a smoldering fire, blackened bones, charred fragments sifting through coils of chain, and the smell of burnt flesh—human flesh—was in my nostrils [88].

The ex-colored man's detailed account displays many of the recurring themes found in accounts of lynchings, such as those describing the real-life lynching of Sam Hose. Johnson's description is also highly symbolic, highlighting the novel's focus on identity. The victim is not merely hung by a rope, but is also burned in order to mutilate and eradicate his black identity. As Canetti notes in regards to those who participate in lynchings, "The brutalities they permit themselves may be explained by the fact that they cannot *eat* the man" (117). The mob desires the erasure of the victim's identity, and as Canetti recognizes, a similar trope emerges in many early American captivity narratives, where cannibalism and this identity erasure are often connected. Furthermore, the crowd cheers as the victim writhes in pain, celebrating the message that is being sent concerning the kind of identity the community desires its black members to adopt, while also demonstrating the punishment awaiting those who do not conform to this identity. Conversely, the lynched man's voice is wiped out as he tries to scream in pain, his eyes bulging in recognition. Chains are mentioned in the passage, a clear reference to slavery and a reference to the subservient, second-class status that is central to the black identity that lynching supporters look to force black citizens to adopt. This imposed identity becomes, via metaphor, the confining chains of a new kind of slavery. In the end, the charred remains provide the crowd with souvenirs, small symbols of the identity they wish to enforce, symbols that they can now control by holding them in their hands, symbols that can likewise be shown to others, passed on as warnings to blacks and affirmation for racist whites. The prowess of the supposed rapist becomes something controlled and co-opted by the lynching community.

The scene leaves the ex-colored man with a clear answer to the identity crisis that he has struggled with throughout the novel, a crisis that surely affected many racially mixed individuals who considered passing because of their light skin color, or who merely passed by adopting a racial identity forced upon them by the white Southern hierarchy. The ex-colored man leaves town immediately, finally making up his mind to "neither disclaim the black race nor claim the white race; but that I would change my name, raise a mustache, and let the world take me for what it would," knowing from his past experience that doing so would allow him to be identified as white (90). He chooses to pass as white out of "unbearable shame": "Shame at being identified with a people that could with impunity be treated worse than animals. For certainly the law would restrain and punish the malicious burning of animals" (90). Johnson here alludes to the misconception, popular during the Modernist era, that aligned black racial identity with the animal world; the ex-colored man knows that self-fashioning a black identity is accepting an identity that normative white society has identified as animalistic, something less than human. He recognizes that failing to fashion and maintain an identity preferred by whites could lead to punishment through crowd violence, violence used by racist whites to further animalize and annihilate black citizens. Canetti also observes this animalizing quality of lynching violence, noting that the victim "differs in looks and behavior from his murderers, and the cleavage these feel or imagine between themselves and him makes it easier to treat him like an animal" (117). As Smith argues, the lynching scene shows the ex-colored man "the extent of black oppression. While formerly he had tried to avoid seeing and identifying himself with both the victims and the perpetrators of such acts of injustice, on this occasion he cannot escape" (99). The ex-colored man's identity, or at least the identity he must adopt in order to survive, is thus settled, and as Goldsby argues, the "decision to pass for white is not made in order to escape that fate, but to historicize the violence" (167). Johnson's novel does not try to convince mixed-race individuals to pass for white or to self-fashion a white identity simply to avoid violence; his purpose is to explore racial identity in an authentic manner, to show that attempts to define racial identity, no matter how violent, do not make these social constructs any more real. Like the reports on lynching violence Johnson authored for the NAACP, Johnson's novel is a report on racial identity and crowd violence in American society.

Johnson's views on lynching and the connection between lynching and identity are clear in the *Autobiography*, but his later work with the NAACP as an activist against lynching also shows his concern for autonomous black identity self-fashioning in the face of threatening mob violence. Furthermore, Johnson's arguments against lynching often involved direct attacks on American notions of progress. Many of Johnson's most effective arguments against lynching invoked the crime's uniqueness to America at the time, and the notion that any country that allowed such lynchings to take place could not be a civilized one. Johnson claimed "lynching and mob violence has got to go or civilization in the United States cannot survive" (*Selected Writings* 2: 44). Johnson often noted that the tolerance of lynching and mob violence devalued America's legal system, arguing that the existence of such violence would "undermine all law and order in our land" (*Selected Writings* 2: 35). Johnson connected these lynchings to crowd violence reported in other areas of the world. The United States would not tolerate this violence in its international relations, and Johnson argues that "if the stories which we hear about mob violence in Russia are true, it is also true that the violence is being directed against those who are considered to be conspiring or acting against the authority of the existing government; but in Washington and Chicago the mobs beat and killed loyal and unoffending American citizens" (*Selected Writings* 1: 237). Johnson clearly saw lynching as a major opposition to American social progress.

Johnson's work with the NAACP against lynching would result in collaboration with Missouri Republican Representative L.C. Dyer on what would be called the Dyer Anti-Lynching Bill, a bill that passed in the U.S. House of Representatives in 1922, only to be defeated in the Senate. In support of the bill, Johnson and others argued "the only effective machinery for stamping out lynching in the United States must be provided by fearless and strict enforcement of an adequate anti-lynching law" (*Selected Writings* 2: 76). The bill called for action in making lynching a federal crime, and in support of the bill, Johnson again pointed out that lynching was thwarting American progress. Part of the reasoning behind the call for harsh punishments for those involved in mob violence involved Johnson's view that lynching was an attempt to overthrow American government:

> The supporters of the bill maintain that lynching is not simple murder, but a conspiracy by the mob that effectually substitutes the anarchy of mob action and mob justice for court trial and due process of law. It is a temporary overthrow of the State. The States are able to deal more or less adequately with simple murder, but are powerless against mob murder [*Selected Writings* 2: 77].

Logically, Johnson and supporters of the bill tried to play upon the general American notion of progress by arguing that lynching was actually impeding this progress, thus hurting *all* Americans, not just African Americans.

After passing in the House of Representatives, the bill would eventually fail, with those opposed to it able to recast the issue of the bill as a matter regarding states' rights. Upon its failure, Johnson would again speak out against lynching by arguing that the existence of the practice severely damages American progress:

> Alone of civilized countries, it permits mob law, lynching and public burning of human beings at the stake. The state and local governments confess themselves helpless to stop this. A bill is presented in the national Congress to prevent lynching by national law. It was not a perfect bill, but it was an attempt, and a sincere attempt to get at crime; the least that a nation of civilized human beings could do was to discuss that bill, to improve it, to remove its weaknesses and to strengthen its deficiencies. On the contrary, the Senate of the United States was not even allowed to discuss it. Can one call this our failure? Quite the contrary. It is the failure and the disgrace of the white people of the United States [*Selected Writings* 2: 41].

While a failure in the legal sense, Johnson's fight to pass legislation against lynching and his depictions of the relationship between identity and lynching in the *Autobiography of an Ex-Colored Man* helped keep these topics alive for debate in American culture, and several Modernist-era American fiction writers would follow Johnson's lead concerning the representations of lynching and identity in their works. Richard Wright, for example, furthered the connection between lynching and identity. Lynchings began to occur less frequently after 1930, the period when Wright's fiction was composed, but Wright's works show that other forms of racial violence were taking place against blacks and, often symbolically, Wright links this racial violence to crowd violence, specifically lynching. In Wright's fiction, lynchings are not always the overtly violent acts they are shown to be in *Autobiography of an Ex-Colored Man*; rather, Wright's fiction shows that systems for the punishment of African Americans have, in the North and throughout the country in general, progressed from the overt brutality of public lynchings to covert and systematic economic, court, and government supported capital violence. This systematic racial violence, as shown by Wright in his most famous novel, *Native Son*, shares obvious similarities with lynching, especially in its focus on defining and enforcing identity, and is discussed in the following chapter.

Wright's earliest work, *Uncle Tom's Children*, deals with lynching in an overt manner similar to Johnson's *Autobiography of an Ex-Colored Man*. Given the nature of Wright's early life, it is not surprising that his fiction is full of depictions of violence, violence that usually involves some kind of racial element. As Houston Baker, Jr., describes in his article "Racial Wisdom and Richard Wright's *Native Son*," Wright's early life was full of violence:

> Hunger, fear, a father who deserted the family, the violence of whites who killed one of his uncles in order to take over his property, the malignity of a sporting "professor" who was courting his aunt and who murdered a white woman with whom he was having an affair and burned the house that contained her lifeless body—there were but a few of the grim elements of Wright's early life.... Violence was omnipresent: there were beatings by whites, black women raped, black men ("bad niggers") fighting back, some of them castrated and lynched. Squalor, fanaticism, and fear characterized the decaying black tenements of southern cities [67].

The presence of such violence in Wright's early life is important to consider, as it in some ways mimics the violence found in his fiction. In addition, it shows the racial violence Wright was surrounded by, racial violence that coincides with the height of American lynch violence. *Uncle Tom's Children* is a collection of short works that are unified into a novel by thematic representations of mob violence, much like William Faulkner's later *Go Down, Moses*, which would appear four years after *Uncle Tom's Children* in 1942.

Uncle Tom's Children is comprised of five short stories, all of which follow Wright's essay "The Ethics of Living Jim Crow," an account of Wright's childhood experiences with racial inequality. Here, Wright begins to outline the various ways that African Americans are often denied the ability to self-fashion their identity, as violent pressure from white racists forces black citizens to adopt certain subservient, second-class identities. Wright describes several events from his life that show the various ways in which, as a black citizen, he was unable to self-fashion his own identity free of the influence of white racism. He opens the essay by describing his life in a segregated neighborhood, where he and his fellow black children have playful wars that include throwing pieces of cinder at each other. One day, when Wright and his companions engage white children in a similar battle, Wright learns that white retaliation for perceived black crimes will always be more violent than the crime itself. The white children, having the advantage of hiding behind "trees, hedges, and the sloping embankments of their lawns," are able to defeat the black children in a barrage that contains glass bottles (225). As Wright explains, he felt the grave injustice of the moment since "it was all right to throw cinders" (225) because "the greatest harm a cinder could do was leave a bruise. But broken bottles were dangerous; they left you cut, bleeding, and helpless" (226). The white children had the additional advantage of the natural cover their neighborhood provided, whereas Wright's black neighborhood contains no such landscaping to hide behind.

When Wright's mother gets home and finds him injured from being hit by one of the white children's bottles, he does not receive the sympathy he was expecting. Instead, his mother tells him that he should "never, never, under any conditions ... fight *white* folks again" (226). Wright learns to internalize this disproportionate approach to justice from this incident, and goes on to explain similar lessons that he learned, often violently, regarding racial inequality. When he tries to receive extra training at his first job in order to achieve a promised promotion, his coworker and supervisor Morrie responds by stating, "Nigger, you think you're *white*, don't you?" (228). At the same job, Wright is later beat up by Morrie and another white coworker for failing to address one of them as "Mister," and Wright states that "they told me that I must never again attempt to exceed my boundaries" (230). These violent encounters with whites continue to enforce an identity upon Wright and other blacks like him, at the same time denying him the ability to self-fashion an identity for himself. Wright is shown attempting to identify himself as an upwardly mobile, hard working man, but the whites around him deny him this identity and impose a different identity upon him.

As Wright notes, his "Jim Crow education" continued at later jobs (230). While working at a clothing store, he witnesses a black woman being beaten. Like lynch violence, this beating serves as a warning to black citizens, as the two men who beat the woman tell Wright "that's what we do to niggers when they don't pay their bills" (230). Wright tells a fellow porter about the event, and the porter responds, "Hell, it's a wonder they didn't lay her when they got through" (231). Sexual violence, always punished severely when an alleged black criminal is involved, is expected of white men in their punishments of black women. Wright goes on to work at a hotel that is often frequented by white prostitutes and their clients, and here white society further fashions and defines his identity, defining him, and all black males, as sexual predators. Wright notes that "one of the bell-boys was caught in bed with a white prostitute. He was castrated and run out of town" (234). Wright later witnesses a naked white prostitute, and the white man she is with tells him to "keep your eyes where they belong, if you want to be healthy" (233). In these ways, Wright's identity, and all black identity, is fashioned by a normative white society. Wright learns that his identity is shameful; "you were not regarded as human" (233). His skin alone "makes him easily recognizable, makes him suspect, converts him into a defenseless target" (232). With these cruelties surrounding him, Wright relates that he "learned to play that dual role which every Negro must play if he wants to eat and live" (235). Wright, while able to recognize the brutal inequalities he faces, must adopt a second-class identity in order to survive in a culture controlled by white interests and enforced by racially motivated crowd violence.

Wright ends "The Ethics of Living Jim Crow" by pointing out the importance of crowd violence in keeping such inequalities in place. Wright supposes that some whites might ask "how do Negroes feel about the way they have to live?" (236), and he answers this question by providing a quotation from one of his black friends: "Lawd, man! Ef it wuzn't fer them polices 'n' them ol' lynch-mobs, there wouldn't be nothin' but uproar down here!" (237). Here, Wright connects this second-class, subservient identity fashioned by white racists and imposed upon African Americans with the threat of crowd violence, and this conclusion to "The Ethics of Living Jim Crow" transitions the reader into the fictional stories that Wright provides in *Uncle Tom's Children*. Like Johnson in *The Autobiography of an Ex-Colored Man*, Wright attempts to provide necessary authenticity to the work of fiction he is about to provide, framing his narrative with the autobiographical "The Ethics of Living Jim Crow." The stories that follow in *Uncle Tom's Children* seem to belong to the same world that Wright has just described in his own autobiographical essay.

Each of the five stories that appear after Wright's essay in *Uncle Tom's Children* contain crowd violence against black characters. In "Big Boy Leaves Home," Big Boy sees his friend Bobo lynched after Big Boy and Bobo, along with two other young black boys, accidentally frighten a white woman near a swimming hole. "Down by the Riverside" is an account of a giant flood that forces the protagonist, a farmer named Mann, to steal a boat to save his family, a family that includes his pregnant wife; the narrative eventually leads to the arrest and shooting of Mann, who has killed a white man that threatened him earlier in the story. In "Long Black Song," a man named Silas kills a white man who has forcibly slept with his wife, causing a white mob to appear at his house and kill him. The next story, "Fire and Cloud," manages a somewhat hopeful ending, as the preacher Taylor, an African American community organizer of sorts, is able to organize his own mob and march through the white controlled community demanding economic aid for his people. Before the march, however, Taylor is captured and badly beaten by a group of white officials hoping to intimidate the preacher and keep the demonstration from happening. The final story, "Bright and Morning Star,"[2] eradicates the hopefulness found in "Fire and Cloud," as a mother and her son are tortured and killed because the son has been involved in Communist activities. *Uncle Tom's Children*, like Faulkner's *Go Down, Moses*, is thus a collection of short stories that can be called a novel because of the stories' shared thematic focus on racial violence, especially mobs and lynching. Like Faulkner and Johnson, Wright's work is full of literal representations of mob violence and its use in enforcing compulsory identity.

In *Uncle Tom's Children*, the best example of this focus on mob violence as a tool for controlling African American identity is found in the story "Big Boy Leaves Home." Big Boy and his adolescent friends, out playing one day, decide to go for a swim in a nearby creek owned by a white man named Harvey who has apparently forbid any blacks from swimming on his property. The boys are aware that by going there, they face violent punishment for transgressing against this white man's rule; when Big Boy first hears of the idea of swimming there, he responds, "N git *lynched*? Hell naw!" (242). Big Boy seems to be the physical leader of the group, and at one point, his friends gang up on him in a wrestling match. Outnumbered three to one, Big Boy wins the match because he is able to get his friend Bobo in a chokehold, forcing Bobo's wrestling partners to submit in order to save him. Big Boy offers them advice in the wake of his victory, telling them that "when a ganga guys jump on yuh, all yuh gotta do is just put that heat on one of them n make im tell the others t let up" (245). The boys fear the white man's swimming hole because of the threat of lynching violence, and from Big Boy's remarks, it is clear that these boys have had to grow up considering what they might need to do to survive crowd violence.

Big Boy is eventually convinced to join his three friends for a swim, and the boys remove their clothing, dive in the water, and begin to splash around. Their playful dialogues and wrestling matches highlight their youthful innocence, but the story takes a serious turn when a white woman appears on the banks and is startled by the sight of the naked boys. The boys seem equally frightened, and as the woman cowers unknowingly near their clothes on the bank, she screams in fear of attack when the boys approach her, attempting only to procure their clothing and escape the scene. The woman screams in fear, and her screams bring to the river her armed companion Jim, who shoots two of the boys before Big Boy wrestles the gun away and shoots the white man in self-defense. With two of their friends killed by the white man, Big Boy and Bobo retreat, and together with their families, they create a plan to escape North where they presume they will be safe. Bobo, however, is caught near the place where he and Big Boy are supposed to meet, and while Big Boy hides, Bobo is lynched in front of him.

The story is full of references that acknowledge the dangers of crowd violence towards African Americans, especially African American males that are suspected of wronging a white woman. The sexual tension of the scene at the river is heightened by the cultural myth of the sexually predatory black male, and by the white woman's apparent shock at the nakedness of the black bodies she encounters. After the boys have alluded to the persistent fear of lynching in their play, they are confronted by the white woman in a way that inverts the racist stereotype of the black beast racist. The boys are innocent and are just as scared of the white woman as she is of them. When they first see her, Big Boy whispers, "Les git outta here!" (249). The first instinct of the boys is to flee, but by fleeing, they only appear more threatening to the woman who unknowingly blocks their path of escape. Big Boy even tells the woman, "Lady, we wanna git our cloes" (250), but she is still frightened by the boys, likely because of the fear of black men that has been instilled in her, and she panics and calls for her protector. As the boys approach her, seeking only their clothing, the contrasts of skin color and nudity are evident, as "Black and naked, Big Boy stopped three feet from her" (250). The bloodbath that follows, including the eventual lynching of Bobo, can all be linked to what Canetti calls the "sexual accusation." According to Canetti, a sexual accusation often fashions the lynching victim as "a dangerous being" (117). Canetti adds that "the association of a black man with a white woman, the vision of their physical proximity, emphasizes the difference between them in the eyes of the avengers, the woman becoming whiter and whiter and the man blacker and blacker" (117). Wright provides this color contrast with the close proximity of Big Boy and the white woman, but in this case, the supposed black predator is the one naked and exposed. It is the white woman, and the social fears ingrained in her, that cause the carnage that follows.

Bobo's lynching, and the circumstances leading up to it, are examples of the literary tradition formed in Modernist-era American fiction regarding portrayals of lynching and mob violence as they relate to identity. The boys are aware that they are not supposed to swim in old man Harvey's swimming hole. They are black, and in the South at this time, blacks are expected to accept their identity as second-class, segregated citizens. Accepting this second-class citizenry means accepting the segregation that defines black identity as a disease, something that can infect its surroundings and make others sick— blacks are to be kept out of local white swimming holes, white schools and churches, even cemeteries where whites are buried. And of course, sexually, they are viewed as diseases as well, carrying black blood that could someday pollute all whiteness if they are permitted to have sexual relations with white women.

Fittingly, given the common accusation used to justify lynching, it is an event involving a white woman that results in the killing of Big Boy's friends. When Big Boy returns to his family and tells them about killing the white man, it is not so much the death of the white man that puts fear into the family, but the fact that a white woman, although unharmed, was somehow involved. Big Boy, his family, and their friends immediately know that any situation involving a white woman will result in a lynching. Big Boy cries, "They gonna kill me; they gonna lynch me!" (258) and "Theys gonna git a mob" (259), and family friend Mr. Peters demands, "Yuh-all better git this boy outta here" because "ef yuh don theres gonna be a lynchin" (260). Once again, a lynching becomes the central tool used by Southern whites to discourage blacks from at all offending or approaching a white woman. Indeed, as Big Boy watches the mob that will lynch Bobo gather, he overhears a white man exclaim, "Ef they git erway notta woman in this town would be safe" (268).

As Canetti argues in relation to sexual accusations and lynching, the woman is perceived as "innocent" since the male attacker is more powerful (117). Again, the black offenders are depicted as sexual beasts, and lynching is used as a way to enforce the black identity whites desired to create. Lynching logic suggests that death is the only way to keep alleged black criminals from repeating these alleged crimes. As Yoshinobu Hakutani puts it, "Not only does his friend Bobo become a scapegoat for the white people's terror, but what happens to him is also given as a lesson for the black men who dare to transgress the taboo" (36). Lynching is used to eradicate the alleged criminal, and to warn other African Americans of the fate they will face if they also transgress.

The lynching scene that follows Bobo's capture, like the events leading up to it, provides many of the same details commonly found in other lynching accounts, literary or otherwise. Bobo is burned alive, and the crowd gathers around him shouting, "LES GIT SOURVINEERS!" (271). The crowd gets their souvenirs by removing Bobo's fingers and ears. Bobo's identity is eradicated by his being branded as a black sexual beast, and his identity is further annihilated through the burning and mutilation of his body. The white mob fears, as Canetti puts it, the lynching victim's "superiority," and because of this, the victim's perceived sexual and physical prowess is "intolerable," forcing the crowd to "unite against him" (117) much in the way that Big Boy's companions banded together against him in their earlier wrestling match. Simultaneously, a message is sent to other blacks, insisting that if they offend whites in any way, brutal crowd punishment awaits them. Canetti argues that the lynching victim is treated "like a wild animal—for has he not mauled a woman?—he is chased and killed by them altogether" (117). The togetherness of this mob is highlighted by Wright's narrative. Big Boy overhears a member of the lynching party proclaim, "We oughta kill ever black bastard in this country!" (267), drawing clear battle lines between white and black citizens. Groups of whites gather, and Big Boy notices that "there were women singing now" (270). The entire community seems to have turned out for the event, and as Canetti relates, the murder of the lynching victim "appears to them both permissible and mandatory, and it fills them with undisguised satisfaction" (117). Indeed, members of the mob proclaim that if the lynching victims get away, "notta woman in this town would be safe" (268). They view the lynching as necessary, and once it occurs, there is singing and the taking of souvenirs.

Big Boy's position as an eyewitness to the lynching highlights the ways lynchings were used to send public messages to black Americans regarding behavior considered by whites as inappropriate. Big Boy witnesses the kind of extreme punishment those who supposedly transgress will face, and while his previous discussions with his adolescent friends showed that he was aware of the danger of lynching violence, his identity, his sense of his position in the world, has certainly been changed. He has learned that any kind of transgression against the subservient and segregated black identity imposed on him by Southern white society could be punished by crowd violence leading to his own brutal death. The unfairness of the situation is obvious, as Hakutani adds, "In terms of crime and punishment, those who are guilty in Wright's story, the lynch mob and the woman who screams, go unpunished, whereas those who are innocent, the four black boys, are physically and psychologically destroyed" (41). This unfairness, however, is an aspect of black identity that black citizens were expected to accept at this time, and in this way, crowd violence in the form of racially motivated lynch mobs provides the clearest connection in Modernist-era society between such violence and identity self-fashioning. Still a young boy in age, thought, and action, Big Boy's ability to self-fashion his identity has been dramatically and permanently negated through crowd violence.

Popularized depictions of lynchings would prove influential on numerous writers during the Modernist era, and many writers of the era would make similar connections between identity self-fashioning and crowd violence. Authors like Johnson and Wright focus a great deal of their writing on racially motivated crowd violence, specifically lynching, and many authors would use the tropes found in depictions of lynchings to depict other ways in which Modernist American culture used crowd violence to control identity. Lynchings, thankfully, would become less and less common by the 1940s, but in the meantime, the struggle between the threat of crowd violence and opportunities for identity self-fashioning were still implicit in American society, and it is this struggle that numerous American fiction writers of the period portray and explicate in their writing.

CHAPTER II

Joe Christmas, Bigger Thomas and Legalized Lynching

James Weldon Johnson and Richard Wright are two important African American Modernist figures who explore the struggle between racially motivated crowd violence and identity self-fashioning in their writing. However, this focus on issues of racial identity and crowd violence is not only unique to African American writers of the period. Importantly, issues of racial identity and crowd violence were explored by white Modernist authors as well. While many of these white authors use literal and figurative portrayals of crowd violence to explore matters of identity not limited to racial identity, William Faulkner further explores the connection between crowd violence and racial identity, especially during the middle phase of his literary career. In Faulkner's *Light in August* especially, he explores a slowly changing legal system in his native American South, a legal system that, at a surface level, appears to be working to avoid the lynching violence of the past, but a legal system that has replaced extralegal lynching violence with what Christopher Waldrep might call "high-tech" lynching violence.[1] Similarly, Wright, in his Chicago epic *Native Son*, portrays a national legal system that has done away with lynching, but as Wright shows, even in the northern United States the legal system still attempts to control African American racial identity through the threat of crowd violence. In this way, Modernist American fiction writers protested against a white normative society that, while slowly eliminating instances of traditional lynching violence, continued to employ the pressures of crowd violence, albeit in a more systematic and state-run fashion, to control African American identity.

Several Faulkner critics have argued that race is the central theme in Faulkner's fiction, while prominent Faulkner critic Noel Polk has argued that "race is ... in Faulkner generally, a mask for very serious matters of sexuality and gender" (139). My own view—similar to Daniel Singal's assertion that identity is a "major subject" of Faulkner's fiction (18)—is that identity, not particularly racial identity, is the central theme of Faulkner's fiction. Furthermore, as explored later in this study, Faulkner systematically examines issues of gender identity, racial identity, and class identity in different periods of his writing throughout his career—gender in his early work, race during the middle stages of his career, and class at the end of his writing career. Faulkner begins to examine issues of gender identity with *The Sound and the Fury* (1929),[2] and does so throughout his next two novels, *As I Lay Dying* (1930) and *Sanctuary* (1931). It is the use of mob imagery to explore gender roles in these novels that I will focus on in the next chapter of this study. Faulkner's second writing phase, a phase that begins with *Light in August* (1932), shows a shift in focus towards matters of race and racial identity, a focus carried on through subsequent works such as *Absalom, Absalom!* (1936), *The Unvanquished* (1938), *Go Down, Moses* (1942), and *Intruder in the Dust* (1948). In all of these novels, matters of racial identity are of central importance, and threats of mob violence and lynching are often used as a tool by normative white society to dictate and enforce black racial identity. Faulkner's final works, especially the novels of the *Snopes Trilogy* (discussed in Chapter V), deal prominently with issues of social class identity. Because of his consistent focus on matters of crowd violence and identity, Faulkner is, as many have already claimed for other reasons, the preeminent Modernist American fiction writer, serving as a prominent example of the Modernist preoccupation with identity self-fashioning and conflicts with crowd forces.

It is in *Light in August* that Faulkner most closely participates in the Modernist-era literary tradition of depicting graphic scenes of mob violence and lynching as they relate to matters of identity. As critics such as Chip Rhodes have noted, modernist writers often "turned to blacks as figural fathers in the formulation of a fiercely independent approach to literature and nationalism" (170) because "black American culture also provided an idiom that seemed characteristically American and unsullied by European sources" (171). It could be argued that Faulkner, perhaps more than any other Modernist American writer, turned to African American culture to understand his region and even his country as a whole, and *Light in August* might be the best example of this literary influence. The plot of the novel follows several different characters, including Lena Grove, the Reverend Gail Hightower, and Byron Bunch, but it is the character of Joe Christmas who seems most important, as he is presented as a bleaker, less worldly, and certainly more violent version of Johnson's ex-colored man, a character who is rumored to, and himself accepts, a mixed-race racial identity. Through his portrayals of Joe Christmas, Faulkner declares that Southern racism and its ever-present threat of collective violence creates violent men like Joe Christmas, rather than sympathetic figures like Johnson's ex-colored man. Likewise, Faulkner shows a Southern community wherein the outright lynching of black criminals has become taboo, replaced instead by crowd violence conducted by state forces.

Joe's crisis of identity is central to the novel, as he suspects that he is of mixed-race heritage, a suspicion that, interestingly enough, is never emphatically confirmed or denied in the novel, by Joe or anyone else with knowledge of his racial past. To many in Faulkner's fictional town of Jefferson, Joe resembles a foreigner, signifying his unspecified difference from them, and at several points in the novel, rumors suggest that Joe may be of Mexican, rather than of African American, descent. The lack of finality regarding Joe's racial identity ultimately questions racial categorization altogether. In spite of the lack of clear evidence surrounding Joe's actual racial descent, Joe is convinced that he is part black, and this blackness becomes part of the racial identity he self-fashions, an identity that Joe views as part white and part black. Like Johnson's ex-colored man, Joe spends a great deal of time traveling the U.S. in search of a community that will either confirm or deny his whiteness or blackness. Similar to Bigger Thomas in Wright's *Native Son*, Joe spends time in both the Northern and Southern United States, and like Bigger Thomas, Joe does not find life in the north to be an improvement when it comes to matters of race. Unable to self-fashion an identity that allows him to connect with any kind of human community, Joe's potentially black parentage ultimately leads to his being branded by Southern white society as a black criminal, and with this racial identity imposed upon him, Joe becomes a prospective victim of racially motivated crowd violence. This violent end to his persistent attempts to understand and self-fashion a racial identity seems inevitable in Faulkner's fatalistic novel. Through his eventual death, a death caused by a kind of lynch violence reserved for black citizens of the Modernist American South, Joe's identity is ultimately defined for him by a white-controlled legal system.

From the earliest descriptions of Joe Christmas in the novel, it is evident that Joe is an individual struggling to gain a sense of his own racial identity. When Joe first appears and begins working at the Jefferson mill, his lack of a discernible racial identity is noticed by those who work with him through a communal narrator obviously concerned, as any small Southern community would be, with matters of racial identity, as it is noted that "he did not look like a professional hobo in his professional rags, but there was something definitely rootless about him, as though no town nor city was his, no street, no walls, no square of earth his home. And that he carried this knowledge with him always as though it were a banner, with a quality ruthless, lonely, and almost proud" (31–32). Upon his first introduction, then, Joe Christmas is a man without a clear racial identity, without origin or home, and his lack of a clear racial identity isolates him from the community of his fellow human beings. As David Minter aptly describes it, "We see Joe Christmas as an isolated, almost hollowed-out person who is one thing and then another and thus seems always, even in clothes and manner, strangely out of place, urban in a rural world and rural in an urban one, we learn to associate him with isolation, barrenness, and artificiality" (89). Immediately, Joe is associated in the novel with matters of racial identity; he struggles to determine his own identity, while those around him aim to define this identity for him. The struggle involves not only who he is and where he comes from, but also *what* he is in a community where individuals can seemingly only be understood as white or black. Whether he is in a white community or a black community, those around Joe always define him as different, as an outsider, and reciprocally, Joe always sees those around him as strange and alien, as unlike himself. Ultimately, Joe accepts his apparent blackness, an aspect of his identity that has been forced upon him all throughout his life, even though he feels alien in and even revolted by the black communities he journeys through. When Joanna Burden asks him, "'What are you?'" Joe responds by telling her "'I got some nigger blood in me'" (196). Thus, Joe eventually learns "that accepting would take the place of knowing and believing" (178). Joe's acceptance can be applied to his understanding of his racial identity—he accepts, and self-fashions, this racial identity, even though he does not know, or believe, that he is either white or black.

Many critics have noted the rather obvious symbolic relationship between Christmas and his likely namesake, Jesus Christ, and this relationship is also important considering the significance of the Christian narrative of the crucifixion of Christ, which serves as the most influential narrative of crowd violence in Western culture. At the beginning of the novel it appears that, like Christ himself, Joe has appeared essentially out of nowhere, adding to the unidentifiable nature of his identity. Joe's identity only begins to materialize when Byron Bunch relates to Gail Hightower that "Christmas is part nigger" (89). Interestingly, but perhaps not unusual given Faulkner's famed nonlinear writing style, the story of Joe Christmas is not related in a straightforward fashion. First, readers learn that Joe has no identity, that he is a mystery without origin. Then, readers learn that Joe is considered by most who know him, including himself, to be at least partly black. Next, readers find out that Joe is suspected of murdering a white woman, a woman who, like Bigger Thomas's victim in Richard Wright's *Native Son*, represents a family that has a long history of attempting to help African Americans seek opportunity and equality. Furthermore, it is noted that Christmas was sexually involved with this white woman, "living with Miss Burden like man and wife for three years" (93) before so violently killing her that "her head had been cut pretty near off" (91). Early in the novel, readers are presented with depictions of Joe Christmas that are also similar to those of Johnson's ex-colored man. Joe, like the ex-colored man, is presented as a man who symbolically represents the confusion over arbitrary racial categories, racist stereotypes regarding black blood's supposed powers of pollution, and exaggerations of black sexual violence towards white women.

In typical Faulknerian fashion, it is only after readers are given this first description of Joe as a man who lacks any identity, except that eventually placed on him by those around him as a predator upon white women, that readers begin to understand Joe's past. Scenes from Joe's childhood are revealed by the middle of the novel, and it becomes evident that Joe has always been conscious of the racial stigma that surrounds him. As a youth, children taunt him for being somehow racially different, and these taunts lead to Joe's eating of the dietician's toothpaste in a childish attempt to whiten himself from the inside. Joe's attempts at whitening fail, making him physically sick and even more psychologically aware of his non-normative racial identity. Eating the toothpaste does not whiten Joe's skin, but rather turns him "in upon himself" (122), forcing him to accept the racial stigma attached to him as something that he cannot rid himself of. Giving up these attempts, he relents, accepts this racial stigma, and tells himself with "passive surrender ... here I am" (122). Joe can only establish that he does exist; *what* he is, black or white, is something he, like those around him, cannot comfortably determine. The novel becomes a tale of his attempts to self-fashion his own racial identity, and a community's attempts to define and control his racial identity through collective force.

Joe grows up to be a man in continual search of a racial community that he can identify with, a common racial identity with either blacks or whites. These attempts, like his efforts with the dietician's toothpaste as a child, ultimately fail. Because whites brand him as black, Joe attempts to wander in black neighborhoods, only to be rejected there and referred to by other African Americans with labels such as "white man" and "whitefolks" (117). Trying to shock a white woman he has slept with, Joe tells her that he considers himself to be black, only to have her reply, "I thought maybe you were just another wop or something" (225). Joe is repulsed by this woman and attacks her, and his life is full of violent confrontations, many of which stem from his own sense of confused racial identity. He fights with white men who call him a Negro before beginning to "fight the negro who called him white" (225). "To be sure," as Daniel Singal asserts, "Joe Christmas is caught up in the familiar southern dilemma of struggling to escape an identity fastened on him by a powerful ancestor" (185). Like Bigger Thomas in Wright's *Native Son*, Joe's search for identity causes violence to be a central event of his life. As is often the case with violent criminals, Joe is a loner, and when his isolation is broken, violence usually ensues. As a youth, he is whipped repeatedly by old man McEachern, Joe's adoptive father, and although McEachern seems unaware of Joe's racial background, the continual beatings and forced labor symbolically reference the South's slave past. Joe's first sexual relationship with a woman, a white prostitute named Bobbie, ends violently when, after Joe has attacked McEachern, the prostitute and her pimps are forced to flee Jefferson. Outraged that Joe has endangered them and their illegal operations, they beat and rob Joe, and his former lover refers to his racial identity upon leaving, screaming, "Bastard! Son of a bitch! Getting me into a jam, that always treated you like you were a white man. A white man!" (217). Joe's eventual murder of Joanna Burden shows him lashing out against a white woman who has attempted, by endeavoring to convince Joe to attend a black college, to clearly define his racial identity for him.

These relationships with women best portray Joe's struggle to understand his own racial identity, as Faulkner unites, as is often the case in narratives involving lynching, tropes related to both racial and gender norms. These relationships usually lead to violent encounters, encounters that separate Joe from any sense of understanding in regards to his own racial identity. Whether he presents himself as black or white, his racial heritage becomes the central matter of importance in his sexual relations. Bobbie, upon the severing of her relationship with Joe, professes to be most disturbed by Joe's apparent mixedrace origins, not his endangering of her career as a prostitute. As Bobbie and her pimp flee after Joe's attack on Mr. McEachern, Bobbie exclaims, "He told me himself he was a nigger! The son of a bitch! Me f. ing for nothing a nigger son of a bitch that would get me in a jam with clodhopper police" even as her accomplices wonder, "*Is he really a nigger? He dont look like one*" (219). Joe does not necessarily look black to the community around him, but whenever the white community cuts its ties with Joe, his potential blackness is always referenced. Similarly, Joe often attempts, as he does with Joanna Burden, to use his racially mixed bloodlines to shock white women he sleeps with, as he continually tries to enforce his own sense of personal isolation through racial difference. When he tries to shock one white lover "still in the (comparatively speaking) south" by telling her he is partly black and she responds receptively, Joe reacts violently. In fact, Joe seems most upset when he encounters white women that don't mind sleeping with African American men. Joe nearly kills this particular woman, is "sick for two years" after the confrontation, and goes on to live "with negroes, shunning white people" (225).

A key aspect of Joe's struggle, then, is his own repulsed reaction to his potential black ancestry. Joe attempts to assimilate himself into a black community, living

> as man and wife with a woman who resembled an ebony carving. At night he would lie in bed beside her, sleepless, beginning to breathe deep and hard. He would do it deliberately, feeling, even watching, his white chest arch deeper and deeper within his ribcage, trying to breathe into himself the dark odor, the dark and inscrutable thinking and being of negroes, with each suspiration trying to expel from himself the white blood and the white thinking and

being. And all the while his nostrils at the odor which he was trying to make his own would whiten and tauten, his whole being writhe and strain with physical outrage and spiritual denial [225–6].

Joe's reactions to the African Americans he encounters show that Joe's inner conflict rages on between the two racial identities that he cannot force to come together. Here, he attempts to fashion a black racial identity for himself, just as he had tried to fashion a white racial identity with the dietician's toothpaste as a youth. Still, his experiences in white communities have conditioned him to loathe his black neighbors, and to especially abhor white women who cross stringent social borders and have consensual sexual relationships with black men. He tries to live in a black community and accept the possibility of his own blackness, but the racism that white normative society has conditioned him to feel has made him unable to accept the humanity of an individual with black skin or blood, accepting them only as he does his black lover referenced above, as symbols of an identity he cannot self-fashion for himself.

Joe's repulsion at being labeled as an African American is a major motivator in his apparent murdering of Joanna Burden. In spite of her good intentions, Joanna, like other members of the white community, attempts to identify Joe as black, forcing this racial identity upon him, and thereby settling his identity crisis for him. Joe's understanding of his presumed racial duality, however, makes it impossible for him to accept Joanna's invitation for him to attend what he calls "a nigger school" (276). She wants him to study law, but he rejects the black racial identity he would have to accept in order to "learn law in the office of a nigger lawyer" or attend "a nigger college" (276). Worse, Joe fears having to "tell niggers that I am a nigger too" (277). Joanna's insistence that he accept this identity, and his resistance to her, serve as his primary motive in her murder.

As is also the case with Bigger Thomas, Joe Christmas's downfall comes after he becomes sexually involved with a white woman, and as the primary suspect in Joanna Burden's murder, Joe is finally assigned a distinctive racial identity by the white Jefferson community, an identity that, through the threat of mob violence, supersedes any identity Joe has been able to fashion for himself. Throughout the novel, he and those around him have questioned Joe's racial identity, but it is only when he is suspected of killing and possibly raping a white woman that his final racial identity as an oversexed, violent, black criminal is imposed upon him with finality. Joe's crime decides his racial identity, and this racial identity becomes central to the violent punishment that awaits him. When news of the crime first spreads through the community, his former friend and bootlegging accomplice Lucas Burch invokes Joe's racial identity, telling the sheriff, "Go on. Accuse me. Accuse the white man that's trying to help you with what he knows. Accuse the white man and let the nigger go free. Accuse the white man and let the nigger run" (97). Burch instantly tries to save himself by branding Joe with this racial identity, and in many ways, this ploy works. After Burch mentions Joe's race, a marshal immediately states, "I always thought there was something funny about that fellow" (99), and law enforcement turn their attention entirely to apprehending Joe Christmas. From that moment on, the surrounding communities begin to refer to Christmas as "that white nigger that did that killing up at Jefferson" (344). Joe even internalizes this identity. It is only through the town's creation of Joe's racial identity as black that Joe is able to "see himself being hunted by white men at last into the black abyss which had been waiting, trying, for thirty years to drown him" (331).

Additionally, Joanna Burden's own whiteness is often invoked in contrast to Joe's blackness by the town, as Faulkner interrogates the cultural view of taboo sexual relations between white women and black men that so often resulted in mob violence against African Americans in the South. Angry whites waiting outside the Jefferson jail desiring to lynch Joe Christmas argue that he did not "give that white woman a fair trial" (354), and thus, they feel they should not give him a fair trial, and that lynching violence is the most appropriate way to punish him for his alleged crime. Surely, he would not be lynched if Joanna Burden had been a black woman, and if Joe was white, the murder of Joanna Burden, always an outsider in the town because of her progressive views on racial equality, may have even been celebrated. As a potentially black criminal, however, Joe's crime is seen as a threat to the entire white community, and especially white women. His prospective black blood is even solely blamed for the killing. The townspeople assume that although Joe "dont look any more like a nigger," it "'must have been the nigger blood in him'" that made him kill, and as they presume, rape, Joanna Burden (349). Although Joanna has been viewed unfavorably by the townspeople her entire life because of her and her family's legacy of kindness towards blacks and their Yankee roots, in death she becomes a symbol, at least to Jefferson and its surrounding towns, of Southern white female purity tainted and destroyed by a black predator. The townspeople in general are depicted as believing in, and even secretly longing for, the black sexual beast myth that James Weldon Johnson and the NAACP fought to undermine in order to stop lynching. Faulkner writes:

> Among them the casual Yankees and the poor whites and even the southerners who had lived for a while in the north, who believed aloud that it was an anonymous negro crime committed not by a negro but by Negro and who knew, believed, and hoped that she had been ravished too: at least once before her throat was cut and at least once afterward [288].

Faulkner, as he does throughout the novel, smartly alludes to the violent, sexually predatory identity that was often assigned to black men during the

Modernist era, noting, as James Baldwin and others have, that this myth may actually say more about whiteness and white fantasies regarding interracial sex than it does about actual black male behavior and sexual desire. Joe Christmas, for most of the novel racially ambiguous, becomes branded as a black killer and rapist, even though no one can confirm his racial identity, and even though his sexual contact with Joanna Burden has been consensual.

Yet the white community, having finally defined Joe Christmas's racial identity for him, enforces this identity through crowd violence which leads to a climatic event full of lynching imagery. A mob appears immediately after word spreads that Joanna Burden's killer could be considered black:

> They were gathering now about the sheriff and the deputy and the negro, with avid eyes upon which the sheer prolongation of empty flames had begun to pall, with faces identical one with another. It was as if all their individual five senses had become one organ of looking, like an apotheosis, the words that flew among them wind- or air engendered *Is that him? ... By God, if that's him, what are we doing, standing around here? Murdering a white woman the black son of a* None of them had ever entered the house. While she was alive they would not have allowed their wives to call on her. When they were younger, children (some of their fathers had done it too) they had called after her on the street, "Nigger lover! Nigger lover!" [291–2].

The suspicion of Joe's crime and of his black racial identity incites a mob as the white community gather's to punish him. Although none of them accepted Joanna Burden into their community, her death has united the white community as they come together to identify and punish Joe for his alleged crime. Joe is eventually able to escape from jail, but in fleeing, he shows a desire to have his identity confirmed by this white normative community, rather than a desire to escape punishment. In his final confrontation in the novel, Joe allows himself to be killed, with a "loaded and unfired pistol in his hand" (449). He does not fight those whose job it is to recapture him, and instead seems to give up his previously violent ways, having finally found a stable racial identity, even though it is forced upon him by the white community and will lead to his death. This racial identity might be forced upon him, but it satisfies the quest he has been on throughout the novel. Denied the ability to self-fashion his own identity, Joe allows the community to fashion his identity for him, seemingly acknowledging that he will always be considered by this society as black, and that this same society will always seek to punish him for being black.

In the end, Joe is not lynched; rather, he is killed in a police standoff full of imagery consistent with many accounts of lynchings. Percy Grimm, a captain in the state national guard, becomes a symbolic representative of the state of Mississippi, a state that saw many African American citizens lynched between 1900 and 1940. Percy Grimm insists that "it might be a good thing if I wear my uniform until this business is settled. So they can see that Uncle Sam is present in more than spirit" (453). Through Percy Grimm, Faulkner depicts a country that has moved on from lynching black victims to punishing them legally through representatives of the government. Percy Grimm and the other guardsmen are supposedly present in order to protect Joe from the possibility of an extra-legal punishment. However, Joe's eventual executioner shares many of the traits common among those who participated in racially motivated lynchings. Percy Grimm is described as having

> a sublime and implicit faith in physical courage and blind obedience, and a belief that the white race is superior to any and all other races and that the American is superior to all other white races and that the American uniform is superior to all man, and that all that would ever be required of him in payment for this belief, this privilege, would be his own life [451].

Importantly, Faulkner's description of Grimm here likely resembles Faulkner's understanding of the state of Mississippi in its treatment of matters of race, racism, and discrimination. Ironically, Faulkner calls attention to what he sees as particularly American beliefs of superiority, destiny, and progress, and Grimm's killing of Joe Christmas is equally symbolic, recalling the mutilation of black lynching victims, especially victims who are suspected of having been sexually involved with a white woman. Christmas does not pose any physical threat to Grimm in their final confrontation or even try to escape once cornered, but when the other officers find Grimm with Christmas recaptured, the events described mirror those found in lynching accounts regarding black rape suspects:

> When they approached to see what he was about, they saw that the man was not dead yet, and when they saw what Grimm was doing one of the men gave a choked cry and stumbled back into the wall and began to vomit. Then Grimm too sprang back, flinging behind him the bloody butcher knife. "Now you'll let white women alone, even in hell," he said. But the man on the floor had not moved [464].

It is not-so-subtly implied that, as was often the case in lynchings of African Americans, Grimm mutilates and removes Joe's sex organs as punishment for Joe's suspected rape of Joanna Burden, a sex crime that Joe likely did not commit. Joe Christmas is not given his day in court, in spite of all of the public posturing by the local law enforcement and Grimm's national guardsmen, all of whom pretend to be present in order to prevent a lynching from occurring. Instead, Joe is killed by a white supremacist and representative of the state who aims to make Joe Christmas's punishment an example that other blacks should be aware of. Joe is essentially lynched, but he is lynched by a legal authority, a representative of the state. As Joel Williamson argues, Joe is "both crucified and lynched," just as "black men had been lynched during the years of Faulkner's youth, not in confusion and chaos, but with clear and passionate purpose. It was done by men who saw their duty, and it was approved by a society that required action. It happened in communities that felt themselves in danger of losing moral virtue" (412). Once again, the punishment of an alleged black criminal involves a violent attempt to define black racial identity.

As Polk argues, regarding race in Faulkner's fiction, "None of Faulkner's fiction offers a solution, certainly, or much hope either" (241). *Light in August* certainly offers no solution to the issues of race and the battle to define racial identity. Rather, as Jay Parini adds, "The enmity and blind fanaticism of southern society crush Joe Christmas, who believes (in his heart of hearts) that he deserves this treatment" because he has accepted a racial identity that society has defined as black, and therefore inferior (182). *Light in August*, rather than attempting to offer solutions, is instead a powerful portrayal of problems Faulkner recognized in Southern race relations, an ironic progress away from extra-legal lynching to state-run violent punishments of suspected black criminals. As Williamson argues, "It was an indictment of Southern culture and particularly of the race and sex roles that were assigned to individuals" (413). Faulkner's indictment becomes clearer when connected with the tradition that includes James Weldon Johnson, Richard Wright, and many others, a tradition that identifies lynching with an attempt by intolerant whites to enforce and punish black identities. Singal also notices a correlation between identity and *Light in August*, arguing that "perhaps the best way to comprehend Faulkner's intentions for *Light in August* is to view the saga of Joe Christmas as an attempt to test the human capacity to achieve personal identity under the most extreme conditions a Modernist author could possibly contrive" (171). As Faulkner shows, crowd violence is often employed to define the stereotypical identity of hyper-sexed black criminals on those who are suspected of having any black ancestry. Joe is not lynched in the traditional manner, but as word of his capture and killing spread, Jefferson is referred to as the town "'where they lynched that nigger'" (497). As Grimm's brutal killing and dismemberment of Joe Christmas show, this new form of lynching is no less violent, and is still concerned with punishing certain identities in order to enforce other, normative identities. After Joe's state-run lynching, Faulkner presents us with the abolitionist Reverend Hightower's memories, and through these memories, Hightower realizes and internalizes the notion that "progress now is still progress, yet it is now indistinguishable from the recent past like the already traversed inches of sand which cling to the turning wheel, raining back with a dry hiss that before this should have warned him" (490).

This ironic progress from lynching violence to a new kind of state-supported mob violence is also a major theme of Wright's *Native Son*. The plot of *Native Son* is familiar, not only because of the fame achieved by the novel, but also because the events that lead to Bigger Thomas's eventual death sentence are familiar; it is a fictional story that has been retold, often in sensationalist fashion, in newspapers and other media reports ever since the Great Migration. Bigger Thomas, an African American, gets involved with a white woman, kills her, is eventually captured by a mob of white police officers and national guardsmen, and is sentenced to death by a white judge and jury. While the essential events of the plot are familiar, Wright uses them in an ironic way to show that although lynchings rarely took place in northern cities like Chicago, and although lynchings were becoming rare even in the South by this time, a new kind of lynching was beginning to take place in the United States, a form of lynching where members of the justice system became the mob in charge of violently punishing and even executing black criminals. As Mikko Juhani Tuhkanen has observed, "The prosecution in Bigger's case advocates what comes very close to lynching" (131).³ In presenting this kind of symbolic lynching, Wright parodies the myth of American racial progress, showing that progress has not led to equality and justice, but rather to a new kind of lynching that gains authority and authenticity through government systems. In essence, Wright shows that the violence of lynching has not been eradicated—it has merely been moved inside to American courtrooms. Although the execution of black criminals would change settings in this way, these executions still played prominent roles in defining African Americans as inferior in a white normative society, enforcing this inferiority through social conditioning, and punishing African Americans for transgressions against these normative identities.

Yet unlike Johnson's ex-colored man and Faulkner's Joe Christmas, Bigger Thomas, like Big Boy and his friends in "Big Boy Leaves Home," has no internal conflict regarding his racial identity. Bigger clearly identifies himself as black and contrasts himself against normative white society. Bigger's conflict is with an external force, against the normative white society that continually assigns him, and other African Americans like him, a second-class and subordinate identity that Bigger can only rebel against through violence. His violence, however, simply provides the crowd force of normative white society with the opportunity to further define his identity, to punish him for his attempts to self-fashion his identity, and ultimately, to execute him in a manner that, as Wright portrays it, is full of the imagery of crowd violence and lynching. Bigger attempts to self-fashion his identity through violence, failing to realize that his violent ways only strengthen the predominantly held notion held by the white society around him that African Americans are inherently violent and oversexed and therefore need to be controlled, punished, an even eradicated by white crowds.

Early in the novel, Bigger is shown struggling against the second-class identity that a white-controlled society has forced upon him. Bigger awakens in the small single bedroom apartment that he shares with his mother, brother, and sister,[4] an apartment where "there was no rug on the floor and the plastering on the walls and ceiling hung loose in many places. There were two worn iron beds, four chairs, an old dresser, and a drop-leaf table on which they ate" (541). This apartment is especially important when contrasted with the opulence of the Dalton residence, a residence inhabited by a rich and powerful white family. The apartment is so small and Bigger and his family live so intimately together that Bigger cannot help witnessing his mother and sister dressing, causing him to feel "ashamed" (447). Before everyone is awake and dressed, a large rat gets loose in the apartment. A violent battle ensues between Bigger and the rat, and as Robert Butler has noted, the rat "is very much like the Thomas family, who are likewise trapped in a squalid room that contains a door leading only into another trap, the ghetto" (32). Like the rat, Bigger and his family are faced with a limited set of choices, a series of equally lethal traps; they can either passively submit to a social structure that forces them to live in such conditions, or they can strike out violently against the systems that oppress them. As Butler puts it, "Such entrapment offers two equally destructive options: paralysis or violence" (43). Bigger, as he does in putting an end to the rat, chooses violence, and at times, he believes that he is in control of his life, able to self-fashion his own identity through his violent actions. Yet, Bigger consistently fails to recognize that even when he responds violently against these social structures, his violence is only making it possible for the state to execute him. As Bigger will learn by the end of the novel, the identity of a trapped rat is very much the same as the identity those in power in Chicago have assigned to black citizens in these ghettos, and trying to change this identity leads to the formation of white mobs and death through mob violence.

The social conditions imposed on Bigger shape his identity, forcing him to hate his own family, the people most like himself. Bigger hates them

> because he knew that they were suffering and that he was powerless to help them. He knew that the moment he allowed himself to feel to its fullness how they lived, the shame and misery of their lives, he would be swept out of himself with fear and despair. So he held toward them an attitude of iron reserve; he lived with them, but behind a wall, a curtain. And toward himself he was even more exacting. He knew that the moment he allowed what his life meant to enter fully into his consciousness, he would either kill himself or someone else [453].

Bigger tries to self-fashion an identity apart from his family, not realizing that the identity that society has imposed upon him denies him the ability to fully love and sympathize with others like himself, and that this forced isolation is one of the most damaging aspects of the identity white society has fashioned for him and other African American citizens. In similar ways, Bigger's self-hate, his hate for the identity fashioned by white society for him and those like him, boils over in his relationships with his friends G.H., Gus, and Jack and his girlfriend Bessie, who he eventually kills because her fear of transgressing against the identity fashioned for her will not allow her to willingly continue as his accomplice.

The identity white society fashions for Bigger is one that promotes this self-hate. For example, images from popular culture condition Bigger that he and other African Americans are inferior to the whites who control most aspects of their society:

> He looked at *Trader Horn* unfold and saw pictures of naked black men and women whirling in wild dances and heard drums beating and then gradually the African scene changed and was replaced by images in his own mind of white men and women dressed in black and white clothes, laughing, talking, drinking, and dancing. Those were smart people; they knew how to get hold of money, millions of it [476].

Such images define African American identity as stagnant, un-evolved, trivial, and animalistic, while likewise identifying white identity as beautiful, luxurious, intelligent, and successful. Bigger recognizes that his second-class identity limits the options he has in life as "it maddened him to think that he did not have a wider choice of action" (456), unlike the "white boys" who "get a chance to do everything" (459). Bigger and others like him are limited in "the vast white world that sprawled and towered in the sun before them" (461). These feelings of limitation and inferiority cause Bigger to feel "fear and emptiness" and "fear and hate" (486) around white people, and he cannot even look Mr. Dalton in the eye when he is first hired as the Dalton's driver because of "an organic conviction in him that this was the way white folks wanted him to be when in their presence" (490). These feelings, feelings that Bigger cannot disassociate from his sense of his own identity, play an important role in Bigger's murder of Mary Dalton. Around Mary and her boyfriend Jan, both of whom seem sympathetic, albeit patronizing, to Bigger's second-class existence, Bigger feels only "foolish" (507) and "naked" (508) as he experiences the sensation that "he had no physical existence at all; he was something hated, the badge of shame which he knew was attached to a black skin" (508). Bigger knows that normative white society views him as "just a black clown" (638). Thus, Bigger is forced to internalize the second-class identity that is imposed on him by normative white society. When he is asked "where the white folks live" he responds, "'Right down here in my stomach'" (464). This identity, however sickening it might be to him, becomes a part of him that he cannot escape. It appears that he even accepts his own supposed inferiority and the supposed superiority of white people; Bigger convinces himself that "if he were white, if he were like them, it would have been different" (509). Bigger has accepted the racial identity imposed upon him, in spite of his violent resistance against it, because he accepts that white people are inherently superior to him.

Bigger's identity is enforced, and further complicated by, the overwhelming presence of whiteness around him, especially in the Dalton home and during his time in jail, and Wright uses the persistent presence of this color symbolism to highlight the crowd force that Bigger faces. Like Joanna Burden, Mrs. Dalton tries to help black citizens, but her whiteness is always deeply contrasted against Bigger's blackness, emphasizing Bigger's difference. Mrs. Dalton is repeatedly described as being "dressed in white" with a "pale face" (562), with "light-grey blind eyes, eyes almost as white as her face and hair and dress" (563). She has a "flowing white presence" and she often appears, as she does in the Dalton's basement full of reporters, "lit up with the white flash of a dozen silver bulbs" (633). Mr. Dalton is similarly described in terms of his whiteness, as Wright's descriptions usually highlight Mr. Dalton's white hair. When Mary's bones are found in the furnace and Bigger flees the scene, Bigger tries to escape from the white crowds that surround him with their superiority and suspicion, yet he still struggles against an all-encompassing whiteness, a suffocating snowstorm where "snow was in his mouth, eyes, ears; snow was seeping down his back.... He struggled against the snow, pushing it away from him" (651). Immediately after this struggle with the snow, it is noted that "he had to get out of this white neighborhood" (652). Like the Daltons, Britten, their private investigator, is often described "with his face pale" (603). Even though Britten seems out to get Bigger, unlike the Daltons, Bigger still sees the whiteness of the Daltons and his other adversaries, a whiteness that irrevocably separates them from him.

Bigger's sense of fear and shame and the all-surrounding whiteness of the world he encounters make it impossible for him to escape from the identity white society has assigned him. Bigger is incapable of escaping "the old feeling, the feeling that he had had all his life: he was black and had done wrong; white men were looking at something with which they would soon accuse him" (650). It is only after his murder of Mary and his subsequent attempt at escape from the predominantly white members of law enforcement that Bigger is able to clearly formulate, in his own head, the crisis of identity he has been facing as an African American in a white-controlled city:

> But what was he after? What did he want? What did he love and what did he hate? He did not know. There was something he *knew* and something he *felt*; something the *world* gave him and something he *himself* had ... and never in all his life, with this black skin of his, had the two worlds, thought and feeling, will and mind, aspiration and satisfaction, been together; never had he felt a sense of wholeness [670].

Because of the strictly enforced identity that has been assigned to him, and other African American citizens, Bigger is unable to completely imagine himself in relation to the world. He does not know what he wants, because he has always been told what to want. Thus, he describes white normative society's attempts to define his identity for him as a kind of rape. He thinks "rape was not what one did to women. Rape was what one felt when one's back was against a wall and one had to strike out, whether one wanted to or not, to keep the pack from killing him" (658).

In order to feel some sense of autonomy, Bigger turns to a life of violent crime in a naive attempt to empower himself with the ability to self-fashion his own identity, to strike against the white pack that he feels is always hunting him. For example, Bigger's gun serves as an integral part of the identity he believes he has self-fashioned for himself, believing it protects him against all rivals, black or white, because "that gun could always make folks stand away and think twice before bothering him" (564). As he learns when he is chased down by the white mob of law enforcement agents, however, his gun is impotent against the sheer number of enemies he must encounter to survive freely. Bigger does not face one or two adversaries that he can simply gun down, as his true enemy is shown to be a crowd force, the entirety of white normative society.

After killing Mary Dalton, his most rebellious criminal act, Bigger believes that he has violently and rebelliously fashioned his own identity. He finds peace in the feeling that "some hand had reached inside of him and had laid a quiet finger of peace upon the restless tossing of his spirit" (570), and in turn, he feels "more alive than he could remember having been; his mind and attention were pointed, focused toward a goal" (583). These feelings empower him in a way he has not felt before, as his taboo acts with a white woman make "him feel alive and gave him a heightened sense of the value of himself" (577). For once in his life, Bigger thinks that he has acted in a way that is outside of the confining paths of action assigned to him by white society. He believes that he has chosen his own path, and this new sense of autonomy brings him peace and reason to live. As a criminal who violently rebels against white normative society, new options seem to become available to Bigger. He believes that "he could run away; he could remain; he could even go down and confess what he had done. The mere thought that these avenues of action were open to him made him feel free, that his life was his, that he held his future in his hands" (622). Bigger thinks these choices offer him potential avenues of freedom and escape, but each choice he imagines keeps him strictly within the boundaries assigned to him by the predominantly white culture that consistently surrounds him. If he flees, he will not be able to get far. If he stays, they will catch him and punish him. If he chooses to confess, as he later does, they will kill him anyway. Bigger is even ignorant enough to believe that his violence is unexpected and surprising, and that the inferior identity imposed upon him will protect him from suspicion since, regarding Mary's apparent kidnapping, "They would think that white men did it; they would never think that a black, timid Negro did that" (620).

In spite of Bigger's growing sense of autonomy after Mary Dalton's murder, the threat of white crowd violence towards African Americans who transgress against normative, white-assigned identities is constantly present, and Bigger eventually realizes that his violent rebellion has only allowed white society to justify crowd violence in order to punish him. Even before Bigger murders Mary Dalton, Bigger is aware that mob violence awaits African Americans who transgress against the normative racial identities concocted by white society. A significant part of Bigger's understanding of his socially fashioned racial identity is his realizing that mob violence is reserved for punishing African American citizens such as himself. When he sees a movie clip of "white girls lolling on the gleaming sands of a beach" and his friend Jack daydreams about being there, Bigger tells him "You can.... But you'd be hanging from a tree" (474). The threat of lynching violence is always present in Bigger's conscience, and it is this threat that immediately enters his mind when he murders Mary Dalton. Instantly after realizing that Mary is dead, "the reality of the room fell from him; the vast city of white people that sprawled outside took its place. She was dead and he had killed her. He was a murderer, a Negro murderer, a black murderer. He had killed a white woman" (527). Realizing his crime, Bigger simultaneously realizes the threat of crowd violence. He knows that if he is caught, "they would kill him" (529). His greatest fear is the electric chair, a new sight for lynchings to occur. When he first kills Mary, "the fear of electrocution had entered his flesh and blood" (583). A key part of the identity that has been forced upon him is the knowledge that transgressions against white authority will be punishable by death.

After Mary's murder, the main representatives of the white justice system that Bigger faces are described as mob forces. When Bigger first comes face to face with Britten, Bigger perceives "what seemed to his excited senses an army of white men" (588). Bigger does not necessarily fear white individuals, but white crowds, mobs intent on defining his identity for him or punishing him for self-fashioning his own identity, are a consistent threat, and a threat that he is accustomed to fearing. In many ways, Britten represents this crowd force. Bigger acknowledges that "Britten was familiar to him; he had met a thousand Brittens in his life" (597). Once Bigger is a clear suspect in the murder, a more concrete, less metaphorical, crowd force emerges. Bigger knows "there would be a thousand white policemen on the South Side searching for him or any black man who looked like him," and he recognizes that against this force "he was alone" (655). Likewise, the various newspaper reports Bigger seeks out all verify the identity that has always been imposed upon him as a black man, while also adding voices to the crowd ready to kill him for his crime. The media, in this instance, joins with the violent crowds shouting for Bigger's death.

Once he is apprehended by law enforcement, Bigger's encounters with the legal system and the media put him in contact with a crowd that is ready to pass a final verdict on his identity and sentence him to death. During his first trip to a courtroom, Bigger notes a "compact array of white faces" (702) that sounds like a lynch mob "determined to make his death mean more than a mere punishment; that they feared and were anxious to keep under control. The atmosphere of the crowd told him that they were going to use his death as a bloody symbol of fear to wave before the eyes of that black world" (703). He sees "white faces along the wall. They are staring at him in surprise" (722). The portrait of the courtroom that Wright provides seems like a scene where mob violence would take place: "Stretching to the four walls of the room was a solid sheet of white faces. Standing with squared shoulders all round were policemen with clubs in hand, silver metal on their chests, faces red and stern" (736-7). Whenever Bigger is paraded past this white crowd, he is always greeted with comments such as, "'Gee, isn't he *black*'" and "'Kill 'im'" (736). Additionally, like Wright's use of snow and his emphasis on the whiteness of the Dalton family, the courtroom Wright describes is full of more oppressing signs of whiteness: "white bones lying atop a table ... white sheets of paper ... Mr. Dalton, white-faced, white-haired" (737), a "court of white men" (785). Adversarial whiteness surrounds Bigger at every turn, and he grows to learn that he cannot escape this violent crowd force.

Once Bigger comes in contact with this white crowd demanding his death, he realizes that the criminally rebellious identity he believes he has self-fashioned for himself has actually been fashioned for him, and that this identity is part of the inferior and subordinate identity that has always been imposed upon him by a predominantly white society. Eventually, Bigger realizes the trap that white society has provided for him in encouraging his violent ways. He acknowledges that "they draw a line and say for you to stay on your side of the line. They don't care if there's no bread over on your side. They don't care if you die. And then they say things like that about you and when you try to come from behind your line they kill you. They feel they ought to kill you then. Everybody wants to kill you then" (774). Bigger acknowledges that he will be punished for his attempt to self-fashion his own identity. He knows that "to live, he had created a new world for himself, and for that he was to die" (710). He further acknowledges that "he had been lured into the open, and trapped, twice trapped; trapped by being in jail for murder, and again trapped by being stripped of emotional resources to go to his death" (785). Bigger, having thought that he had managed to free himself of this white-assigned identity, ends up with the same emotions that he felt before Mary's murder, as "fear and dread were the only possible feelings he could have in that court room" (799).

In the end, like Joe Christmas in his final confrontation with Percy Grimm,

Bigger Thomas must stand against a state force, "the People of the State of Illinois" (791), as those who conduct lynchings become empowered by government sanction. Buckley, the man who argues for Bigger to be put to death, is referred to by the judge as "Mr. State's Attorney" and as Max puts it, "the State whets the appetite of the mob" (795). Indeed, Max's final defense of Bigger Thomas provides one of the clearest explications of the relationship between crowd violence and racial identity in all of American literature. Max notes that "the complex forces of society have isolated here for us a symbol" (804), as Bigger Thomas becomes a symbol the state can torture and eradicate in order to warn other African Americans. Max notes that the jury is "not of his peers, but of an alien and hostile race" who have been "conditioned by the press of the nation; a press which has already reached a decision as to his guilt" (805). Max notices the ironic progress away from lynching and towards state-endorsed capital punishment, noting ironically that under these conditions, "an outright lynching would be more honest" (805). He goes on to describe the ways in which the white crowd has perpetually attempted to define African American identity, creating "a mode of *life*" that is "stunted and distorted ... an existence of men growing out of the soil prepared by the collective but blind will of a hundred million people" (809). Max argues that white society has told Bigger "what to do; where to live; how much schooling he could get; where he could eat; where and what kind of work he could do" (815). Max recognizes that issues of identity are central to this matter, that "men can starve from a lack of self-realization" (821), and that by allowing Bigger to go to prison rather than being executed, Bigger would finally develop an "identity" since "sending him to prison would be the first recognition of his personality he has ever had" (825). Buckley, meanwhile, relies on the same arguments used to justify lynching as he refers to Bigger as a "half-human black ape" who "may be climbing through the windows of our homes to rape, murder, and burn our daughters" (829). He further defines Bigger as a "sub-human killer" (830) and a "treacherous beast" (832). In spite of his attempts to escape from this white-assigned racial identity, Bigger is once again defined by antagonistic whites who label him as inferior, even animalistic.

Buckley's argument, in the end, persuades the court to pass its final verdict, a final verdict from the legal system that seconds the persistent suggestions shouted from the white crowds who demand that Bigger be lynched. The judge announces that "Bigger Thomas shall die on or before midnight of Friday, March third, in a manner prescribed by the laws of this State" (837). This legal lynching shows that American racial progress has only been made in an ironic and sardonic sense, and I am not the first to notice Wright's attempts to refute national progress myths in *Native Son*. Butler notices the presence of the Alger myth in Wright's novel, arguing that Wright "came to see how the Alger myth was little more than a cruel joke for black people, since the doors of American opportunity were systematically closed to blacks because of their skin color. *Native Son* is therefore a conscious parody of the Alger novels" (97). The novel is likewise a parody of American racial progress. Bigger is given a good job by Mr. Dalton, a super-rich man who, along with his wife, seems to be interested in helping poor and uneducated blacks. Unlike the typical stories that make up the Alger myth, Bigger's opportunity to work with the rich leads not to social advancement, but to his eventual death. Butler goes on to add that *Native Son* "generates many of its most powerful meanings by consciously echoing and then ironically inverting the conventions of the Alger myth" (98). Butler sees this subversion of the Alger myth as a major theme of the novel, noting that "Wright clearly stresses that American capitalism does not work for blacks and other minorities" (101).

The Alger myth, and other notions of the American dream, are also parodied in Wright's attack on the myth of American progress. As Harris argues in her essay "Native Sons and Foreign Daughters," "Wright sets up an opposition in the novel between the native and the foreign, between the American Dream and American ideals in the abstract and Afro-Americans trying to find their place among those ideals" (63). The American Dream, with its notions concerning the possibility of progress for all, is shown to be a myth in *Native Son* by Wright's portrayal of how this dream works for those who are poor, black, or worst of all, both. The American Dream, as the myth goes, is supposed to exist for all Americans, but as Harris notes, "Bigger is indeed American and native, then, in his expression of individuality, but the paradox is that the structure was never intended to include him" (84). As he does with the Alger myth, Wright uses the novel as a way to question the American Dream, and as previously noted, the Alger myth and the notion of the American Dream are two key components involved in ideas surrounding American progress.

Indeed, the only kind of progress seen in Wright's representation of America near the close of the Modernist era is a kind of ironic progress made, in the North and elsewhere, regarding the way that African Americans are accused of crimes, convicted, and punished. Unlike those who are accused of crimes, captured by violent mobs, and immediately lynched in Johnson's *Autobiography*, Faulkner's *Light in August*, and Wright's *Uncle Tom's Children*, Bigger Thomas is hunted down by a mob, but this mob is made up of police officers, National Guard forces, and other figures of the state, and when they apprehend him, they do not kill him immediately. Bigger is instead brought to jail and placed on trial, although the fairness of his trial is questionable, and is made up of the kinds of anti-black rhetoric often used to enrage crowds before a lynching. The burning cross that is present when he is arrested and the crowd waiting outside the jailhouse all but seal Bigger's fate. As is the case in most lynchings, Bigger's trial, conviction, and death sentence will be used as an example, a warning to all African American citizens regarding the subservient and second-class racial identity they are expected to adopt. This process of arrest, detention, and prosecution takes the place of lynching. As Waldrep notes, "In the first decades of the twentieth century the number of times white men lynched black men decreased at just the time when the numbers of legal executions of black men skyrocketed" (162). It is this growing problem, this replacing of old-fashioned lynching with high-tech lynching, that Wright presents in his novel, showing that the American espousal of progress is still being undermined, only now by a new form of mob violence against African Americans, a legal form involving policemen, lawyers, juries, and judges.

In the process, Bigger Thomas becomes the embodiment of a key Modernist-era literary figure, an individual whose own identity is mutilated and violently destroyed by literal and/or symbolic crowd violence aimed at eradicating the individual's identity altogether or forcing the individual to conform to the identity espoused by dominant society. For Bigger Thomas, "the actual killing of Mary and Bessie was not what concerned him most; it was knowing and feeling that he could never make anybody know what had driven him to it" (732-3). As Bigger's lawyer valiantly asserts, and many critics have echoed, it is Bigger's lack of identity, his inability to create an individual identity independent of the power structures put in place controlling his blackness, that leads him to commit the crimes he is executed for. Bigger can never make those around him understand his motives because those around him cannot see him, at least not independently from the identity they have assigned him. Unable to self-fashion his own identity, Bigger's identity becomes that of an animalistic street criminal, a black murderer and rapist, a "black ape" (757). Bigger's trial is thus not progress, but rather a reenactment of Southern lynch violence, a more sophisticated form of identity-shaping mob violence.

Johnson's *Autobiography*, Faulkner's *Light in August*, and Wright's *Uncle Tom's Children* and *Native Son* all represent the ways that writers during the Modernist era interrogated issues of identity through depictions of mob violence. In the cases of these works, assaults on black racial identity are represented through scenes of lynchings, whether these lynchings are of the traditional Southern variety or the more modern, legalized version depicted in *Native Son*, where a black criminal is put to death for his crimes against a white woman, crimes that include an alleged rape, an alleged rape that becomes the key reason for his execution. Of course, gender and racially motivated lynching violence have always been connected, whether the lynching takes place in an extra-legal or legal fashion, just as matters of equal rights for women and African Americans have often been championed together. In this way, the African American literary tradition, through, among other things, the common trope of racially motivated lynching violence, inspired U.S. Modernist-era authors to explore the struggle between identity self-fashioning and crowd violence, especially as this struggle related to post–World War I gender roles. The most prominent American Modernists investigated gender roles that were, like certain second-class racial identities, imposed on their subjects by coercion through mob violence. Importantly, these writers do so by depicting white women as the victims of a kind of metaphoric, figurative lynching violence aimed at defining womanhood and setting boundaries for women that were enforced by crowd threats.

CHAPTER III

Female Identity, Southern Womanhood and Crowd Narration in Faulkner's Fiction

As gender roles changed following World War I, and racial violence and lynching continued to be prominent in the American South, it is not surprising that a Southern writer connected mob violence and lynching with the precarious nature of female identity in United States society. William Faulkner, like many Modernist American fiction writers, has been criticized for failing to display a deep level of political consciousness in his work, for creating his art while conforming to the Modernist mantra of "art for art's sake" rather than directly engaging with the key social issues of his time. Faulkner, like Ernest Hemingway, F. Scott Fitzgerald, and other writers commonly referred to as Modernists, is often charged with having ignored the social issues taken up in the writing of their more overtly political contemporaries, a group that includes Sinclair Lewis, Mike Gold, Upton Sinclair, John Steinbeck, and Richard Wright. Often the charges levied against these canonized but allegedly apolitical authors are rather harsh; as Ted Atkinson observes, "Authors associated with high modernism and literary formalism were charged with emphasizing artistic self-reliance, berated as relics of egocentric bourgeois individualism, and deemed supportive of an oppressive capitalist system" (42). Accusations such as those noted by Atkinson depict these writers as not merely ambivalent towards, but actually supportive of, political oppression and social inequality.

Given the increasingly overt political stance of most post-formalist literary criticism, it is not surprising that efforts to reform and diversify the literary canon have perpetuated the myth that Faulkner, Hemingway, Fitzgerald, and other canonical writers typically referred to as "high Modernists" lacked appropriate social consciousness in their writing. Throughout this book, I argue that all of these writers, Faulkner especially, produced works that confronted, rather than avoided, serious social, cultural, and political issues. This chapter will focus on the ways in which Faulkner uses imagery suggestive of crowd violence to challenge traditional gender roles, especially traditional notions of Southern womanhood. Faulkner's use of crowd violence and mob imagery in his famous portrayals of Southern women like Caddy Compson and Addie Bundren likens their suffering to that suffered by Joe Christmas in *Light in August*, as all of these characters face a perpetual cycle of crowd violence aimed at denying them the opportunity to self-fashion non-normative identities.

Defending or attacking Faulkner's political and social consciousness, or lack thereof, has been a popular topic in Faulkner studies. Recently, Atkinson has argued that

> for the most part, Faulkner's place in 1930s culture has been defined in terms of alienation, from both contemporaneous and retrospective points of view. During the Depression, Faulkner's fiction appeared out of touch with what many influential denizens of the literary establishment, energized by leftist activism, considered relevant and worthwhile [2].

Atkinson adds that "readers of Faulkner's novels and stories could find virtually no explicit references to matters deemed essential to enlightened social consciousness" (8). On the opposite side of those readers mentioned by Atkinson are readers like David Minter, who believes that

> Faulkner, as compellingly as any writer of his time, and more compellingly than most, also engaged grave social and political issues that were at the time grave personal and moral issues. These problematic issues included, among other things, the force of race and class, gender and sexuality, poverty and abundance, as well as failure and success in privileging and disadvantaging and thus shaping and misshaping human beings [3].

Noel Polk has noted both Faulkner's preoccupation with race and his preoccupation with issues of gender and sexuality, arguing, as Atkinson, Minter, and others have, that Faulkner consistently critiques social and political matters. Agreeing with such readings of Faulkner, I assert that identity is the central focus of most of Faulkner's fiction, and that in different periods of his writing career, he focused on gender identity, racial identity, and class identity. Furthermore, Faulkner's focus on identity is often shown through depictions of crowd violence, whether he is focusing on racial identity, as discussed in the previous chapter, class identity, as will be discussed in Chapter V, or gender identity, the focus of this chapter.

Faulkner's representations of women especially have generated many critical discussions, and Faulkner has at times been read as a sexist and misogynistic writer. As Minter observes, "Several readers have felt that Faulkner's sympathies as a fictionist lay more with men than with women" (44). Certainly,

Faulkner's male characters portray misogynistic behaviors. Gail Mortimer does not describe the male treatment of women in Faulkner's fiction with favorable terms, arguing that "Faulkner's male characters tend to perceive women as containing spaces, places that (1) when benevolent, offer serenity, security, and peace and (2) when threatening—that is, sexual—seem capable of devouring the man who gets too close" (123). Mortimer adds that Faulkner's imagination may have failed in creating female characters, noting that "most of Faulkner's fictive women tend to be parodies: sexually intense physical presences, desiccating spinsters, faded housewives, or venerated old ladies. When he does attempt to draw a fully rounded, strong female character, he can conceive of strength only in masculine terms" (124). As Polk has argued, "Much of Faulkner's work is marked by gynophobia if not always outright misogyny. Women in his fiction are nearly always associated not just with sex and shame but also with filth, excrement, pain, and death" (150). These statements, all from prominent Faulkner critics, certainly cast a shadow on Faulkner's views of women, both personally and in his fiction.

Faulkner's depictions of women, while rarely flattering, echo the cultural assumptions concerning women found prominently in the Mississippi that he tried to recreate in his fiction, and his representations are, in my opinion, a direct attack on cultural assumptions that Faulkner realized were limiting and endangered. Life is rarely easy for anyone in Faulkner's fiction, and his portrayals of the difficulties facing women, especially in the geographical region he is most concerned with, are not without historical basis. From a historical perspective, Don H. Doyle notes that from the time it was settled, Mississippi was a tough place for women to live:

> Mississippi was a frontier of promise and adventure for young white men aspiring to gain a place for themselves in a new country full of opportunity. But male ambition to move west often came at the expense of the domestic comforts and social ties women valued most. The West was often a lonely place for white women, cast amid a heavily masculine population and a society that offered little to compensate for the kinship and friendship they left behind [103].

Doyle's description of Mississippi, as it was first settled, is echoed in Joel Williamson's account of love and marriage in Faulkner's fiction, showing the connection between Faulkner's writing and its historical sources:

> Faulkner's major characters lived and moved upon a marital and sexual landscape that was in shambles. It was littered with the fragments left by a destructive social order—love without consummation, sex without love or marriage, adultery, rape, attempted rape, rape with an inanimate object, rape using another male, incest, miscegenation, prostitution, homosexuality, androgyny, bestiality, voyeurism, nymphomania, pedophilia, necrophilia, impotence, and, finally, frigidity, both male and female. Moreover, sex of any kind was very often associated directly with physical violence [369].

III. Southern Womanhood and Crowd Narration in Faulkner

It is true that Faulkner's fiction provides us with few examples of heroic women, but it should be noted that Faulkner's fiction usually lacks heroes of any kind, male or female. Furthermore, Faulkner's men rarely fare better than their female counterparts do when it comes to love, sex, and marriage. In fact, as is the case in *The Sound and the Fury* and *As I Lay Dying*, Faulkner's men are often rendered impotent, showing the dying off of their cultural power and control while conversely, Faulkner's women continually struggle with the burdens imposed on them by normative notions of womanhood and motherhood. In Faulkner's fiction, women are not inherently un-heroic, overly sexual, or devilishly sinful; rather, they appear to be the products of patriarchal social systems that often cause them to be highly dysfunctional in their roles as daughters, sexual partners, and mothers.

Relationships between men and women, especially sexual ones, seemed to be unnaturally complicated because of the traditional roles expected of women. Gender roles existed (and continue to exist) for women everywhere, but in the South, gender roles for females were even more strictly defined. As Williamson notes, "Historians have sometimes argued that white men in the South painted themselves into a sexual corner," explaining that Southern white men " took advantage of black women and so pedestalized white women as to render physical and sexual relations with their wives unusually difficult. The southern wife was pious and pure, the angel, the conduit of God, and accessible physically only for procreation" (382). Perhaps this self-inflicted conundrum explains why, in Faulkner's fiction, Williamson "finds among the leading characters no reasonably perfect union—nor even, one might add, a reasonably happy couple outside of marriage" (367). Faulkner shows sexual relationships between men and women to be unnaturally encumbered by a variety of sexist views that strictly limited all aspects of traditional male/female relationships.

Faulkner, writing his most renowned works of fiction in the 1920s and 1930s, does not seem to depict women as progressing socially, as the national myths of the Roaring Twenties and the flapper popular cultural persona might have pronounced, instead displaying an intricate patriarchal system that has not been at all lessened by the Jazz Age's common stereotype of the liberated woman. As John T. Matthews posits,

> Though the celebrated flapper became the jazz age icon of the newly liberated woman, women made few serious gains during the decade. The Nineteenth Amendment, passed by the House in 1918 but blocked in the Senate for a year by southerners, had provided the right to vote for women beginning in August 1920. Women may have behaved with less restraint during the twenties, but there was virtually no improvement in their economic, political, or social status. Only perhaps in their personal life did they realize some improvement; birth control methods, electrical appliances, processed foods, and relaxed divorce laws furthered women's control over their own lives [6].

Note that the "improvements" Matthews mentions, while certainly making domestic life less work-intensive, still involved traditional normative roles that fashioned female identity as synonymous with motherhood and domestic servitude. In spite of popular culture depictions of newly liberated women smoking, drinking, and enjoying casual sex, traditional gender roles regarding female identity still pervaded throughout the U.S., and especially in the South.

As several literary critics and historians have noted, the strict identities assigned to women and the forms of social control used to regulate these identities were often similar to the expectations and obstacles facing black Americans, and there is plenty of evidence in Faulkner's fiction of his awareness of the correlation between social attitudes towards blacks and women. As Matthews has noted, "In Faulkner's world, both women and blacks suffer as objects of various sorts of oppression" (64). While African Americans were overtly threatened with violent punishments involving crowd violence, women in the United States faced more covert, but often equally heinous, forms of social control. Diane Roberts adds that "women, along with blacks, are the objects of the South's most careful defining and categorizing" (xiv), and it is this denial of the opportunity to self-fashion identity that often links Faulkner's African American characters and his female characters. Mortimer provides a theoretical basis for the similarities between the treatment of blacks and women, noting that "in Faulkner's stories the black person and the female evoke strikingly similar emotions in characters to whom they represent all that is 'other' than the self" (15). Faulkner's women share many commonalities with characters who are oppressed because of their race, characters such as Joe Christmas.

In each year from 1929 to 1931, Faulkner produced a novel (*The Sound and the Fury* in 1929, *As I Lay Dying* in 1930, and *Sanctuary* in 1931) that dealt specifically with issues of Southern womanhood, especially the challenges a patriarchal system imposed on women. Fittingly, given the observations noted above regarding the similarities between the ways women and African Americans are treated in Faulkner's fiction, Faulkner uses images of crowd violence and even lynching to show that women were also victims of collective violence, albeit in more covert forms, violence aimed at defining their identities and punishing them for transgressing against these normative identities. Although this crowd violence does not always lead directly to death, this violence does usually lead to physical and emotional trauma. Some readers have questioned Faulkner's ability to enter the consciousnesses of his female characters, yet Faulkner's fiction, and especially *The Sound and the Fury*, *As I Lay Dying*, and *Sanctuary*, persistently questions the desire of the dominant patriarchy to enforce specific roles for female identity. As Polk observes, "Life for women is not always significantly better in the fiction of the later years, but it is particularly terrifying in these crucial years" (74).

As is the case with many of his novels, identity is the central theme of *The Sound and the Fury*. Walter Benn Michaels argues, "*The Sound and the Fury* repeatedly insists that what people and things do or mean is a function of what they are; it insists, that is, on identity as the determining ground of action or significance" (1). Although shifting perspectives were often used in Faulkner's prior novels, *The Sound and the Fury* was Faulkner's first attempt to use multiple narrators, all of whom relate their story through stream-of-consciousness narration. These individual narrators, the Compson brothers (Benjy, Quentin, and Jason), focus their thoughts on their sister, Caddy. Caddy is the absent center, as many readers have noted, of the novel—she is never given the opportunity to tell her own story, and instead her story is narrated through the collective voices of her brothers. Likewise, as an author, Faulkner avoids narrating from Caddy's perspective, defining her, as her culture might, from the outside only, denying her fictional character any autonomy, any identity self-fashioning. Caddy's identity is constantly defined by the mob that is made up of her brothers and the other men around her. Caddy's brothers project on her the identity they desire her to adopt, and each of the respective identities they construct fits their own unique needs and personalities; as Minter puts it, "It is in Caddy that each brother's discontent finds its focus, as we see in their various evocations of her" (42). This narrative style allows Faulkner to recreate the normative female identities he sees men fashioning for women in his native South, a region where women, even more so than elsewhere, are denied the ability to construct their own subjectivities by the overarching, patriarchal social system that defines their identity for them.

Caddy is the central focus of not just any family, but the Compson family, a symbolic Southern family whose past glory is, like the Old South itself, outdated and crumbling in the present. As Daniel Singal asserts, "The Compsons, with a governor and three generals to their credit, clearly fall within the Cavalier tradition, but it is also apparent that that tradition has become threadbare" (117). The Compson family has fallen greatly from its prior prominence as a favored Southern family, and as Doreen Fowler notes, Caddy's name is representative of this fall: "Derived from the Latin word *cadere*, to fall, her name may refer not only to her state as a fallen woman but also to the original fall from a state of plentitude" (32). Caddy, through the course of the novel, becomes viewed by all of the males around her as a fallen woman, the reason for their family decline, but importantly, Faulkner creates Caddy as a symbol of their failed attitudes. The fall is not to be blamed on Caddy or any other female character (except perhaps by the misogynist, Jason); instead, the blame lies strictly on the attitudes towards women Faulkner portrays through the Compson brothers.

With an alcoholic father figure who eventually drinks himself to death and an ineffectual and hypochondriac mother who usually spends the day in bed, the Compson family seems doomed to fail. Their failure, however, only becomes complete through the mistakes brought about by the family's patriarchal attitudes. Mr. Compson is clearly portrayed, mainly in Quentin's section but elsewhere as well, as the source of much of this patriarchal thinking, with Karl F. Zender noting that Mr. Compson is "both a parent and an embodiment of a pervasive and insidious cultural attitude" (16). Mr. Compson, as a failed father, represents the continually failing patriarchal system, a system that ruins women like Caddy while also making men dysfunctional in their sexual and familial relationships with women. As a family in decline, a family representative of the South, it becomes apparent that the South's slave past and the destruction wrought by the Civil War are not the only causes of the region's, or the Compson family's, decline. Rather, the decline of the Compsons, and symbolically the South, is also rooted in the treatment of Southern women. As Roberts notes, as is the case with the Southern patriarchy, "Female 'honor,' that is, chastity, as a verifier of family status, is a Compson fixation" (112). This fixation leads to the denial of female subjectivity in *The Sound and the Fury* by the Compson brothers, and ultimately, the complete collapse of the Compson family.

Benjy, Quentin, and Jason combine to form a mob that attempts to define Caddy's identity, often through violence. Given Faulkner's own temporal and geographical contexts in Mississippi, it is not surprising that he chooses to examine some of his favorite themes (the fall of the South, time, identity) in *The Sound and the Fury* with mob and lynching imagery. As Faulkner biographer Joseph Blotner points out, "Lynchings and burnings were reported in the *Eagle* every year" (235), and the presence of these events in the local newspapers certainly caught Faulkner's eye. Benjy, Quentin, and Jason are all very different individuals, as is noted by Matthews, who observes that

> you can hardly imagine three more extreme world visions: the dumb, mentally retarded, and castrated youngest brother, Benjy; the idealistic, gentlemanly, eldest son of a southern aristocratic family and a student at the Yankee Harvard University, Quentin; the resentful, paranoiac, and mean-spirited middle brother, hardware store clerk and small-town southern bigot, Jason [33–4].

The three brothers represent three different versions of Southern patriarchy: through Benjy, the Oedipal desire for maternal companionship, through Quentin the desire to uphold gentlemanly values, and through Jason the desire to violently control an "other." In spite of the differences in the brothers' attitudes, and even their mental capacities, Faulkner shows that the Compson brothers, and by implication many Southern men, view women, and especially female sexuality, as things that should be strictly controlled by the ruling patriarchy.

Caddy's importance to Benjy, and Benjy's obsession with Caddy, is apparent from the novel's opening page, when Benjy hears golfers who play on a course bordering the Compson land shouting, "Here, caddie" (1), causing Benjy to break into one of his outbursts of moaning and sobbing. Michaels notes that

> the word "caddie" appears to Benjy less as the use than as the misuse of her name; uttered on the land that was sold to pay for her wedding, it marks not the fact that she's "here" but the fact that she's *not* here. Which is why, hearing the word that he understands only as a name, and hearing the name as a reference to the absence rather than the presence of the person named, Benjy starts bellowing [3–4].

Caddy becomes the novel's absent center in Benjy's section, often present only in the minds of her brothers. Her own sense of personal identity is completely lacking in the novel; her character is a void that is filled by the projections of her brothers. For Benjy, as Matthews argues, "From the first indirectly spoken word of the novel—'caddie'/ Caddy—Benjy's world reels with the loss of his sister" (38). To Benjy, Caddy is a mother figure, a figure like the black servant Dilsey who provides him with the comfort and solace he does not get from his own mother, a mother who, although certainly not a sympathetic figure, is bed-ridden, likely because of the hardships she has already endured at the hands of the Compson males. It is Caddy who tries to carry Benjy as if he is her child, since Mrs. Compson refuses, telling Caddy, "A five year old child. No, no. Not in my lap" (63). To this rejection, Caddy responds to her mother, "'You dont need to bother with him ... I like to take care of him'" (63). It is Caddy who sleeps with Benjy at night to calm him, and Caddy who defends Benjy, attacking Jason with scissors when he purposefully cuts up Benjy's paper dolls. In her relationship with Benjy, Caddy attempts to take on the maternal role vacated by Mrs. Compson as Caddy attempts to fashion a mothering identity that her society encourages.

Benjy's moments with Caddy are the calming moments that he holds to, creating Caddy as his Oedipal mother, his caretaker and, from a Freudian standpoint, his only sexual desire. Minter notes that "all instinctively, he tries to hold fast to those moments in which Caddy meets his need for tenderness" (45). This tenderness, as Roberts notes, contains sexual elements as well. Roberts argues, "Sexuality—both his and Caddy's—is at the center of Benjy's section. Without knowing the words for it, Benjy is just as obsessed with her virginity as Jason, Quentin, and Mrs. Compson. However, Caddy's virginity is not, for Benjy, part of an economic or social system" (115).[1] Benjy, just like his brothers, attempts to guard his sister's sexual identity, conforming to a rigorous patriarchal social standard that Benjy can sense even if he cannot understand. Benjy's desire, however, is derived from purely sexual motivations—he wants her for himself to fill roles as both mother and lover. Benjy moans when Caddy smells different after she becomes sexually active; he cries and pulls on Caddy's dress when she is sitting on the swing with her boyfriend Charlie;

and he objects to Caddy wearing perfume as a teenager, forcing her to relent and give the perfume away to Dilsey. Benjy's interactions with Caddy in *The Sound and the Fury* continually repeat these patterns; Benjy has one of his fits whenever he is ignored by Caddy or threatened sexually by Caddy's sexual activity with other men. When Caddy relents and attempts to pacify Benjy, she gives him her sole attention, and Benjy stops crying and begins to function as close to normally as he can. When Caddy becomes sexually active, Benjy can only try to control her, to keep her from having sex and keep her in his own bed. His sexual desire for his sister, who is also symbolically his mother, leads to unconcealed attempts to control, and punish through his fits and outbursts, her sexual identity. Yet Benjy cannot act upon any of his sexual desires, as his mental disability renders him essentially impotent in his Southern community. He will forever live in the Compson house, isolated from society, and if he ever leaves the Compson home, it will be to fulfill Jason's threats to have Benjy sent to the state mental hospital.

An opposite of Benjy, Quentin is the most intelligent and perceptive of the Compson brothers. In fact, he is all too aware of his own desire to repress his sister's sexual identity, and he recognizes the patriarchal cultural forces that provoke this treatment of women. Quentin's actions towards his sister, like the South's actions towards women in Faulkner's view, as Fowler puts it, all "seem to culminate in failure" (37). In his relationship with his sister, Quentin seems to act out a role Southern society has taught him even though he recognizes this role only complicates relationships between men and women. Quentin's physical challenge to Dalton Ames ends in impotent embarrassment. His urges to act on his own sexual desire for Caddy always fail, and even when he tries to feign incest with his sister by lying to his father, he fails to be convincing. His desire to kill Caddy, since he cannot aptly guard her purity or have her for himself, also fails even though Caddy demands that he "push" the knife at her throat "like this" (152). Quentin cannot even control the symbolic, phallic object of the knife without giving Caddy uncharacteristic control. As is often the case in Faulkner's fiction, male characters are empowered by a patriarchal social system even when these men themselves are not powerful. Caddy, perhaps to a fault, has the will to act that her brother lacks, while Quentin too often only imagines. Even his good intentions to guide "Sister," the lost immigrant girl he meets on the day of his suicide, ends with his being physically attacked and almost imprisoned under the suspicion of being a child molester or kidnapper. Ironically, Quentin has the desire to molest his own sister, and to make her a prisoner protected from the sexual desires of other men, yet he is tormented by his own paralysis, his own inability to protect her in any meaningful way. He is Faulkner's version of Eliot's Prufrock.

Quentin's failures all seem to stem from his belief in the outdated notions toward women that he recognizes in himself, but cannot overcome. Singal notes that Quentin is "a keen observer of the world around him" and that "he knows all too well that his values have become outmoded and his defense of them quixotic, but he can envision no alternative standard of meaning" (119). Quentin, like most Southern men, has been given no alternative way to understand women. He longs to define Caddy's identity for her, yet he cannot conceive of any identity other than that of the pious, angelic, and un-sexual version of womanhood his culture has provided him with, an unrealistic identity that Caddy obviously rejects. While Quentin is failing to enforce an identity upon her, Caddy is attempting to create an identity for herself, one that, as Zender observes, "Quentin discerns, even as he abhors," an identity that is based on her "sexual boldness and transgression of racial and class boundaries" (14). Caddy, it seems, rebels in a manner similar to Joe Christmas and Bigger Thomas. She rebels against the collective male forces that try to assign her identity, and her rebellion leads to her own destruction.

Quentin's attempts to control Caddy's sex life are complicated by his own sexual desires for her. Likewise, Faulkner comments on the South's fixation on its daughters' sexual activities, linking this obsession with a Freudian impulse towards incest. Southern men have been conditioned to think that they are meant to protect the objects of their own sexual desire, creating an unsustainable angel/whore dichotomy. Caddy, however, rejects Quentin, and through her actions, rejects Southern patriarchal attitudes. Although she acts on her sexual desires in a way that causes her scorn in Faulkner's South, Caddy does not seem mentally unbalanced or unusually sexually voracious. Her rejections of Quentin, and the impotence of both his actions and desires, cause Quentin to begin to see Caddy as a figure of death as he realizes his own inability to control her in the ways society expects him, as a male, to do. Minter argues that "Caddy begins to merge with 'Little Sister Death'—that is, with an incestuous love forbidden on threat of death. Rendered impotent by that threat, Quentin comes to love not the body of his sister, nor even some concept of Compson honor, but death itself" (47).

For Quentin and Southern patriarchal definitions of womanhood, death is an inevitable result of an unsustainable system. First, Quentin mistakenly thinks that, by killing both himself and Caddy in the branch with the knife, the dilemma of patriarchal gender roles for women will be resolved. It is only when Quentin arrives at Harvard that he is able to distance himself from the Compson home and contextualize his father's ideas concerning women. His father's ideas are the Southern patriarchy's ideas of women having an "affinity for evil" (96), of there only being two identities for a woman ("a lady or not" [103]), of women being nothing more than a "delicate equilibrium of periodical filth between two moons balanced" (128). From this distance, Quentin is able to see his errors, the errors of his culture's views of women. At Harvard, around Northern men his own age who talk about women as if they are "all bitches" (92), Quentin realizes that the patriarchal system, not women, must be changed.

Having come to this realization, Quentin decides to kill himself, but his meticulous planning on the day of his suicide is interrupted by his socially conditioned desire to protect women. He meets a lost Italian immigrant girl and immediately brands her with the Southern moniker of "little sister." He tries to escape what he has been trained to think of as his responsibility as a Southern gentleman by giving her a coin and walking away. Quentin, however, is unable to escape the notions concerning the protective control of women that he has been indoctrinated with, joining up with the little girl again and lamenting, "You're just a girl. Poor kid" (138), showing that Quentin is aware of the suffering awaiting the girl in a world that tries to so strictly define female identity, but again failing to realize the problematic nature of his desire to protect such girls.

Quentin's section ends with his death, a suicide clearly motivated by his inability to navigate the complex relations between men and women that he has grown up with, all of which are symbolized through his relationship with Caddy. As Polk argues, "His memories evolve out of scenes of trauma, all centered in his loss of Caddy: her wedding, his conversation with Herbert Head, the husband his parents trapped for Caddy; her love affair with Dalton Ames and his humiliating inability to defend her honor; and his long conversation with his father" (110). As was often the case with lynchings, Quentin desires to define Caddy's identity with finality by killing her, as he attempts to do during the scene in the branch. Failing to do so, Quentin reaches the decision that, at least symbolically, makes sense for Faulkner; in order for women to gain the power of self-fashioning their identities, the representatives of the strict patriarchal system of the South must, and will eventually, destroy themselves.

Although Benjy and Quentin Compson are culturally conditioned to think of women in sexist and misogynistic ways, they are generally sympathetic figures, shown to be confused by and struggling with these attitudes. Jason Compson, the third and final brother to narrate in *The Sound and the Fury*, is not a sympathetic character. He accepts these attitudes as truths and desires the control these cultural attitudes empower him with. Benjy desires natural motherly love and sexual satisfaction. Quentin also desires sexual satisfaction, but he also intends to uphold Southern gender roles that define both women and men. Jason, however, is Faulkner's finest example in the novel of the destructive nature of his society's outlook on women, as Jason represents the completely bigoted, misogynistic, racist, and paranoid kind of men that Faulkner recognized and despised in the culture that surrounded him. Jason is an extremely cruel man, the kind of man Faulkner liked to mock in his writing, and much of Jason's cruelty is aimed at women, leading Matthews to claim that "Jason's cruelty magnifies the assumptions of patriarchal social systems" (95).

Jason's section—his rant—is full of hatred, and it is in his section that Faulkner links the patriarchal assumptions found in the novel's earlier sections with outright misogyny, which is also shown to be related to other forms of hatred such as racism, xenophobia, and class envy. From his opening statement, "Once a bitch always a bitch" (180), it is clear that Jason, unlike his brothers, treats women with a pure hatred that he also reserves for blacks, Jews, and essentially anyone not like himself. When Jason refers to Caddy's behavior and his treatment of her with the statement, "When people act like niggers, no matter who they are the only thing to do is treat them like a nigger" (181), Faulkner makes his most overt reference in the novel to the relationship between the violence Southerners enforced upon African Americans, their supposed social inferior, and upon women, another group that Southern, male-dominated society considered inferiors. As Matthews notes, the "catalog of Jason's enemies suggests that Faulkner in part wants to explore the psychology of a 1920s southern small-town bigot" (64). This bigot wishes to violently punish both blacks and women who transgress against his ideas regarding racial and gender identity.

In Jason's world, both African American and female citizens are viewed by white, male normative society as subservient individuals meant to react to the whims of the Southern white patriarchy. Likewise, Jason tries to control Caddy and her daughter Quentin in the same way he tries to control Dilsey and his other African American household servants. As Faulkner explores the psychology of a bigot, he finds a direct correlation between racist and misogynist attitudes. When Caddy and her daughter Quentin reject the subservient identity that Jason tries to force upon them, he can only reply simplistically that one or the other is "going on like a nigger wench" (189).

Jason's monologue also furthers Faulkner's exploration of the socioeconomic forces behind racist and misogynist attitudes. Polk has categorized Jason's section as "a long loud agonizing cry" (116), and Polk adds that "clearly Jason is in pain" (120). Jason is indeed troubled throughout his monologue, but the source of his trouble is not African American, Jewish, or female, as he himself seems to claim, but rather money. Money is central to Jason's identity, and it is the money he thinks he is losing because of the black servants in his family and the female members of his family that causes his hate towards them. As Fowler argues, this obsession with money is clear in Jason's relationships with women, since "money helps him to counter his feelings of anxiety about his masculine identity.... Money is Jason's substitute for potency: appropriately, then, he selects for a girlfriend a prostitute, choosing a relationship that is clearly based on his ability to pay rather than on any other ability" (38). Like those who supported the lynching of African Americans based in part on the economic competition emerging between poor whites and the newly freed black population, Jason seems to support the social control of women such as Caddy and her daughter Quentin in order to affirm his own financial potential. By the end of the novel, Jason's main relationship with Caddy is one of financial competition, as he continually creates elaborate ways to steal the money Caddy sends home to support Quentin.

Jason's monologue is also the most straightforward section of the novel, and it is Faulkner's clearest expression of repulsion towards the kinds of values Jason manifests. Few readers can encounter Jason's section without developing a strong dislike for its narrator. Luckily, for most readers, Jason's actions, like those of Quentin and Benjy, always end in failure. By the end of the novel, Jason has lost a good deal of money, the only thing he truly values, because the women in his family have outsmarted him. The women and minorities that he shows so much hatred toward seem to prosper in comparison. Unlike Quentin and Benjy, Jason tries to handle the family problems with what he would call logic, but as Polk notes, "for all the apparent 'logic' of his outpourings, he too is driven by irrational forces buried deep within his unconscious that are battering at the boundaries of articulation" (116). The main source of these irrational forces is Jason's belief, handed down to him by his father and by Southern culture, that he is superior to all African American citizens and all women, and therefore, he feels responsible for their control. His attempts to define their identity, especially the identities of his sister and his niece, only lead to his own downfall. As Matthews surmises, "Jason's preoccupations as he experiences them are illustrated in Jason's remarks on gender and family. We have seen that Jason's world identifies force with masculine authority, yet his section repeatedly demonstrates the impotence of such a set of values in the moment of crisis" (73).

Benjy, Quentin, and Jason Compson together form a representative mob that continually tries to enforce a specific identity onto their sister Caddy. Each brother represents a different aspect of the patriarchal society that seeks to define and enforce normative female identities. The threat of real violence, and other forms of abuse, are consistently employed in their attempts to define Caddy as a Southern lady. Benjy represents underlying psychological male desires for a Freudian mother. Quentin, meanwhile, represents the Cavalier tradition and it's outdated notions of female protection, a protection that is at odds with his sexual desires. Jason most obviously represents outright misogynist attitudes that continued to prevail in Southern culture's outlook on gender. In spite of these pressures, from an early age, Caddy seems uninterested in wholly adopting the behaviors that are expected of her. Faulkner said of his novel that "the story is all there, in the first section as Benjy told it.... When I realized that the story might be printed, I took three more sections, all longer than Benjy's, to try to clarify it" ("Two Introductions to *The Sound and the Fury*" 295). Indeed, Benjy's section provides the central scene of the novel. As Caddy climbs the pear tree, ignoring the warnings from her brothers, the three of them catch a glimpse of her muddied drawers as she discovers death, witnessing a family funeral taking place in her home. Here, Caddie sees and begins to understand a concept that her brothers cannot. The reactions of her brothers all encompass the behaviors of the members of communities often found at Southern lynchings. Benjy, dumb and mute, can only watch the scene, a voyeur, a silent, tongue-tied witness, unable to communicate the emotions spawned by the symbolic image of her muddied drawers. Quentin becomes obsessed with the image of his sister's soiled underwear, remembering until the day of his suicide the sexual connotations involved, and forever wanting to violently blot out her sexuality to, in his mind, cleanse her. Moreover, Jason, demanding what he thinks is justice, demanding a punishment that exceeds the crime, can only tattle on Caddy, telling Dilsey, "I told her not to climb up that tree" (45). The brothers form three key groups of spectators in most lynching scenes: the voyeurs, those concerned with the sexual nature of crime and punishment, and the sadistic torturer.

It is important to remember, however, that there are no heroes or martyrs, in Faulkner's fiction, yet Caddy and her daughter Quentin do display some heroic tendencies. According to Roberts, through Caddy "the cherished binary of virgin and whore are challenged" (117). Matthews argues, "Caddy's simple physical appetite for sexual pleasure endangers the elaborate code of purity and property upon which the patriarchy depends" (91). Caddy indeed challenges the codes and roles that make up the identity she is supposed to adopt as a Southern woman, showing that changes in normative gender roles are on the horizon. Nevertheless, as Matthews adds, "Caddy's choices, of course, hardly set her perfectly free; she suffers the continuing effects of social restriction" (92). In Faulkner's fiction, women can, and often do, challenge the identities that are assigned to them. Rarely, though, do they successfully create their own identities because of these challenges. These women challenge the identities assigned to them, but they rarely escape the punishment that awaits such challenges. Faced with the virgin/whore binary mentioned by Roberts and others, Southern society has given Caddy, as a woman, only one way to rebel, to seek her own identity. As Singal argues, "Caddy's tragedy ... is that she can discover no suitable identity to replace the one she rejects" (131). The whore identity, as Caddy finds, is an extremely limited one as well, with Matthews noting that "there is no room for female desire, and so there is no space for Caddy's subjectivity, her version of her story" (91). Caddy's identity is always defined by the males around her, even when she rebels against the identity they wish to assign her. Her rebellion against one male-assigned identity, the male-fabricated identity of Southern lady, only allows the males around her to identify her and craft her identity as a whore. Failing to formulate her own identity, she is left to struggle in a male dominated world, one that cheats her out of her desires in a manner similar to the way Jason cheats her out of money.[2] While her own choices led her up the tree, it is the desires of her brothers that cause her ongoing subjection to violence whenever she transgresses their notions of female identity, of motherhood, sisterhood, and Southern womanhood.

Immediately after writing *The Sound and the Fury*, Faulkner began working on *As I Lay Dying*. The two novels, written so closely together, share a thematic space as well, with Faulkner creating a female character in Addie Bundren who is also central to the novel in spite of her absence, and who is also defined by the male members of her family and her community. As Polk observes, "Addie and Caddy have much in common besides their rhyming names.... They share a certain masochistic urge" (35). This urge, best described as a desire to overthrow the identities that patriarchal authority has assigned them, leads to their punishment at the hands of vengeful male mobs. Caddy, only suffering from threats of physical abuse in *The Sound and the Fury*, actually seems to fare better than Addie does. Addie, in a novel full of mob and lynching imagery, dies rather publicly, at the center of multiple, mostly male gazes, before having her body mutilated in an epic trek to her final resting place.

Whereas *The Sound and the Fury* focused on the identity crises facing daughters and sisters in the patriarchal South, *As I Lay Dying* explores the identity of Southern motherhood in the same male-dominated region. Faulkner again uses multiple narrators, and again, these narrators are predominantly male[3] and focused on defining the identity of a relatively absent female figure. The similarities in the narrative styles of *The Sound and the Fury* and *As I Lay Dying* have been noticed before; as Atkinson observes, "As in *The Sound and the Fury*, the modernist form of *As I Lay Dying* features an incisive social vision that emerges from the fractured subjective positions and experiences of individual characters to expose and comment on social, economic, and political issues active on a range that encompasses text and context" (176). In *As I Lay Dying*, issues of female identity and motherhood are the central social, economic, and political issues Faulkner dissects.

The title Faulkner chose for *As I Lay Dying* portrays the novel's focus on issues of patriarchy and motherhood. Fowler notes that the title alludes to a line in a speech by Agamemnon from *The Odyssey* and that "scholars have frequently observed that Agamemnon's speech stresses the indignity of death, a theme certainly evident in *As I Lay Dying*" (48). Fowler elaborates on the significance of this allusion to Homer's epic, arguing that "in *As I Lay Dying*, Clytemnestra reappears in the form of Addie Bundren, another murdered mother who demands a price for her death" (48). Fowler's description of Addie Bundren's death as a murder at the hands of the Bundren men might initially seem to put too much blame on the family for her death, but Fowler's description closely matches the description provided in an early section of the novel narrated by Cora Tull, one of the few sections of the novel narrated from a female perspective. Cora describes Addie's face as having "wasted away" at "the mercy and the ministration of four men and a tom-boy girl" (8). Upon first hearing of the death, Peabody, the family doctor, similarly remarks that Anse must have "wore her out at last" (41). Singal argues that "since the characters speak from their own limited vantage points, reflecting their needs and biases, the reader cannot possibly arrive at any assured, objective truth about them" (145), yet Cora Tull's and Peabody's descriptions of Addie's death at the hands of her family are consistent with the physical abuses that her dead body suffers as the Bundren family journeys to bury her. Their viewpoints, coming from outside the family, seem to objectively imply that Addie's death has come only after years of group-enforced suffering and even violence.

As Roberts and others have observed, like Caddy Compson, Addie "is the central obsession of the Bundren family and the novel ... a personality powerful in its (apparent) absence" (198). Each male member of the Bundren family (Addie's husband, Anse, and their sons, Cash, Jewel, Darl, and Vardaman) is obsessed with defining their mother, and as David Williams asserts, Addie, "like Caddy" in *The Sound and the Fury*, "prompts them to speak out" (111). Fittingly, the only Bundren who is not obsessed with Addie is seventeen-year-old Dewey Dell, who has her own approaching, and unwanted, motherhood to worry about. The Bundren men are obsessed with defining Addie as a loving mother, an identity that she repeatedly and openly rejects while alive. Addie's rejection of this identity leads to her punishment at the hands of the symbolic lynch mob made up of the men in her family, men who, as Fowler asserts and Cora Tull narrates, are her torturers and killers. This killing takes place publicly as they parade her dead body through the countryside. Along the way, Addie's body will be continually mutilated, as the death of Addie Bundren becomes deeply infused with lynching imagery.

Anse leads the Bundren mob that lynches Addie, and he and his sons are portrayed by Faulkner as representatives of poor, ignorant Southern whites. In some ways, Anse is himself a sympathetic figure, and again it is important to note, as Singal does, that "*As I Lay Dying* eschews heroes and villains" (145). Anse and the Bundren sons are too ignorant to have created, or to rebel against, the systemic patriarchy of the South—they only participate in it. Darl narrates in an early section that "Pa's feet are badly splayed, his toes cramped and bent and warped, with no toenail on his little toes, from working so hard in the wet in homemade shoes when he was a boy" (11), and it is noted later in the novel that Anse possibly suffers from a disease that endangers his life if he sweats, although it is unclear if this is to be taken seriously, or if this disease is just an excuse for him to avoid manual labor. Anse is also depicted as a toothless hunchback, a physically and mentally grotesque figure. In the South

Faulkner is portraying, however, these traits do not keep men like Anse from having the ability to choose a wife and subsequently control her identity. Men, even ignorant and physically weak ones like Anse, still have power over the women in Faulkner's South.

Anse's sons are all given sympathetic traits as well. Cash is a hard worker who takes pride in constructing a coffin to bury his mother in. Darl, as Cora Tull notes, appears to have the most love for his mother, and although he is considered by many to be strange and possibly even mentally ill, the sections Darl narrates are often the clearest and the most poetic. Jewel, as is shown in the only section he narrates, seems to care deeply for his mother and desires a peaceful death for her, wishing that he could protect her from the noise of Cash's buzzing saw and the annoyance of Dewey Dell's fanning her. Vardaman, the youngest son, is surely a sympathetic figure, a confused and perhaps mentally disabled child who cannot understand his mother's death. Each of these characters at one time or another receives sympathy from the reader, yet they all focus intently on making the journey to bury Addie for selfish reasons. For each of them, the trip represents a way to define Addie's identity as a loving mother, the loving mother that their society has told them she is *supposed* to be, rather than the cold wife and mother who has at some time or another rejected them all. For this rejection of the identity patriarchal society forces her to adopt, Addie is punished by death and by the mutilation and indignity her corpse suffers.

From the only section narrated by Addie in the novel, it is clear that she has rejected all traditional formulations of motherhood in an attempt to self-fashion her identity. Narrating events prior to her marriage, Addie describes life as a single woman who needs to work. She takes a job as a schoolteacher, one of the few jobs available to women, even though she dislikes children. Addie states, "In the afternoon when school was out and the last one had left with his little dirty snuffling nose, instead of going home I would go down the hill to the spring when I could be quiet and hate them" (169). She adds that her father, the first patriarchal figure in her life, had told her "that the reason for living was to get ready to stay dead a long time" (169), but that this way of living, having to work with children, was not an ideal way to live or to get ready to stay dead:

> And when I would have to look at them day after day, each with his and her secret and selfish thought, and blood strange to each other blood and strange to mine, and think that this seemed to be the only way I could get ready to stay dead, I would hate my father for having ever planted me. I would look forward to times when they faulted, so I could whip them. When the switch fell I could feel it upon my flesh; when it welted and ridged it was my blood that ran, and I would think with each blow of the switch: Now you are aware of me! Now I am something in your secret and selfish life, who have marked your blood with my own for ever and ever [169–70].

Addie feels trapped in this kind of employment, and she blames her father, her sole symbol of the patriarchal hierarchy at the time of her employment as a schoolteacher, for placing her in this situation. Fittingly, she does not blame her mother, seeming to already sense at this time that her mother is not to blame for her being born, her later relationship with Anse convincing her that children are something men force upon women. Full of anger, Addie takes pleasure in punishing the children she teaches in part because it makes them aware of her and the anti-mother identity she has tried to construct for herself. She repeats the idea that the children are full of "secret and selfish" thoughts, projecting on them the thoughts she sees in her everyday adult life, the "secret and selfish thoughts" she recognizes in the male figures around her. These "secret and selfish thoughts" are evident in the sections narrated by her children.

To escape her job in the schoolhouse, Addie chooses to take Anse as a husband after learning that he has "a house and a good farm" (171). From her experiences as a single woman, Addie learns the importance of choosing a husband not so much out of love but out of a sense of economic need. Without any living kin to rely on, and as a woman who will always have limited financial options, Addie sees this move as her best choice, but she realizes her mistake upon having her first child, relating that "when I knew that I had Cash, I knew that living was terrible and that this was the answer to it" (171). The answer to living is death, and Addie correlates motherhood with death, a reversal of the common notion that motherhood is life, that being a parent gives a mother something to live for. She realizes "that motherhood was invented by someone who had to have a word for it because the ones that had the children didn't care whether there was a word for it or not" (171–2). As Roberts argues, "Motherhood is a male construct, designed to contain women in an unreal role" (201), and immediately upon becoming a mother, Addie realizes this deception.

One of Addie's biggest complaints regarding motherhood is its invasion of her privacy, as she relates that her "aloneness had to be violated over and over each day" (172), a violation that she notes as specific to motherhood, a violation that was not caused "by Anse in the nights" (172). Addie is not a sexual prude or a simple hater of men; she does not complain about sex or men in general—only motherhood. Social expectations of motherhood create expectations for Addie that she is coerced to fulfill. When she finds that she is pregnant with Darl, she thinks she might "kill Anse" (172). After thinking about it more, however, she decides that she "had been tricked by words older than Anse or love" (172), referring to the patriarchal social order that was in place long before Anse arrived, a social order that defined her identity for her and had systems in place to punish her if she attempted to assume an identity outside of these confines.

Nevertheless, Addie attempts two different paths of escape in hopes of removing herself from the role of mother, but both paths of escape, like those taken by Caddy Compson, fail miserably. First, she has an affair, an affair that, rather than leading to an escape from motherhood, leads only to her impregnation with another child. Addie's intimate contact with men forces motherhood upon her, and the same fate apparently awaits her daughter Dewey Dell. Yet Jewel, the child born from this affair, becomes her favored child because he represents this attempt at escape and the identity she tried to self-fashion. This affair, however, leads to two more children, as she gives Anse "Dewey Dell to negative Jewel" and "Vardaman to replace the child I had robbed him of" (176). Addie also tries to escape from her identity as the mother in the Bundren household by asking Anse to take her body to Jefferson when she dies so that she can be buried with her own family; in her own family, Addie was not forced to take on the role of motherhood. This attempt at escaping her family also backfires, leading to her body's mutilation as her husband and children journey to bury her body.

The first mutilation that Addie's body undergoes on this journey is caused by Vardaman and his confusion over the death of his mother. Watching Cash finish placing Addie in the homemade coffin, Vardaman shows his confusion and concern, asking, "'Are you going to nail it shut, Cash? Nail it? *Nail* it?'" (65). Vardaman is confused about the physical state of death, and is concerned that his mother will not be able to breathe in the coffin. To remedy this, Vardaman bores holes in the coffin to allow the corpse to breath, with Vernon Tull narrating, "the next morning they found him in his shirt tail, laying asleep on the floor like a felled steer, and the top of the box bored clean full of holes and Cash's new auger broke off in the last one. When they taken the lid off they found that two of them had bored on into her face" (73). The first assault on Addie's dead body mutilates her face, the clearest physical form of an individual's identity. Vardaman's confusion, his belief that his "mother is a fish" (84), further highlights the destruction of her identity. Vardaman is rightfully confused by his mother's changing identity. The anti-mother identity that Addie attempted to self-fashion for herself will slowly be eradicated upon her death, replaced by her husband and sons' desires to identify her as a loving wife and mother whose dying wish must be met.

The next mutilation of Addie's body occurs during the river crossing scene, as her coffin falls in the water, water described by Darl as "the thick dark current" (141). The Bundrens come close to losing her body altogether, but, as Vardaman relates, "Darl was strong and steady holding her under the water even if she did fight he would not let her go he was seeing me and he would hold her and it was all right now it was all right now it was all right" (151). Jewel, the favored son, finally recovers Addie's coffin from the water, and the family is again on its way. Importantly, Canetti identifies rivers, along with other forms of water such as the sea and rain, as crowd symbols. Canetti writes:

> The unresting and uninterrupted flow of its waters, the definiteness of its main direction—even if this changes in detail—the determination with which it makes towards the sea, its absorption of other, smaller streams—all this has an undeniably crowd-like character. And thus the river has become a symbol for the crowd [83].

Canetti goes on to add that rivers "stand for processions" (83), and this crowd symbolism is readily apparent in Faulkner's novel. The Bundrens march in their funeral procession, unyielding in their direction no matter what obstacles they encounter. Their journey, and Addie's literal absorption into the river, represents the absorption and dissolution of the identity she has tried to fashion for herself by rejecting motherhood. Likewise, Canetti notes that "a river is the crowd in its vanity, the crowd exhibiting itself" (83). While at times the Bundren family seems embarrassed by their poverty and their ineptitude in the struggle they have chosen to undertake, they display their vanity as well, with each family member secretly wanting to make the journey to bury Addie for their own individual and selfish reasons. Most obviously, Anse has undertaken the journey for the vain purpose of getting new teeth. Likewise, the family's vanity is fed as they seek to publicly define their mother as a loving individual who they will honor through their journey. In doing so, they try to redefine themselves as her loving family not at all responsible for her death.

The final mutilation of Addie's body occurs when Darl, sensing that Addie "wants Him to hide her away from the sight of man" (215), burns down Gillespie's barn. Darl's act seems to be one of mercy, an attempt to end the family's tragic trek, but, as is the case with Anse's motivations for bringing Addie to Jefferson, Darl's true motivations are questionable. Perhaps more than any of his brothers, he desires to have Addie be his loving mother. As Williams argues, "Darl's feeling that he is not a part of his mother is more than an expression of sibling rivalry. Addie's rejection of him is absolute; it is the most terrible thing she does" (114). Darl's attempt to save his mother from further disgrace is also an attempt by him, even though she is already dead, to gain favor, to be the beloved son, and to earn his mother's love. His attempt to burn her, to enforce further her identity as his mother, provides the final mutilation of her body as Faulkner correlates Addie's mutilations with the burnings used to enforce black identity at lynchings. Fittingly, fire is one of the main symbols of the crowd explored by Canetti.

The Bundrens, with buzzards following them and circling the corpse of Addie, parade Addie's mutilated body, trying to claim a family identity that portrays a loving mother, a dedicated husband bent on meeting his wife's dying wish, and sons united to fulfill their mother's command. All the while, it can be assumed that Addie's body, exposed to water and to heat, is decomposing rapidly, all in an effort on her family's part to satisfy their own longings. Kevin Railey argues, "Disguised by the trappings of loss and bereavement, the journey serves to fulfill each one's secret, selfish, and individual desire" (92). Railey asserts that each member of the family is truly concerned with material gain, but the Bundrens want more than material gain; they desire to claim a traditional family identity, an identity that they hope will gain them admiration in spite of their poverty. They want to be seen as a family that meets their mother's dying wish, a family so loved by their matriarch that they would do anything for her. They all seem to sense, however, that even by getting Addie's body to its final resting place, they still will not truly be a family. Their actions will not change the fact that their mother did not love them. Nevertheless, their actions will perhaps make onlookers believe that their mother loved them dearly, and that they are interested in repaying this love by satisfying her dying wish. The male Bundrens wish to create this image, and this image parodies Southern attempts to create an image of female purity and motherhood and the image of honorable gentleman cultivating and protecting this identity.

Throughout the novel, the Bundrens are greatly concerned with how others view them. Anse must rely on the goodwill of his neighbors to survive, and he is concerned with his physical appearance, especially his lack of teeth. Cash is obviously most concerned with his craft, his work as a carpenter—he makes a display of his building of Addie's coffin to showcase his hard work and ability. Jewel's horse is a clear status symbol, and young Vardaman desires the opportunities had by the town boys, such as having bananas to eat and toy trains to play with. The Bundrens try to replace Addie's love with the things they hope to find in Jefferson. They know that getting her body to Jefferson will not change the fact that she did not love them, but it will make others see them as a traditional family—it will make Addie be identified as a loving mother, the identity she rejected. For the most part, they are content with parading her mutilated body around in order to solidify this identity.

Just as white Southerners created notions of womanhood that simultaneously complicated sexual relationships, the Bundren crowd, in their attempts to define their mother and their family, render themselves impotent, meaning their ideas concerning traditional motherhood will eventually die out. Anse's impotence is highlighted by his ineffectiveness and inactivity. Cash, crippled by the river accident and lacking proper medical care, will be unable to continue his carpentry work, his main source of pride and his only economically viable skill. Jewel's horse, a symbol of his sexual potential, is sold by Anse to allow them to afford their journey. Darl is removed from society and institutionalized, and Vardaman displays psychological issues that make him similar to Darl and Benjy Compson. Again, Faulkner's male characters are unable to reproduce the crowd they will need to sustain their patriarchal structures. Women who do become pregnant, like Caddy Compson, Addie Bundren, and Dewey Dell Bundren, must be tricked and coerced.

Canetti consistently emphasizes the necessary reciprocity of double crowds, writing that "the two crowds keep each other alive," and he identifies men and women as "the first and most striking" (64) of these double crowds. Like Faulkner, however, Canetti realizes that one of these groups cannot become too superior, that "the superiority on the side of the enemy must not be too great " (63). A patriarchal system built upon notions of male superiority and female inferiority cannot be permanently sustained, and through the impotence of these male characters and their destructive treatment of women, Faulkner shows this system failing.

The impotence of Faulkner's male characters in *The Sound and the Fury* and *As I Lay Dying*, and in other works such as his next novel, *Sanctuary*, will ultimately deny them the ability to sustain this system. Canetti notes that humans reproduce relatively slowly, "coming singly and taking a long time to arrive" (107) and that "it is certain that man, as soon as he was a man, wanted to be more" (108). Faulkner's Southern society was influenced more than any other geographical region of the United States by notions of crowds of ancestors, the invisible crowd identified by Canetti as the posterity crowd, the desire for "large numbers, unbroken succession ... and unity" (46). Faulkner's male characters in these novels are depicted as dying breeds, reiterating Faulkner's point that this patriarchal crowd is responsible not only for the unjust treatment of women, but for the South's many other dying legacies. Faulkner sees the wrongs of this patriarchal system threatening all social systems, from marriages and families to governments and courts. Undermining all of these systems is the mob-like crowd violence taking place against women as men seek to define their identities. Women in Faulkner's fiction, especially *The Sound and the Fury* and *As I Lay Dying*, are constantly subjected to mob pressures and even violence in order to control their identities as daughters, sisters, wives, and mothers.

The Sound and the Fury and *As I Lay Dying* represent a specific period in Faulkner's career when the concerns he showed throughout his writing regarding mob violence are used to interrogate the identities that were forcefully assigned to Southern women. Faulkner's fictional women are often surrounded by multiple, identity-enforcing men, a fact made most obvious in these two novels. In this way, women in Faulkner's fiction are usually outnumbered. Examples of such women later in his fiction include Temple Drake in *Sanctuary* (one of the men surrounding her is the impotent Popeye), the love triangle involving Laverne Shumann in *Pylon*, Judith Sutpen in *Absalom, Absalom!*, Charlotte Rittenmeyer in *The Wild Palms* (*If I Forget Thee, Jerusalem*), and Eula Varner Snopes in the Snopes trilogy (*The Hamlet*, *The Town*, and *The Mansion*).

These women, like Caddy Compson and Addie Bundren, seek to self-fashion their identities, and even though Singal argues that "if anything, Faulknerian women from the late 1930s onward are *more* formidable and admirable than their male counterparts" (158), these women are not able to create new, unchallenged identities for themselves. Charlotte Rittenmeyer's death, caused by her lover's attempt to abort her pregnancy, is one example of the danger Faulkner's women face when seeking their own identities, identities free from the burdens of motherhood. As Railey puts it in regards to the domestic sphere, "When women stepped out of that sphere, they were hurt or punished" (45). Identity is always formed by the social pressures surrounding individuals in Faulkner's fiction; individuals, especially women, are never able to define themselves. When women attempt to do so, they do so at great risk.

CHAPTER IV

The Crowd at War and at Home in Hemingway's and Fitzgerald's Fiction

In the fiction of F. Scott Fitzgerald and Ernest Hemingway, issues of race, especially African Americans' struggles for equality in the U.S., are rarely a central focus of their work. When Modernist-era America's racial problems are referred to in their fiction, Fitzgerald and Hemingway fail to give these issues prominence. The absence of race as an overt, central concern in Fitzgerald's and Hemingway's fiction extends to the literary criticism and the prominent biographies that focus on these authors. However, matters of race play an important, if often concealed, role in their fiction through their use of allusions to mob violence. In their most important works, such as Hemingway's *The Sun Also Rises*, *A Farewell to Arms*, and *For Whom the Bell Tolls*, and Fitzgerald's *The Great Gatsby* and *Tender Is the Night*, Fitzgerald and Hemingway provide several covert references to issues of racial inequality, and their persistent use of mob violence, specifically in their analysis of social norms regarding male gender roles and masculinity, reflects the prevalence of mob violence and lynching in the U.S. while they are writing. Likewise, both authors use portrayals of mob violence as ways to question masculine gender roles, both at war and in domestic spaces.

Like Faulkner, Hemingway and Fitzgerald have often been criticized for what some perceive as their lack of concern with the contemporary social issues of their day, including racial inequality. As James F. Light has observed, "Criticism has largely ignored Fitzgerald's political consciousness" (137). Hemingway, having prospered as a writer and national figure during the 1920s, was later criticized during the Great Depression for ignoring America's economic troubles in his fiction, with Robert Gajdusek noting, "During the thirties, a sudden demand for socialist and egalitarian assumptions created an atmosphere in which Hemingway was viewed with disfavor" (4–5). The same can certainly be said of Fitzgerald. Regarding their portrayals of gender, Fitzgerald's depictions have been read as misogynist,[1] while Hemingway's apparent espousal of traditional gender roles has led to charges that he thought of women in purely stereotypical terms.[2]

Despite these criticisms, changes in gender roles between World War I and World War II are significant foci in Fitzgerald's and Hemingway's fiction, as both writers are chiefly concerned with the effects these changes have on normative conceptions of masculinity. Several critics have noted this focus, especially in regards to Hemingway. As Nancy R. Comley and Robert Scholes assert, "There are many indications in his writing that gender was a conscious preoccupation for Hemingway" (ix). Comley and Scholes go on to cite Hemingway's "attention to impotence, abortion, and sexual transgression" (80-1), arguing that his "best writing about sexuality involves divorce, castration, impotence, male and female homosexuality, transvestism, and transsexuality" (81). Peter B. Messent notes a similar importance placed on gender and sexuality in Hemingway's fiction, positing that

> the inversion of sexual roles in his fiction, the uncertainty of his male protagonists' sense of their own manhood, and the divided and contradictory nature of his discourse of sexuality and gender in general are all markers of a deep concern about masculine identity and its relation to the feminine "other" in a culture where gender roles are in transition and where traditional versions of masculinity are under acute threat [*Ernest Hemingway* 87].

Likewise, Carol H. Smith observes the importance of gender roles in Hemingway's fiction and the prominence of his female characters:

> When we read about the Hemingway hero—Lt. Henry or Jake Barnes or Robert Jordan—we are often told that he is the man who stands alone against the universe, who preserves his sanity and his integrity by a silent rebellion and a private armistice. Yet on close inspection it is clear that he is seldom entirely alone; he stands armed against the forces of nature with his woman at his side: Catherine or Maria or even Brett [129].

The observations of these critics provide ample opposition to claims that Hemingway was unconcerned with *all* of the social issues of his day, while also asserting his focus on the changing nature of gender, and masculine identity in particular. Normative notions of gender are constantly being challenged in Hemingway's fiction.

Fitzgerald's preoccupation with masculine identity has also been noted by readers, but not nearly as frequently as Hemingway's. Fitzgerald is perhaps best known as a chronicler of the 1920s Jazz Age, and one of the most frequently recalled images of this era is the flapper, the female who drinks, smokes, dresses and dances provocatively, and is sexually active. Fitzgerald depicts several of these of characters, and in some ways can be read as a historical writer capturing the changing gender roles of the time. As Sarah Frye Beebe observes,

> F. Scott Fitzgerald lived and wrote in an era of momentous social change, particularly for upper middle-class American women, and he was emphatically alert to the revolution taking place all around him. Many critics have noted that Fitzgerald had an uncanny knack for recording social history in his stories and novels, which reflect the slowly shifting status of women during the two decades between World War I and World War II [1].

While Fitzgerald's women, and their responses to these changing gender expectations, have been the subject of much critical exploration, the effects of these changes on normative social definitions of masculinity have received less attention.

For different reasons, Hemingway and Fitzgerald consistently explore gender roles in their contemporary culture, and both writers are particularly concerned with their society's changing definition of masculinity, so concerned in fact that their male characters are often shown as being subjected to crowd violence when breakdowns of traditionally masculine gender expectations occur. This focus on crowd violence also shows their awareness of America's particular history of mob violence and lynching, and their recognition of this violence's importance in understanding American identity. Although many critics have begun to recognize Hemingway's and Fitzgerald's fictional treatment of gender roles, none has recognized their use of crowd imagery and mob violence as a way to portray these roles. However, their use of this trope further aligns them with other Modernist-era American fiction writers.

This focus on the changing status of masculinity through depictions of mob violence does not mean, however, that black characters are absent from, or wholly unimportant in, Fitzgerald's and Hemingway's texts. Black characters, or references to the situation facing African Americans during the Modernist era, can be found throughout Hemingway's and Fitzgerald's texts, and these appearances and references usually take place in violent and/or sexual contexts. This undercurrent adds credence to the notion that, while racial violence was not a central concern of their fiction, this violence did inform their understanding of the society they lived in, especially the pressure their society exerted on individuals and the fashioning of identity. Great writers are in part celebrated for their ability to decode society, their ability to look at the underlying consequences of overt social problems. Both of these authors link racial issues with sex and violence, and with issues of masculinity. Hemingway's *In Our Time*, for example, is a collection of short stories, and each story is presented with a preface full of violent images.[3] In the preface to "Big Two-Hearted River: Part II," Hemingway describes the hanging of five men, three of them black. Upon entering a Paris club early in Hemingway's *The Sun Also Rises*, Brett is familiarly greeted by a black drummer, a drummer who she relates is "a great friend of mine" (69); it can be assumed, given the nature of most of Brett's friendships with men, that she has a sexual history with the drummer, a relationship that Jake Barnes is unable to replicate. This possible relationship is meant to provide further evidence of Brett's promiscuous sexual behavior, her breaking of the sexual taboos of the period. In *For Whom the Bell Tolls*, Pilar's story of the mob violence started by Pablo at the beginning of the revolution is interrupted by Robert Jordan's brief story of a lynching he witnessed as a child, thus linking the two acts of crowd violence.

Depictions of black characters and America's racial disputes linger in Fitzgerald's fiction as well. Nick Carraway, Fitzgerald's narrator throughout *The Great Gatsby*, portrays racist attitudes not only in his descriptions of Gatsby's Jewish associate Meyer Wolfsheim, but also in his descriptions of a limousine "driven by a white chauffeur, in which sat three modish Negroes, two bucks and a girl" (73). Tom Buchanan is depicted as being even more overtly racist. With his racist fears heightened after reading *The Rise of the Coloured Empires*,[4] Buchanan fears that "the white race will be—will be utterly submerged" by the black race and argues that "it's up to us who are the dominant race to watch out or these other races will have control of things" (17). In *Tender Is the Night*, justice for black characters is shown to be fallacious. When Abe North gets involved in an altercation involving Jules Peterson, a man described as "a small, respectable Negro" (106), the result is Peterson's dead body being found in Rosemary's room, causing Dick Diver to comfort her by stating that "its only some nigger scrap" (110).

These examples show that, while hardly the central concern of any of Hemingway's or Fitzgerald's works, racial issues are certainly present in their fiction. Hemingway's and Fitzgerald's texts thus seem to be ripe with what Morrison calls the "Africanist presence." Although neither author is especially concerned with racial issues, a fact that each author can justly be criticized for, Hemingway and Fitzgerald use popular images of crowd violence and racial violence to show the war-like atmosphere they see surrounding the formation and enforcement of masculine identity. In this way, they equate the strictness of masculine gender roles with the threats of mob violence facing African Americans.

In the three Hemingway novels discussed here—*The Sun Also Rises*, *A Farewell to Arms*, and *For Whom the Bell Tolls*—war creates new conceptions of masculine identity while also serving as the central context for moments of mob violence. Tiffany Joseph explains that "the time after any war ... is often spent reorganizing domestic and economic spheres to conform to gender ideals, but the situation after World War I was especially volatile" (64–5), adding that the era "is marked by an intensified attention to gender issues that, in the eyes of many, worked to overturn repressive gender identities" (64). Hemingway's fiction often deals with these postwar periods and the challenges war often poses to normative conceptions of gender, and Hemingway's best analysis of these changes involve his attempts to understand gender, especially the expectations of masculinity, through depictions of mob violence.

The postwar period was not the only time that gender roles were challenged. World War I was not, as the traditional myth regarding war went, a place for unrivaled displays of masculinity, and instead challenged traditional roles of masculinity. As seen in Hemingway's fiction, the war cripples the masculinity of individuals such as Jake Barnes and Frederic Henry. War had traditionally been seen as a kind of proving ground for masculinity, but Joseph adds that many soldiers had this illusion shattered upon arriving at the battlefield:

> At first, the Great War seemed the ideal opportunity for American men to reestablish their masculinity. Here, perhaps, was the chance to reclaim manliness on the battlefield. However, instead of becoming heroes, soldiers often found themselves reduced to anonymous bodies in trenches, where life and death seemed the result of dumb luck rather than bravery, skill, or cunning [65].

The passive nature of modern warfare described by Joseph leads to a new kind of conflict that denies soldiers' chances to achieve heroic masculine identities, subjecting them instead to the passive whims of chance. War becomes a passive experience, rather than a heroically active, masculine one. Alex Vernon notes that World War I was, for many soldiers, a particularly emasculating experience because of this new kind of warfare:

> One historical consensus about World War I is the unprecedented degree to which its soldiers were rendered passive by the new technology of machine guns, indirect fire artillery, and mustard gas. Soldiers rarely had the opportunity to fight the enemy, not in the classic sense in which one's own agency and skill might affect the outcome. Instead, bullets from great distance sprayed them, bombs dropped on them, and gas invaded their lungs, and they were powerless to prevent it [74].

Vernon adds that while the passive nature of the new warfare was a major challenge to male masculinity during the period, Hemingway's work shows that war was hardly the *only* challenge to traditional male roles:

> The emasculating effects of the new warfare occurred in the context of other assaults on the nineteenth-century conception of the autonomous, self-constructed male self, such as the challenges to white masculinity posed by industrialization (and urbanization and immigration), first wave feminism, and the general loosening of gender strictures in the first thirty years of the new century. Male Americans responded with hypermasculine cultural productions like western novels and Edgar Rice Burroughs's *Tarzan* (1912), as well as the invention of Mother's Day (an effort to put women in their place disguised as a celebration) by the U.S. Congress. Hemingway thus began writing in the

middle of a culture desperately struggling to make sense of its new and still unfolding experiences of both war and gender [22–23].

These issues become constant themes in Hemingway's fiction, and his male characters often show a level of passivity that mirrors the new passive nature of warfare and industrialized society in general.

The Sun Also Rises, considered by many to be Hemingway's best novel, is also his best portrayal of the passivity and damaged masculine identity that Vernon and Joseph outline. Jake Barnes is physically and psychologically scarred by his war experiences, and his passivity is directly linked to the physical damage he suffered in the First World War. From an unnamed injury suffered during the war Jake is rendered unable to perform sexually, and this injury leads to passivity in his relationship with Brett, the woman he loves, and a woman whose sexual behavior also challenges traditional gender roles. The novel's focus on these two characters places gender identity at the forefront of the narrative, wherein, as Messent argues, "gender roles have lost all stability" (*New Readings* 112). Brett's openly promiscuous sexual behavior shows her acting in a way that traditionally has been defined as masculine. Meanwhile, Jake's perpetual impotence and his increasingly passive behavior problematizes traditional depictions of masculinity, a fact that is highlighted by the crowds of sexually able men that Jake encounters throughout the novel. The war and Jake's injury do not make him a masculine war hero, and instead, his war experience makes him a passive actor, especially in his relationships with women.

The plot of *The Sun Also Rises* consists of three settings that Jake Barnes passively moves through: a Paris full of American expatriates drinking aimlessly, a relaxing fishing trip to the Spanish countryside, and a visit to Pamplona to watch the bullfighting. Each adventure highlights Jake's damaged masculinity and his new passive identity. The novel opens in Paris as Jake narrates the time he spends drinking with his friends and the woman he loves, Brett Ashley. Although Brett relates to Jake, "I simply turn to jelly when you touch me," an apparent declaration of her desire, Jake is unable to have traditional sex with her, telling her "there's not a damn thing we could do." Jake's inability to perform sexually with her is a roadblock to their relationship. Brett goes on to tell him, "It isn't all that you know," in reference to sex, but Jake responds, "No, but it always gets to be" (34). From this exchange, it appears that Jake is the person in the relationship who is unable to move beyond his sexual dysfunction. Jake cannot satisfy Brett or himself through sex, so Jake attempts to satisfy Brett by setting her up with other sex partners. Ironically, during this first section of expatriate revelry Jake describes his friend Robert Cohn as being emasculated by Cohn's wife, Frances, who Jake states "led" Cohn "quite a life" (15). Jake is describing Cohn's supposed weakness here, his inability to assert himself with his wife, yet Jake allows Brett to control his life through her sexual desires for other men. Brett desires and acts while Jake merely follows and observes.

Robert Cohn becomes Jake's sexually performing foil, especially once Cohn becomes involved in a sexual relationship with Brett. Likewise, the nightclubs and the bars of Paris that Jake frequents are full of sexual activity that he cannot participate in. Jake becomes an outsider in these crowds; as the patrons of these bars and clubs seek and find sexual partners, Jake can only watch as an outsider. Jake's identity is fashioned by this collective force, as he is constantly surrounded by individuals whose sexual prowess highlights his own impotence. Thomas F. Strychacz has noted Jake's position as an onlooker, stating that "his role as observer-participant dominates the novel's narrative trajectory, constantly drawing attention to the multiple acts of watching that shape his identity and that lead, ultimately, to his psychological travail in the arenas where men demonstrate their potency" (76–77). As a solitary onlooker, Jake becomes an "other," an individual apart from the crowd because, as Gajdusek puts it, he is physically "dephallused" (332). Jake is psychologically sterile as well, and he exhibits homophobic tendencies upon encountering a group of homosexual males at a Paris club, an act that Comley and Scholes connect with his own dysfunctional identity:

> He cannot perform, though he desires to do so, while the homosexuals can perform and yet do not desire "normal" heterosexual sex. The sexually fragmented Jake is thus linked to men he perceives in fragments as unmanly because he has himself been unmanned. Indeed, his wound has put him in the passive feminine position of lack and has put Brett in the active position of finding men to provide the apparatus that Jake has lost [44].

This group of homosexuals represents the context that surrounds Jake, a context that singles him out as different, a sexual exile. The group of homosexuals, traditionally a conservative symbol of sexual abnormality, are more sexually normal than Jake. Jake is surrounded by a crowd of sexually functioning individuals, while he is forever sexually frustrated. Jake's identity becomes defined by his relationship with, or rather, his separation from, the crowd that consistently surrounds him.

Because of this outsider status, Jake quickly loses interest in these Paris parties, stating, "This whole show makes me sick" (29). Jake's sickness is most pronounced when he is placed in opposition to the naturally functioning group, and their "show" of this prowess makes Jake painfully aware of his dysfunction. Jake's only escape is to retreat to the Spanish countryside, where he enjoys a restful and solitary fishing trip, accompanied only by Bill Groton. Together, they participate in the masculine ritual of fishing, a ritual that, unlike sex, Jake is able to participate in. These fishing scenes with Bill provide Jake with an escape, but he cannot stay away too long because of his desire for Brett. Unable to resist her, Jake rejoins the mob of friends who, by their sexual relationships with Brett, or at the least their potential for sexual relationships with Brett, define Jake's identity as one that is emasculated. Robert Cohn is able to perform in an affair with Brett in San Sebastian; Mike Campbell is her future husband, a position impotent Jake is unable to satisfy; and Bill provides another male that could potentially satisfy Brett's sexual cravings. Upon rejoining his friends for the bullfighting in Pamplona, Jake's identity is again enforced by the mob of friends he travels with, as well as the anonymous sexually active individuals who create the novel's persistent backdrop. Jake can only try to heal his masculinity by participating in normative masculine activities such as drinking, fishing, and becoming a bullfighting *aficionado*.

Even Robert Cohn, who becomes a figure of scorn in Pamplona because he continues to follow Brett after she has ended their relationship, becomes a sexual rival to Jake. Again the irony is clear, as Jake is essentially doing the same thing, constantly following Brett, or coming to her rescue, as he does at the end of the novel. When Cohn and Jake come to blows over Brett, it is only Cohn who is able to land a punch; knocked "down on the pavement" (195), Jake tries to rise, to assert his masculinity, only to be knocked down again. Jake is literally unable to get up, to assert himself in situations that demand that he be active. For all his social awkwardness, Cohn is Jake's sexual rival, a rival who is able to perform in ways Jake cannot.

Jake's weakness is further highlighted in Pamplona by his passion for bullfighting. Jake is a self-proclaimed bullfighting *aficionado*, but he is unable to be a bullfighter himself. Instead, he must watch the bullfighters at work, and he takes great interest in trying to get Brett to enjoy the fights as well. He succeeds in getting her so interested that she becomes sexually involved with Pedro Romero, a young and fantastic bullfighter who is an obvious symbol of sexual virility. As Strychacz observes, "it is unclear" whether Jake's passing of Brett to Romero "refers to a contract fashioned between men—a kind of transfer of Brett from impotent watcher to potent matador—or to Jake's understanding of Brett's desires" (83). In either case, Jake must share Brett with another because he lacks the traditional masculine precursor to satisfy her himself. The crowds that witness Pedro Romero cheer for him and admire him, and Pedro preens and performs for the crowd in a display of his masculinity, while Brett is likewise drawn to Pedro through his ability to perform. Jake seems forever doomed to repeat this pattern, his injury forcing him to passively accept his lover's sexual adventures with other men. Once again, Jake is relegated to the position of voyeur, apart from the crowd, while others perform the deeds he cannot.

Brett's heightened sexuality makes her the key member of the mob that defines and enforces Jake's emasculated identity, and she becomes representative of the post–World War I gender battle.[5] As Comley and Scholes note, "Brett is 'unfeminine' in her usurping of the male prerogative of promiscuity on her own terms" (43). Smith reads Brett as "dangerous and untrustworthy in her need," and threatening to "the male code of honor and stoicism" (130), adding, "She is a threat to men because she forces them to recognize the primitiveness of their desire and the fragility of male bonding when threatened by lust, sexual need, or competition for a woman" (132).[6] The characteristics critics have noted show that Brett is an especially hazardous woman for Jake, or any other man,[7] to fall in love with—her ability to control men with her traditionally masculine traits heightens Jake's own lack of control and his inability to pleasure Brett in a sexual relationship. Jake's war injury makes him a domestic failure, an individual who is subjected to a figurative mob that constantly defines his masculine identity as lacking. Given the physical and psychological crippling Jake suffers from his war injury, it is hard to imagine him ever being able to self-fashion a more assertive identity.

The protagonist of *A Farewell to Arms*, much like Jake Barnes, has his masculine identity defined, and eventually undermined, because of an injury that takes place on the battlefield. Messent argues that "the question of selfhood and autonomy is a deeply troubled one in Hemingway's work" (*Ernest Hemingway* 45), and Messent's observation rightly describes Frederic Henry's dilemma in *A Farewell to Arms*. The novel is full of questions surrounding the nature of masculinity making the novel, as Berman calls it, "a central intellectual document of the decade" (*Fitzgerald, Hemingway, and the Twenties* 9). Although Henry's injury, unlike the injury suffered by Jake Barnes, does not cost him the ability to have sexual intercourse, Henry's masculinity is also defined by circumstances surrounding the war, and he leaves the battlefield after witnessing, and almost falling victim to, a scene of crowd violence.

Masculine stoicism, as it does in much of Hemingway's fiction, plays an important role in *A Farewell to Arms*. The novel often displays the mass killing and death that is occurring at the front, while relating these deaths in an understated tone that seems to minimize the importance of individual life. As Canetti recognizes, any war "has to do with killing," adding that the aim of all war "is to transform a dangerous crowd of live adversaries into a heap of dead" (68). Scenes of death and war are often presented with passive emotion in Hemingway's fiction, a tone that mimics Hemingway's representations of the new passive nature of warfare and the clear, unsentimental goal of war, the production of mass death. The opening pages of *A Farewell to Arms*, for example, describe a cholera outbreak that takes place at the front, relating that "it was checked and in the end only seven thousand died of it in the army" (4). These deaths are described through Hemingway's famous journalistic narration, and his reporting of journalistic facts is a form of this masculine stoicism that opens the novel. As Millicent Bell argues, "Hemingway's style, his realist prose, suggests, guilefully, that much more has been borrowed directly from experience than is actually the case" (108), making the events seem real, the characters' reactions stoically unreal. This stoic brand of narration is important throughout the novel. For example, when Aymo is shot by his fellow Italians, Henry stoically narrates that "he looked very dead," and that "I had liked him as well as any one I ever knew" (214). In spite of this liking, no further emotion is shown, or thought given, regarding Aymo's death. A war is going on, but at the beginning of the novel, the war and the numerous deaths resulting from the war are a mere background for other conflicts.

The central conflict taking place in A *Farewell to Arms* is not the war itself, but the contested nature of masculinity. Males in the novel consistently battle both verbally and physically to define each other's masculinity. In A *Farewell to Arms*, male rivalry and sexual prowess seem to be at the heart of all war. The men in Henry's mess continually make fun of the priest's celibacy, teasing him about masturbation when they joke, "Every night priest five against one" (9). The men go to whorehouses to satisfy their lust, and they assume that the emasculated, celibate priest must masturbate instead. The priest's identity, like Jake's identity in *The Sun Also Rises*, is in part defined by his sexual inactivity. The implication is that one cannot be a man without being sexually active. Meanwhile, Henry's roommate Rinaldi teases Henry about homosexuality when Henry states that he likes the preacher's company. Rinaldi responds, "Oh, I knew it. Sometimes I think you are a little that way. You know" (65). Sexually inactive and a noncombatant in the war, the priest becomes a symbol of homosexuality as the men around him struggle to define his identity. Earlier, an argument between Passini and Manera about the purpose of the war involves Manera's justifications that defeat means that the enemy will "take your home" and "take your sister" (50). The purpose of the war, following this line of thinking, is for men to fulfill their masculine responsibility of protecting women and domesticity, while also sexually exploiting the losing side. This line of thinking seems similar to the stated, and unstated, justifications often provided for lynching. Failure to serve in the war is perceived as a failure in masculinity, a failure to aptly protect women. Taking such a protective stance will become even more important for Henry, since his relationship with Catherine Barkley and her subsequent pregnancy cause him to shift his focus to domestic matters, rather than matters of warfare. Traditional notions of manhood are questioned as well, as noted by Comley and Scholes, who argue that "Frederic Henry's childish status is reiterated throughout. His roommate Rinaldi's favorite epithet for him is Baby, and the priest and Catherine, among others, call him a good boy or urge him to be one" (38). Serving at the warfront as a nurse rather than a soldier, these questions regarding normative social definitions of masculinity become important in any consideration of Frederic Henry's identity.

Such themes reverberate throughout the novel, as critics have noticed.

Bell describes Henry's time in the hospital as another flaw in his masculine facade, arguing,

> far from the war's inordinate demand upon his responses, he has been converted to feeling in the isolation of his hospital bed, where, like a baby in its bassinet, he is totally passive, tended and comforted by female caretakers, the nurses, and particularly by this one. The image is regressive, and the ministering of Catherine, who looks after all his needs, including sexual, while he lies passive, is more maternal than connubial [114].

Bell notices Henry's general passivity, and it is important to note that Henry's war injury does not occur during heroic, masculinized warfare, but during a passive and domesticated moment that has him cooking for his men while enjoying cheese and wine. Like Jake's injury in *The Sun Also Rises*, Henry's injury leads to further questioning of his masculinity. As Vernon observes, even Henry's wartime role can lead to questions of his masculinity, noting, "war posters clearly depicted Red Cross work as a feminine endeavor" (69).

Questions surrounding the concept of masculinity, and specifically those pertaining to Henry's masculine identity, are raised throughout the book, and especially in the active war zone. Identity is central to understanding *A Farewell to Arms* and its protagonist. As Messent notes, "The text initially withholds the name of this central protagonist" (57), and this withholding operates as one of the formal tools Hemingway uses to highlight his focus on identity in the novel, a strategy similar to that used by James Weldon Johnson in *Autobiography of an Ex-Colored Man*. A key scene for any reading of the novel, but especially for a reading of masculine identity in the novel, takes place during the retreat. Here, the simple goals of war as noted by Canetti, and normative concepts of soldierly masculinity, begin to breakdown. Instead of fighting, the Italian forces retreat from battle, and in retreating they transform into a confused and violent mob. Likewise, individuals involved in the war suddenly lose their sense of identity as the masculine structure of the battlefield and the goal of creating dead enemies becomes confused and random. Canetti states that "every participant in the war belongs simultaneously to two crowds," the crowd of the living and the crowd of the potentially dead (71). Before the retreat, Henry claims his abhorrence for "abstract words such as glory, honor, courage, or hallow" (185), all of which historically imply some level of masculine heroism. As the retreat begins, Henry sees the emptiness of these words fully, as he learns that during a retreat many of the wounded will be left behind, since they only "take as many as they can and leave the rest" (187). The retreat signals a breakdown in masculinity, a refutation of masculine abstractions such as heroism. Additionally, the retreat causes a mass loss of identity among the soldiers. Military discipline, previously rigidly enforced, becomes a chaotic situation where individuals worry only about saving themselves. Henry no longer belongs to a clear side in the war, and in his attempt to leave the military, he becomes an individual hunted by, and defined by, the crowd that will shoot him if he is caught. The retreat is a massive movement easily undermined by disorder, and Malcolm Cowley notes the allegorical meaning of the retreat, observing, "Hemingway describes not an army but a whole people in motion" (45). The retreat is made up of the defeated, those whose masculinity has failed in the masculine proving-ground of war, and this failure in masculinity leads to chaos as members of the defeated side try to redefine their masculinity by turning against each other. Henry notes that "all that was needed was for a few men to leave their trucks or a few horses be killed to tie up completely the movement on the road" (199), and the fact that this chaos occurs signals a failing in masculine military discipline.

At first, Henry and his companions try to enforce military discipline, shooting a soldier Henry outranks because the soldier refuses the order to cut brush and attempts to desert. Henry's attempts to maintain military etiquette are not enough. Before long, the retreat is in complete disarray, and many of the Italian soldiers begin thinking and acting with a mob mentality. Henry notes that it is these same Italian soldiers who shoot his friend Aymo, and that he and his companions are "in more danger from Italians than Germans" (214). Quickly, the mob mentality of the retreat has confused prior distinctions between enemy and ally. The mob of retreating Italians are noted as being "frightened and firing on anything they saw" (216), demanding death in retribution for their own failed war effort and their own overcome masculinity. The killing during the retreat represents that of an angered mob, killing "suddenly and unreasonably" (218) in an attempt to recover the vestiges of a heroic masculine identity. When threatened, the mob acts as all mobs seem to act, using violence to reinforce their position and to define the identity of an enemy.

Henry is soon confronted by those members of the retreat who have resorted to such mob violence. The retreat leads to heightened suspicion and paranoia regarding spies and betrayers, and Henry is apprehended by a mob simply because "he speaks Italian with an accent" (222). The members of this mob have no interest in justice, and instead look to reinforce their own masculinity by effectively lynching a perceived threat. Their positions as members of the mob create a safety-in-numbers mob mentality that is observed by Henry, who notes that "the questioners had all the efficiency, coldness and command of themselves of Italians who are firing and are not being fired on" (223). Henry further highlights the mindless nationalism of the mob, stating, "I saw how their minds worked; if they had minds and if they worked. They were all young men and they were saving their country" (224), operating with "that beautiful detachment and devotion to stern justice of men dealing in death without being in danger of it" (224–5). Hemingway's description of this mob echoes the U.S. literary tradition of lynch mob representations, and Henry, facing this unreasonable mob, is left with no other choice but to desert from the Italian cause.

In spite of his honorable actions during the war, which include helping his injured companions while suffering his own injuries in the bunker, this mob is the final factor in defining Henry's masculine identity. Instead of continuing in the war effort, fighting, drinking, and frequenting whorehouses, Henry attempts to escape to the domestic sphere where definitions of masculinity might be more stable, returning to Catherine and removing to Switzerland with her and their unborn child. Attempting to "forget the war" and "make a separate peace" (243), Henry takes up the masculine rituals of sports and following the war in the papers. Catherine's death in childbirth at the end of the novel, however, suggests that this attempt is also doomed to fail. Berman notes that "throughout the story men believe that if they stop fighting—if they throw away their rifles—then peace will arrive. More important, if the war is stopped, then life can resume its norms" (*Fitzgerald, Hemingway, and the Twenties* 113). The war, however, has changed notions of masculinity, and Berman adds that "the reason why Hemingway ends this novel in chaos, disorder, and accident is that when they are elevated to the status of principles they make as much sense as their opposites" (*Fitzgerald, Hemingway, and the Twenties* 114). These principles, it appears, will be adopted by Henry now that he has witnessed the failure in masculinity during the war, and now that he faces the postwar world[8] that will present continuing challenges to traditional notions of masculinity.

Like *A Farewell to Arms*, Hemingway's *For Whom the Bell Tolls* is a novel concerned with war and masculine identity, and once again, a scene of crowd violence is central in defining masculinity, while at the same time exploring the myths of masculine identity. Much of the novel's focus deals with comparing the traditionally masculine and heroic soldier (Robert Jordan) and the traditionally cowardly and un-heroic soldier (Pablo). The novel is mostly concerned with Robert Jordan and his masculine ideals surrounding the way a war should be fought and Pablo serves as his foil, an undisciplined guerrilla soldier who appears to have given up hope after years of fighting for what he has grown to believe is a lost cause. Jordan, mainly through Pilar's tale of Pablo's mob-leading actions at the beginning of the war, seems to be favored by critics as Hemingway's ideal of an honorable, truly masculine character. The novel's ending, however, where Jordan is killed and Pablo escapes with Jordan's lover in tow, serves to muddy this simple delineation of masculinity, making Hemingway's questioning of traditional masculinity central to any reading of the text.

Many of the abstract terms despised by Frederic Henry could be used to describe Robert Jordan, Jordan's dedication to carrying out his orders, and his commitment to the antifascist Spanish rebellion. Although Jordan resents the orders he is given to blow up a bridge because of "what they could do to him" and shows a concern that "they were bad orders all right for those who would have to carry them out," he convinces himself that the orders must be carried out since "that bridge can be the point on which the future of the human race can turn. As it can turn on everything that happens in this war" (43). Later Jordan relates to Pilar, the matriarch of the Spanish guerrillas, that he does not fear death, and instead only fears "not doing my duty as I should" (91). Jordan knows that part of his duty involves killing fascists in combat, but he does not enjoy the killing, does not do it savagely, and goes about the killing as part of his duty, realizing the humanity of those he kills and killing them only to serve the cause he believes in. He is convinced that "no man has a right to take another man's life unless it is to prevent something worse happening to other people" (304), and his actions seem to be guided by this moral principle. After meticulously planning to blow up the bridge and successfully doing so, Jordan risks his own life in order to assure that all of the members of his party safely cross a tank-guarded road before he attempts to do so himself, knowing that by the time he attempts to cross, the tank will surely have its sights on him. Eventually wounded and left for dead, Jordan calmly lies in wait at the end of the novel with his pistol in hand, aiming at an approaching fascist officer, still upholding his heroic masculine identity.

Jordan's adherence to military policy, his leadership and bravery, his grace under fire and pressure, and his self-sacrifice, make him one of Hemingway's most fully realized and complete hyper-masculine characters. Jordan is a traditionally ideal solider, a traditionally ideal man, and his work as a soldier is not the only aspect that makes him a figure of traditional masculinity. He is described as having *cajones*, a masculine ideal that is symbolically highlighted by the two large sacks of explosives he carries. In his relationship with Maria, he plays a paternalistic and protective role while also satisfying her as a lover. He has the emotional strength to mercifully shoot his old friend and fellow soldier Kashkin, a friend who is seriously wounded and wishes to be put out of his misery. He worships his grandfather, who was a successful soldier, while dismissing his father, who committed suicide, an act Jordan clearly sees as cowardly.

All of these aspects add to Jordan's masculinity, but his masculinity is perhaps best shown through comparison with Pablo, Jordan's foil. From the first moment of Pablo's appearance in the text, his masculinity is questioned, especially in comparison to Jordan's. Pablo is described by the other guerrillas with words such as "ugly" and "barbarous," and they even refer to him as "flaccid" (26), a clear reference to Pablo's lacking masculinity, especially in comparison with Jordan's *cajones*. It is noted that while he was "something in the beginning" of the war, he is now "very much afraid to die" (26). Throughout the novel, Pablo lives up to these cowardly descriptions, eventually stealing

Jordan's detonators in order to avoid Jordan's mission, an act that does not dissuade Jordan and instead only complicates the destruction of the bridge. Although he returns at the end of the novel to help with the bridge, bringing some reinforcements as well, it is suspected that he shoots these reinforcements when he no longer needs them so that there will be enough horses for him and his companions to escape on.

Robert Jordan's idealized masculinity is defined through negation by Pablo's behavior, but it is Pilar's tale of Pablo's actions earlier in the war, at the revolution in Pablo's hometown, that clearly defines Pablo's identity as Jordan's savage opposite. Fittingly, immediately before Pilar gets very far into her story of mob violence, Jordan relates that he had seen "a Negro ... hanged to a lamp post and later burned" when he was a child in Ohio (116).[9] Pilar's story of Pablo's mob is meant to recall the brutalities of Southern lynch mobs, the barbarity and unjust nature of collective violence against the helpless. This type of collective violence becomes the opposite of traditional heroic masculinity in the novel. After attacking a fascist barracks and ordering the fascists to surrender, Pablo shoots some of the fascists as they are lined up against a wall, an act clearly in contrast to Jordan's declaration that he has "avoided killing those who are unarmed" (304). Pablo orders the remainder of the fascists to be "beaten to death with flails and thrown from the top of the cliff into the river" (103). The crowd carries out Pablo's orders reluctantly at first, but after becoming drunk and covered in blood, they transform into a mob that is frenzied and torturous. Pilar relates that Pablo's initial orders break down, that "there were no more lines but only a mob" (121) of individuals who "neither understand nor believe in anything" (120).

The narrative of Pablo's mob-inciting violence defines him as the coward he is described as by the guerrillas, an un-masculine man who is emboldened to fight only when he is part of a large group or at a clear advantage, like those who question Frederic Henry in *A Farewell to Arms*. Pablo's characterization further idealizes Robert Jordan's. As Cooper notes, "Pablo is a walking illustration of the lack of discipline that Jordan often laments. On the other hand, he is an illustration of the danger and difficulty of trying to use a questionable means to achieve some good purpose" (108). Jordan consistently acts with discipline and seeks to achieve the purpose of winning the war through a traditionally masculine code of honor. As Berman notes in regard to Hemingway, "Manner, he thought, was not only a way of doing things but of setting up barriers, of doing them in the one way that was right—sometimes, of not doing them at all. In his work, rules that come from somewhere govern eating, drinking, and hunting—things stylistically larger than they seem to be" (*Modernity and Progress* 32). Jordan is certainly a Hemingway character who strongly adheres to these traditional rules of manhood and masculinity.

As Cooper observes, however, if Hemingway's "background taught him a set of ideals (duty to others, self-reliance, freedom, democracy), the second great influence on his political development—his experiences in World War I and postwar Europe—taught him to be skeptical of ideals" (133). By 1940, the year *For Whom the Bell Tolls* was published, Hemingway had certainly had time to realize that many old ideals, such as those regarding gender roles and masculinity, could be severely flawed. At the end of *For Whom the Bell Tolls*, it is Robert Jordan bleeding to death, waiting to take out one last fascist officer before dying himself. Meanwhile, Pablo rides off into the proverbial sunset. Hemingway's ending makes it clear that while he admires the traditional, idealized versions of masculinity that Robert Jordan represents, these older versions of masculinity are not meant to endure in the modern world. War leaves Hemingway's characters dead, as is the case with Robert Jordan, or alive but struggling in the postwar world, as is the case with Jake Barnes. Questioning Jordan's idealized masculinity is not an endorsement of Pablo's behavior—Pablo is a brutish coward throughout—but Hemingway does ponder the fate of individuals like Robert Jordan in a world where traditional conceptions of masculinity are being questioned. Traditional notions of masculinity are often left, like Jordan, to bleed out in Hemingway's fiction.

Like Hemingway, F. Scott Fitzgerald's most often discussed novels use references to crowd violence in their depictions of gender expectations related to masculinity in the post–World War I era. Unlike Hemingway, Fitzgerald's novels typically explore gender roles and notions of masculinity in domestic spaces, as he does in *The Great Gatsby*. Like Robert Jordan, Fitzgerald's Jay Gatsby is a character who tries to mimic a traditional and idealized version of male masculinity, in Gatsby's case, a specifically *American* version of male masculinity that involves aspects of the American Dream, such as a dedication to hard work and the accumulation of wealth. Ultimately, Gatsby invites a crowd to surround himself in an attempt to attract and retain Daisy Buchanan's love, only to see this crowd transform into a mob that will turn on him and ultimately abandon him because he cannot compete with Tom Buchanan's overpowering masculinity. In this way, Fitzgerald uses crowd violence as Hemingway often does, as a way to explore changing gender roles.

Given Fitzgerald's often forgotten Southern roots, it is not surprising that Fitzgerald turns to lynching imagery to end Jay Gatsby's story in *The Great Gatsby*. As Bruccoli notes, Fitzgerald "grew up listening to his father's stories of the war and the lost South" (14) and "thought of himself as a courtesy Southerner by virtue of his father's pedigree" (37). Fitzgerald's interest in the South and its particular struggles are especially prominent in his short story collections *Flappers and Philosophers* and *Six Tales of the Jazz Age*, and it may be surprising to many that Fitzgerald, a national symbol and symbol maker of the Jazz Age, wrote as often about the South and Southerners as he did about jazz, drinking, and flappers. Fitzgerald is as much a chronicler of relations between the North and the South as he is a chronicler of the Jazz Age.

Although *The Great Gatsby* cannot be classified as a Southern novel, Fitzgerald was interested in the South throughout his life, and this interest is shown through his use of mob imagery in portraying Gatsby's fate. As was often the case with African Americans lynched in the South, Jay Gatsby's main rival is a racist white man at a time when, as Walter Benn Michaels notes, "Klan membership was at its all-time peak," and Michaels adds that the "Klan's style of racism finds a nonironic spokesman in *Gatsby*'s Tom Buchanan" (23). Michaels also notes the racial elements found in the struggle between Tom and Gatsby, adding that Gatsby "isn't quite white, and Tom's identification of him as in some sense black suggests the power of the expanded notion of the alien. Gatsby's love for Daisy seems to Tom the expression of something like miscegenation" (25). In *The Great Gatsby*, then, Fitzgerald has set up an obvious conflict between Gatsby and a white supremacist tormenter.

Indeed, Tom Buchanan is consistently described in reference to his physical body, and he also represents a body of individuals whose wealth and power gives them the social clout to define the identity of their inferiors and to punish those who dare transgress against these identities. Just as Jason Compson represents white supremacist attitudes in the post–Civil War South in Faulkner's *The Sound and the Fury*, Tom Buchanan represents a group of wealthy white Americans in the country's northern half, a group that is dually empowered by its skin color and its untouchable wealth. Nick Carraway's first description of Tom references "the enormous power of that body," "a body capable of enormous leverage—a cruel body" (11). Tom's body is not only large and strong in appearance—the body he represents is also capable of great physical and social leverage, the ability to move and shape others, because Tom's body represents the body, or group, of wealthy white Americans who view themselves as the gatekeepers of white normative society. Tom is not afraid to use his physical leverage to manipulate others. He breaks Myrtle Wilson's nose when she dares to speak of his wife Daisy, and he later picks up her husband "like a doll" (148). Later, Tom is described as blocking out doors "with his thick body" (122), and it is his physical body, and the representative body of individuals like himself, that closes doors for individuals like Gatsby.

Although Michaels aptly notices the racially fused elements of the struggle between Tom Buchanan and Jay Gatsby over Daisy, Michaels does not mention the presence of mob and lynching violence in the novel. Tom Buchanan and Jay Gatsby offer two opposing versions of male masculinity. Tom Buchanan is a man of both vast physical and financial strength. Nick Carraway relates that Buchanan "had been one of the most powerful ends that ever played football at New Haven—a national figure in a way" (10), a statement that immediately joins Tom's physical ability with the ability afforded by his elite social status. This description also defines Tom as a symbol of his country's normative attitudes. His speaking voice is noted as "paternal," a voice that Carraway sees as implying, "Now, don't think my opinion on these matters is final ... just because I am stronger and more of a man than you are" (11).

Tom's voice is not the only aspect of his character that could be described as paternal. Tom's views on women also seem to mimic those voiced by Faulkner's Jason Compson. In regard to Jordan Baker, Tom tells Nick that "she's a nice girl," but "they oughtn't to let her run around the country this way" (23). When Mrs. Wilson, a woman Tom is having an affair with, mentions Daisy's name, Tom makes "a short deft movement" that "broke her nose with his open hand" (41). And when Tom finds out about Daisy and Gatsby's past, and the possibility of their potential future, he rants, "I suppose the latest thing is to sit back and let Mr. Nobody from Nowhere make love to your wife. Well, if that's the idea, you can count me out.... Nowadays people begin by sneering at family life and family institutions and next they'll throw everything overboard and have intermarriage between black and white" (137). Tom is a man who, in spite of his physical and financial strength, has many fears, all relating to issues of gender, race, and class. He is, like Jason Compson, a representative of outdated attitudes of paternalism towards women and blacks, a paternalism whose paranoia cannot help linking issues of race and gender with the perceived threat of miscegenation. Tom's rant on family values especially recalls Southern hypocrisy in regards to miscegenation, a hypocrisy involving white males' sexual relationships with black women and the violent lynching punishments imposed on black men who were suspected of having sex with white women. Tom Buchanan is a man resistant to change, and he feels that it is his masculine duty to maintain a social order that clearly defines the roles of women and men, blacks and whites.

Tom's paternal, racist, and class-motivated desires are one version of American masculinity, as he seems intent on defending his privileged position as a member of one of the country's traditionally rich families. Jay Gatsby, a character many critics read as an embodiment of the American Dream, is representative of another version of American masculinity. Gatsby's past is, like the pasts of many American immigrant groups and especially African Americans, unclear and certainly not as historically well-defined as Tom Buchanan's. Gatsby's wealth is new and self-made; he is clearly a member of the *noveau riche* that upper-class men like Tom Buchanan fear, and this fear is compounded by the suspicion that Gatsby's wealth was not accumulated legally. Adding to all of this, as Michaels notes above, is the distinct fear on the part of Tom Buchanan that individuals without clear bloodlines are especially threatening because they may in fact have some black blood in their lineage.

Gatsby and Tom's struggle over Daisy, a battle supposedly over her love but truly over the wealth and privilege she represents, actually takes place by means of a philosophical and ideological struggle regarding what the U.S. is and should be. As Berman argues, "The Buchanans lead American lives of no moral or existential significance. They remind us of characters we have seen before in political and philosophical discourse who refuse to make choices or even to recognize the necessity for doing so" (*Fitzgerald, Hemingway, and the Twenties* 12). Daisy, lacking a literally powerful physical body, still, like Tom, represents a body of individuals that have the power to define others. She and Tom "moved with a fast crowd, all of them young and rich and wild" (82). She is at first attracted to Tom and his "wholesome bulkiness" and "his position" (159). This position, specifically his position as one of the country's historically wealthy, allows them to be a part of a crowd of "careless people" who "smashed up things and creatures and then retreated back into their money or their vast carelessness or whatever it was that kept them together, and let other people clean up the mess they had made" (188). It is Tom's position that he uses for leverage to retain Daisy as his wife when he realizes Gatsby's challenge.

The Buchanans represent the old guard in the United States, and Tom Buchanan is representative of the old guard's paternalistic masculinity. Berman adds, however, that "a character like that of Tom Buchanan is a compendium of American failures. He is rich with no conscience, moralistic without being moral, exclusionary, racist, and, above all, untrue to any self-conception" (*Fitzgerald, Hemingway, and the Twenties* 56). Tom Buchanan is representative of a version of American masculinity that is responsible for many American failings (slavery, paternalism, patriarchy, class enslavement), but his financial and physical strength allow him to maintain his prominent social standing. Tom seems most concerned with changing social norms regarding race and gender. He fears that "the white race will be—will be utterly submerged" (17), showing his own recognition of the power of the crowd, of massive bodies, that might overwhelm individuals. Tom believes that "it's up to us who are the dominant race to watch out or these other races will have control of things" (17). Tom uses his massive strength to do so.

Jay Gatsby tries to fashion an identity for himself within society that can equal that of Tom Buchanan and the crowd that Buchanan represents, but this identity is denied by Tom Buchanan and the crowds that prey on Gatsby's *nouveau riche* social standing. Fitzgerald sees both Tom's old version of masculinity and Gatsby's new version of masculinity as limited; but Gatsby's death, as Robert Jordan's death does for Hemingway, shows which version of masculinity Fitzgerald sees as maintaining its power during a period of rapid social change. In order to compete with the traditionally rich, in this case specifically for Daisy's love, Gatsby must subject himself to crowds and the inherent dangers involved in doing so. Gatsby's elaborate parties, designed in hopes of somehow connecting with Daisy and then impressing her, create a carnival, mob-like atmosphere. Nick relates, "People were not invited—they went there," and once at Gatsby's parties, "they conducted themselves according to the rules of behavior associated with amusement parks" (45).

Gatsby's parties are consistently described in terms of crowds. At one party, Nick recognizes "the already violent confusion of the scene" (58), and later that same night, references "the crowd—it was now a crowd" that gathers when a drunken individual tears off the wheel of his car as he tried to leave Gatsby's party (59). As more and more free alcohol is consumed at these parties, the parties turn from merely disorderly, carnivalesque gatherings to scenes of absolute mayhem. Canetti defines such crowds as "feast crowds," crowds where

> there is more of everything than everyone together can consume and, in order to consume it, more and more people come streaming in. As long as there is anything there they partake of it, and it looks as though there would be no end to it. There is an abundance of women for the men, and an abundance of men for the women.... Many prohibitions and distinctions are waived, and unaccustomed advances are not only permitted but smiled on [62].

For Gatsby, these parties represent a breaking away from these prohibitions and distinctions mentioned by Canetti, as he is able to entertain and socialize with individuals who may view themselves as distinctly different from Gatsby because of their inherited wealth. These parties, Gatsby thinks, are his best way of connecting with Daisy's crowd, and ultimately, Daisy herself. Without this crowd, Gatsby is usually described as a pathetic, solitary figure. When Gatsby's parties clear out, Nick relates, "A sudden emptiness seemed to flow now from the windows and the great doors, endowing with complete isolation the figure of the host who stood on the porch" (60). Gatsby tries to win Daisy's heart back, and to gain entry into the world of the super wealthy, by surrounding himself with a crowd that he believes might be like her, and therefore, that he believes will bring him closer to her. In effect, he tries to join the crowd that she is a part of, a crowd that individuals like Tom Buchanan define, in hopes of becoming a valid sexual rival.

However, his union with the crowd is always temporary. Gatsby cannot fully join the crowd because his wealth is not the same as Tom Buchanan's wealth, and this fact keeps Gatsby from self-fashioning the identity he so deeply desires in order to win Daisy's love. As Gatsby's dreams crumble, Nick realizes the crowd that Gatsby has been up against is "a rotten crowd" (162). In the end, Gatsby is left out of this crowd: "the lawn and drive had been crowded with the faces of those who guessed at his corruption—and he had stood on those steps, concealing his incorruptible dream, as he waved them goodbye" (162). As evidenced by the emptiness of his funeral, he is never able to truly join this crowd, and he is left a solitary individual defined by the crowd as an outsider, as someone who does not belong. As much as he tries to self-fashion himself differently, Gatsby is always an individual apart from the crowd that Tom and Daisy are a part of.

At the end of the novel, Gatsby is essentially lynched, unjustly killed without trial for a crime that he did not commit, a crime involving a woman whose love is forbidden to him in part because of his unclear racial past. He is killed by George Wilson because of Tom Buchanan, whose own version of masculinity still controls America and is threatened by new versions such as those inspired by the American Dream Gatsby partially represents. As Messent argues, "Nick converts Gatsby's story into an old American narrative: the failure of the dream of perfection" (*New Readings of the American Novel* 42). Fitzgerald's purpose in presenting Gatsby's failed dream, and the purpose of the novel itself, is not to simply show the failure of the American Dream, but to show the American Dream as being defeated by the old patriarchal and racist masculinity of individuals such as Tom Buchanan, individuals who are a part of a dominant and norm-defining crowd. Individuals, as Fitzgerald shows in *The Great Gatsby*, cannot truly attain the American dream because a crowd of superwealthy whites fight vigorously to maintain their exclusive social position.

In *Tender Is the Night*, Fitzgerald produces another version of failing masculinity in Dick Diver, and Diver's fall, like Gatsby's, is partly blamed on the feasting crowd that Dick surrounds himself with. Gajdusek has noticed the similarities, positing that "Dick Diver dissolves in or becomes a cycled victim of waters he cannot master; the effeminization he well understands yet fears is his undoing. Gatsby lies dead, floating at last on the waters destined to claim him" (291). Dick Diver's fall can be blamed on many factors: his neglected career, his financial reliance on his wife Nicole, Nicole's mental illness, his affair with the actress Rosemary Hoyt, and his alcoholism, to name a few. As Bruccoli argues, "Diver is the victim of corrupting influences, but he is corrupted because he is corruptible. On the simplest level he is ruined by the rich" (336). Interestingly, however, Bruccoli claims that Dick's major weakness is "his need to be loved and admired, which compels him to squander his emotional capital" (336). Diver, like Gatsby, ultimately fails because of his inability to sustain the crowds that feed upon him like a feast crowd. He builds his power on the basis of the crowd's acceptance and even celebration of him, but when the crowd abandons him he is left in ruins.

In spite of the numerous biographical links between Fitzgerald and Dick Diver, "Fitzgerald's original intent" in *Tender Is the Night*, as stated by Light, is to "emphasize social criticism" (136). The main emphasis of this social criticism, as several critics have noted, is a battle of the sexes. Gajdusek posits, "The dominant undercurrent of the surface action of *Tender Is the Night* is a state of undeclared war" (278). Tiffany Joseph reads the novel as a critique of "patriarchal power even as it often seems to lament the loss or challenge to such power in the wake of the war" (68), adding that Diver's "decline represents, on one level, the corresponding decline in masculine power perceived by many men after the Great War" (69). As Milton R. Stern has argued, "Overtones of war permeate the book's language in almost every event" (74), and Stern cites the "breakdown of sexual identities" as "a sign of the breakdown of moral identities, one with metaphors of war and combat as signs of the breakdown of a civilization" (41). Furthermore, Stern's description of *Tender Is the Night* sounds as if he is describing the actual warfare often seen in Hemingway's novels, as he notes that "in *Tender Is the Night* the warfare between the sexes and the breakdown of sexual identities, like the warfare among nations and the breakdown of national identities, are a dimension of the exploded old decalogues" (38). The persistent presence of international war in Fitzgerald's world is mirrored in the battles over gender roles taking place in the domestic spaces of his fiction.

As is seen through the case of Dick Diver, ground in this domestic war is being won for women, albeit slowly; ideals regarding masculinity are slowly changing, which is why at the end of the novel Rosemary Hoyt is a successful and independent actress and Nicole is able to leave Dick, signaling her own growing independence in response to his history of paternalism. Dick's defeat comes about in a manner similar to Gatsby's; the people he has surrounded himself with, upon his decline, turn into a crowd that defines his fallen identity at the end of the novel.

Dick Diver's masculine identity is not based on war action, like that of Hemingway's Frederic Henry and Robert Jordan, or on wealth, old or new, as is the case with Tom Buchanan and Jay Gatsby. Rather, Diver's masculinity is based on his social and domestic abilities, specifically his ability to gather and entertain small groups of people and his understanding of social etiquette. This ability makes him attractive to women, as he is able to attract wealthier women such as Nicole Warren and younger women such as Rosemary Hoyt. Indeed, Dick's ability to entertain, manage, and manipulate a group is what first attracts Rosemary. She first notices Dick "giving a quiet little performance" for his group on the beach (6). He is later seen "going from umbrella to umbrella carrying a bottle and little glasses in his hands," causing his friends to grow "livelier and closer together," an act that Rosemary observes "even the children knew" as they notice the excitement "generating under the umbrella" (11).

Dick's domestic masculinity, his presence in any group as the alpha-male and center of attention, positions him, at least at the outset of the novel, as a symbol of control and potential. Rosemary observes that "he seemed kind and charming—his voice promised that he would take care of her, and that a little later he would open up whole new worlds for her, unroll an endless succession of magnificent possibilities" (16). The Divers' daily routine, orchestrated by Dick, adds to the effect noticed by Rosemary:

The Divers' day was spaced like the day of the older civilizations to yield the utmost from the materials at hand, and to give all transitions their full value, and she did not know that there would be another transition presently from the utter absorption of the swim to the garrulity of the Provencal lunch hour. But again she had the sense that Dick was taking care of her [21].

Rosemary, young and inexperienced, a newly made celebrity, is not the only one to notice Dick's ability, his consistent sense of proper etiquette that makes all of those around him seem important and included in his world of leisure. At a later party, it is noted that Dick made "the group into so bright a unit that Rosemary felt an impatient disregard for all who were not at their table" (52). Dick becomes attractive because of his ability to draw a crowd and to then lead the crowd.

Dick's charm, his control of etiquette and manners, begins to diminish as his own personal life crumbles, and it is then that the small groups he has created begin to turn against him. Losing his power to control these groups, Dick simultaneously begins to lose his prior, enchanting masculinity. Joseph notes that Dick becomes "repeatedly feminized" (72) and traumatized by his "failing to live up to a socially dictated gender ideal" (72). Dick's fall, caused by his failing marriage, his drinking, and his own growing sense of mortality, causes him to lose control over not only his little parties, but over all aspects of his life. Baby Warren, Nicole's sister, begins to dictate Dick's financial endeavors, his drinking ruins his ability to function professionally, and his love interests, Nicole and Rosemary, begin to take control of their own lives, completing Dick's defeat by gaining their own independence from him.[10]

Dick's fall becomes final through a scene of mob violence when the "passionate impatience" of his failings causes him to lose his prior control (224), and he strikes a taxi driver, causing a mob to take aim at him:

> They surged about him, threatening, waving their arms, trying ineffectually to close in on him—with his back against the wall Dick hit out clumsily, laughing a little and for a few minutes the mock fight, an affair of foiled rushes and padded, glancing blows, swayed back and forth in front of the door. Then Dick tripped and fell; he was hurt somewhere but he struggled up again wrestling in arms that suddenly broke apart. There was a new voice and a new argument but he leaned against the wall, panting and furious at the indignity of his position [224–5].

Dick is not killed by this mob, but he is beaten badly, and he suffers the eradication of his masculine dignity in domestic spaces. Once renowned for his social control, Dick now loses control, and this loss of control over his own life and identity subjects him to mob violence. Taken to the police station, he incites another mob, and he is attacked by a group of Italian carabinieri who also beat him for his indiscretions:

He was clubbed down, and fists and boots beat on him in a savage tattoo. He felt his nose break like a shingle and his eyes jerk as if they had snapped back on a rubber band into his head. A rib splintered under a stamping heel. Momentarily he lost consciousness.... Still he was dragged along through the bloody haze, choking and sobbing, over vague irregular surfaces into some small place where he was dropped upon a stone floor. The men went out, a door clanged, he was alone [226].

The beatings Dick receives completely annihilate whatever shreds of alpha-male masculinity that he had previously maintained, the identity that he had self-fashioned and that had allowed him to be successful. He is left a victim of mob violence, battered and beaten, with his physical appearance and his sense of identity maimed. No longer does he demonstrate his previous control, his grasp of manner and etiquette, his power over women. His last attempt to impress young Rosemary only ends in further public humiliation, another metaphorical removal of his masculinity, as he is left "exhausted and expressionless" from attempting water sport stunts he no longer has the vitality to carry out (285). The mob that usually surrounds Dick, by recognizing his deteriorated masculinity in all domestic matters, defines his new identity as lacking. He goes from being someone the group admires and allows to lead to being someone the group finds pathetic and unqualified to lead. The crowd he has always found his power in now deserts him, leaving him alone and subject to their whims. Dick has always defined himself by these little crowds, but at the end of the novel, they define him.

Like Jay Gatsby, Dick's damaged masculinity fails to live up to the masculinity of his sexual rival, in this case Tommy Barban. Likewise, Tommy, recalling Tom Buchanan, uses his powerful masculinity to settle the battle for Nicole Diver, taking her from Dick and leaving Dick powerless to object. Tommy simply tells Dick, as Buchanan tells Gatsby regarding Daisy, that Nicole "does not love you ... she loves me" (308). Throughout the brief discussion, Tommy Barban takes control, ending the conversation by commanding Dick to "let it be understood that from his moment ... I stand in the position of Nicole's protector until details can be arranged" (310). Susann Cokal notes the disparity in the masculine stances of Dick and Tommy, arguing, "Dick fades away in the face of Nicole's marriage with an adulterer who becomes another father-figure; Tommy Barban is a soldier, just as Papa Warren is a captain of industry, and he dominates Nicole much more thoroughly than Dick ever has" (94). Because of this disparity, Dick can only respond to Tommy's demands that "I never did go in for making love to dry loins," a clear admission of his own diminished abilities and inability to sexually stimulate his wife (310). Like Jake Barnes, Dick, now lacking the prerequisite masculine abilities, instead can only pass on his lover to another man. Furthermore, Dick lacks the military masculinity of Tommy and the domestic financial success of

Nicole's father. His masculine ability was based on his presence in social settings, a presence that is no longer accepted.

Unlike Gatsby or Hemingway's Robert Jordan, Dick is not killed by a mob at the end of *Tender Is the Night*; but his behavior in the novel shows that, without making drastic changes, he may very well be on his way to being killed by an angry mob, much like the fate suffered by his alcoholic friend Abe North. Fitzgerald, while not always considered a political writer and often criticized for not being one, shows intense concern in *The Great Gatsby* and *Tender Is the Night* for changing gender roles, especially normative definitions of masculinity. These novels, and their focus on America's changing gender landscape, show that Fitzgerald commonly uses images of crowd violence to understand these changing roles. Fitzgerald's questioning of masculine identity through characters such as Tom Buchanan, Jay Gatsby, and Dick Diver shows his intent to reevaluate gender roles in the postwar domestic spaces he inhabits. Like several other writers from the Modernist era, Fitzgerald does so by connecting mob violence with identity.

Hemingway, in spite of his popular culture reputation as a masculine icon, likewise criticizes various forms of masculinity in his fiction as a way to display postwar changes in gender expectations. In *The Sun Also Rises*, *A Farewell to Arms*, and *For Whom the Bell Tolls*, Hemingway is not endorsing a particular version of idealized masculinity, and is instead showing the various failings of traditional masculine identity. Hemingway is often portrayed as endorsing certain masculine characteristics, even criticized for doing so, yet his major fiction is full of unsuccessful versions of masculinity. For Hemingway and Fitzgerald, progress is especially questionable, as neither writer is able to imagine a functional version of masculine identity in the modern world.

CHAPTER V

The Great Depression and Migrating Crowds in Steinbeck's and Faulkner's Fiction

As was the case following World War I, the Great Depression served as the catalyst for multiple changes—economic, political, and cultural—to the American way of life. One such change involved an abrupt shift in American ideology, among politicians and literary authors alike, from an adherence to the old rugged individualism of Thomas Jefferson and Ralph Waldo Emerson to the New Deal politics of Franklin D. Roosevelt and John Steinbeck. This dramatic change in American consciousness is reflected in United States literature. In general, there is a shift away from the Modernist trope of the tortured individual as American authors began to focus on groups and collective bodies as catalysts for social change during, and in the years following, the Great Depression. Mirroring these ideological and literary shifts, Depression-era socioeconomic conditions caused massive population migration as well, as displaced Midwestern farmers migrated to California and rural farmers across the nation increasingly gave up farm life and moved into nearby towns and cities to explore other occupations. These ideological, literary, and demographical shifts are readily apparent in much of John Steinbeck's fiction and in William Faulkner's Snopes trilogy as Modernist authors continued to interrogate matters of identity within the contexts of crowd violence.

In William Faulkner's late novels, and especially in the Snopes trilogy comprised of *The Hamlet*, *The Town*, and *The Mansion*, one of U.S. Modernism's prominent writers turned his attention away from the tortured, representational individual subjects of his earlier fiction. Instead, his trilogy focuses on the movement of a group, in this case poor sharecroppers, away from their agrarian roots and into American capitalist culture, the same capitalist culture that is seen invading even small rural areas such as Faulkner's Jefferson, Mississippi. At the same time, John Steinbeck focuses on group dynamics in numerous works of fiction, especially *In Dubious Battle* and *The Grapes of Wrath*. Steinbeck's lifelong focus and Faulkner's late career focus on economic conditions mirror American social and political culture, displaying an ideological shift away from the subject of the individual tortured by a cruel and sadistic mob force, and focusing instead on the ways that groups are often oppressed by cruel and powerful individuals. In these novels, then, the Modernist-era tendency to portray the individual as the oppressed and the crowd or mob as the oppressor is reversed.

Steinbeck's portrayals and analysis of crowd dynamics has garnered much critical attention, but Faulkner's own work in this area has generally been ignored, overlooked, or misinterpreted. Faulkner is often mistakenly read as a writer who always advances individualism over collectivism. For example, Lawrence H. Schwartz argues that Faulkner's critical reputation was first championed by New Critic intellectuals seeking a literary embodiment of American individuality.[1] Much of the misunderstanding regarding Faulkner's treatment of the masses, and economic issues as a whole, stems from a general critical tendency to regard Faulkner's fictional Flem Snopes and his Snopes clan as merely greedy, opportunistic, animalistic, or worse. As Daniel J. Singal asserts, "From the moment Flem emerged in print, critics have taken great delight in construing him and his fellow Snopeses as subhuman" (254). Such critical readings of the Snopes clan, and especially Flem Snopes, ignore the similarities between Faulkner's Snopeses and Steinbeck's numerous collective bodies, such as the "Okies" of *The Grapes of Wrath*. Faulkner's Snopeses have much in common with Steinbeck's Joads, as both clans are representative of economically disadvantaged families whose migratory journeys center on economic survival within the American capitalist system. The mob becomes not merely a group of violent individuals working collectively to define an individual subject's identity, but a collective group of Americans who often suffer at the hands of the powerful few Americans who control the country's capitalist enterprises and are therefore able to define the group's identity.

Many critics and historians read the ideological shift in the U.S. around the Great Depression as a political swing away from conservative, right-wing individualism to progressive, left-wing collectivism. For example, Ted Atkinson argues:

> While the Great Depression pushed the Right to the margins of political discourse, the Left experienced a time of unprecedented vibrancy—socioeconomic conditions that made its political concerns more relevant and appealing than at any other time in the nation's history. Marginalized during the bacchanalian reign of capitalism in the twenties, the Left viewed the despair of the thirties as an opportunity to advance an agenda of fundamental reform in American social, economic, and political life [33].

Atkinson's brief historical narrative of America's changing political perspective signals a broader change in American thinking, and these political changes, brought about by dramatic changes in the country's economic conditions, had vast social and cultural implications, one being that U.S. authors generally began to overtly deal with social and political issues, even when dealing with such issues led to critical disparagement. Steinbeck's place in the canon, for example, has, as Louis Owens argues, "undoubtedly suffered from the fact that he was too easily and often simplistically labeled 'proletarian,'" and Owens adds that since the thirties, "Steinbeck has never been warmly embraced by America's critical establishment" (xi). This dismissive attitude is similar to that taken towards Faulkner's later work, work that is often compared unfavorably with earlier novels such as *The Sound and the Fury*, *As I Lay Dying*, and *Absalom, Absalom!*. Thus, Faulkner's Snopes trilogy, especially *The Town* and *The Mansion*, have failed to receive the critical attention they deserve in comparison to these earlier novels. Parini observes that as the effects of the Great Depression loomed, "the subject of politics was now pushed to the front by the sharp economic and social inequities of American life," and "the Depression played a key role in this shift of consciousness" (162). The most important aspect of the Snopes trilogy is the way these three novels capture America's changing economic, political, and social dynamics leading up to the Great Depression. In doing so, these novels merge with the writing of Steinbeck and other U.S. fiction writers of the Great Depression in turning to political writing that focuses on economically oppressed crowds.

Throughout his writing career, Steinbeck consistently explores the subjects of crowd dynamics, mob violence, and collective identity. Often, Steinbeck's depictions of this violence echo the depictions found in the fiction of other Modernist-era writers discussed throughout this book. In all of his depictions, Steinbeck portrays crowds as potential forces for positive social change, and even mob violence is often represented as a necessary evil in this regard, an effective strategy to use in conflicts with powerful individuals. Steinbeck, in spite of his consistent portrayals of the potential of collective force to inspire social change, also shows numerous examples of mobs reacting with irrational and counterproductive violence. Steinbeck's fiction implies that mobs can be used for positive social change, but Steinbeck also argues that any mob, even a mob being used to create positive social change, is capable of losing control and committing senseless acts of violence. When Steinbeck's mobs work together as a collective, organized unit, they are able to achieve progress, but when these groups devolve into violence and chaos, their progress is thwarted.

Mobs, whether organized towards a common social goal or merely enacting violent punishments, are seen throughout Steinbeck's work. In *Of Mice and Men*, a lynch mob is gathered to track down Lennie Small, the big-hearted, slow-minded migrant farmer whose innocent indiscretion with Curley's wife, the flirtatious daughter-in-law of a ranch owner, leads to her accidental death. The novel's fame derives in part from its depiction of Lennie and his companion George Milton, two migrant workers who represent a larger class of Americans lost amidst Depression-era economic turmoil and forced to bounce from odd job to odd job in order to survive. Lennie and George are part of a larger social class oppressed, and in Lennie's case threatened with lynching, by wealthy individual landowners such as Curley and his father.

Several stories found in Steinbeck's famous short story collection *The Long Valley* involve mob violence as well. In "Flight," young Pepé is hunted down by a mob because he has killed a man in self-defense during a drunken fight. When Pepé is killed at the end of the story, it is noted that the mob has demolished his previous identity; he falls after being fatally shot, and an "avalanche slid slowly down and covered up his head" (48). In "The Raid," Dick and Root, two Communist strike agitators, are attacked by a group of men who identify them as Reds. And in "The Vigilante," Mike, having just passively participated in the lynching of a young black man, is left feeling "a cold loneliness" after the "terrible and important affair" (94), a story that "reflects" what Owens identifies as "Steinbeck's acute interest during the thirties in the phenomenon of group-man" (127). Mob violence, and its connection with identity, is frequently explored in Steinbeck's fiction.

Steinbeck's *The Pearl*, like "Flight," follows Kino, who after finding "the Pearl of the World" (21), must deal with the mob of neighbors who try to rob him, as well as the mob that hunts him and kills his son after he has killed a man in self-defense. *The Pearl* seems to condemn mob action when the reaction to Kino's finding the large pearl is described:

> It is wonderful the way a little town keeps track of itself and of all its units. If every single man and woman, child and baby, acts and conducts itself in a known pattern and breaks no walls and differs with no one and experiments in no way and is not sick and does not endanger the ease and peace of mind or steady unbroken flow of the town, then that unit can disappear and never be heard of. But let one man step out of the regular thought or the known and trusted pattern, and the nerves of the townspeople ring with nervousness and communication travels over the nerve lines of the town. Then every unit communicates to the whole [41].

The mob that attacks Kino is clearly formed to enforce conformity to a certain localized identity. Steinbeck's last novel, the semiautobiographical *East of Eden*, a text that represents a radical departure from Steinbeck's earlier novels, describes a public execution of "the golden man" who "did dreadful things— things only a fiend could think of" (177). Later in the novel, anti–German community members are noted as having "tarred and feathered a Pole they thought was a German" because "he had an accent" (516), another case connecting mob violence with identity.

Crowds and collective violence are a constant presence in Steinbeck's fiction, but his portrayals of mobs and other collective entities are not always negative, and this is one way that Steinbeck differs from many of his Modernist forbearers. As John Ditsky has argued,

> Readers of Steinbeck are familiar with his earlier usage, "group man," to describe humanity in small or large masses functioning, for whatever internal or external reason, as a unit—very much as fish in schools and birds in flocks do. In such units, individual members developed specialized abilities in order to perform functions required by the needs of the unit, or group, particularly to substitute for a cell or member of which (or whom) the unit or group has been deprived, rather in the manner in which the body compensates for the loss of a limb or adjusts to the loss of brain cells. This theory, in other words, derives from Darwinian notions of species survival, and it is also therefore morally neutral [180–81].

Tortilla Flat is Steinbeck's first examination of this group mentality, and the novel follows Danny and his paisano friends through their lighthearted, irresponsible, and collective alternative to capitalistic social standards. In this novel, the mob is not a source of abuse—rather, Danny and his friends are victims of abusive social standards that encourage only individualistic goals, such as the accumulation of money and property. Published in 1935 but taking place shortly after World War I, the events of *Tortilla Flat* provide an early insight into Steinbeck's interest in group dynamics, especially the dynamics of a group that, while large in number, is still defined and punished by a dominant bourgeois society whose standards are set by wealthy individuals. Here, the group is punished by wealthy standard-setters, but Steinbeck portrays friendship, community, and collectivity as potential alternatives to restrictive bourgeois standards.

Tortilla Flat presents a new version of mob-like behavior in Modernist-era fiction, as Danny and his friends represent the collective, communal, anti-individualist kind of social group that Steinbeck would explore further in *In Dubious Battle* and *The Grapes of Wrath*. One explanation for Steinbeck's examination of mobs as protagonists rather than antagonists is discussed by Brian E. Railsback, who argues that "Steinbeck wrote not in the tradition of the liberal arts, but more in the tradition of the sciences" (7), and because of this change in focus, "Steinbeck's contribution to American literature is unique, for he offers dramatizations of biological principles" (7). Often influenced by nineteenth-century versions of romanticized individuals struggling against larger cultural forces, many Modernist-era writers, especially those who overtly align themselves with the aesthetic principles of Modernism, generally take the side of the individual in conflicts between individual and community forces. Steinbeck, however, shifts from focusing on romanticized individuals, instead taking a more objective and scientific look at humanity as a species. Unlike most Modernists, Steinbeck's focus is on the group, not the individual, and his writing is more influenced by biology and sociology, rather than individual psychology. Railsback states that "much of Steinbeck's fiction challenges our notions of the exalted human position, reminding us that we answer to many of the same natural laws and conditions that the occupants of the tide pool do" (41), and adds that this Darwinist position "tries to stand outside humanity and examine it as a biologist would any other species" (44). It is this position that Steinbeck attempts to take in much of his fiction, and therefore his authorial focus is often on groups (the paisanos of *Tortilla Flat*, the workers of *In Dubious Battle*, the "Okies" of *The Grapes of Wrath*) rather than on individual characters.

Parini seems to be in agreement with Railsback in regard to Steinbeck's scientific approach:

> Steinbeck's work anticipates many current developments in thinking about the natural world, including bioregionalism and the ecology movement; viewing all parts of nature as a united whole, he saw clearly that the existence of any single part is dependent upon all other parts. He thought it useless to study people outside their natural setting, understanding that even the smallest of human interactions are, on some level, governed by an individual's place within his or her physical context. The underlying drive in all of Steinbeck's fiction (and much of the nonfiction) was to locate patterns, or gestalten, within apparently random circumstances [*John Steinbeck* xvii].

Thus, understanding Steinbeck's work seems essential in an attempt to understand American binaries of collectivism and self-reliance, democracy and individualism, crowd dynamics, and individual identity. Steinbeck consistently attempts to locate these "patterns" in his fiction in order to understand group dynamics. These attempts usually show a pattern wherein mobs and mob violence are a powerful force that can be used for positive social change, but a force that is often undermined by individual interests, disorganization, and violent urges. Steinbeck's interest, especially in *In Dubious Battle* and *The Grapes of Wrath*, lies in trying to understand human group dynamics, specifically the ways in which collective human action might work to oppose individualized and privatized systems of political and economic control. In these novels, his basic approach to group action becomes clear, as groups are seen as powerful entities capable of changing unfair conditions, but lacking in cohesiveness, organization, and control. As is the case with Wright, Faulkner, Hemingway, and Fitzgerald, images and scenes of mob violence are found throughout Steinbeck's fiction. Uniquely, however, Steinbeck approaches the issue of mob violence in a scientific manner that explores both the strengths and weaknesses of the mob mentality, rather than simply dismissing collective action as a threat to individualized expression.

In Dubious Battle, written in 1936, attempts to analyze the potential value of crowds as a tool for social change, making it an important work on the subject of crowds and identity. The novel focuses on an attempt by Mac and Jim, two American Communist Party[2] members, to organize a strike among fruit pickers in California. Mac and Jim are representatives of one collective organization, "the Party," that is trying to rally and inspire the California fruit pickers into a frenzied mob that will force higher wages and better working conditions. The plot of the novel focuses on Steinbeck's own assessment of mobs as agents for change, examining the potential of mobs as such agents while also studying their weaknesses. Like Doc Burton, the medical doctor that Jim and Mac employ in order to uphold sanitary conditions in the camp of striking fruit pickers, Steinbeck attempts to examine the mob objectively, showing the ways that mobs can act with irrational violence while also showing that mobs can provide the strength of collective action necessary to influence individuals whose power would otherwise go unchallenged. In the novel, Steinbeck can be seen exploring the correlation between this potential social usefulness and this potential violence in the same way that Canetti outlines in *Crowds and Power*, noting,

> The strikers are men who have suddenly denied themselves the normal activity of their hands.... As soon as they feel the unity of their stand threatened, they incline towards destruction, and particularly towards destruction in the sphere of their own familiar activity. It is here that the most important task of the organization begins [57].

Canetti, theorizing decades after *In Dubious Battle* first appeared, essentially outlines the central problem of crowd organization that Steinbeck examines in his novel.

From the novel's beginning, Jim and Mac lack any identity outside of their party affiliation; although the novel focuses on them, they do not see themselves as individuals, and instead serve a larger social movement. Mac appears to have no past outside of his participation in Communist politics, and Jim's past offers only a glimpse of his former life. Jim and Mac are two men who allow their individual identities to become submerged into the Communist Party. Jim, for example, wonders at the beginning of the novel "if I ought to change my name" (11). For Jim and Mac, their service to the party is their only identity, and their unified goal involves creating a mob of men who see things the same way, getting "the men to find out how strong they are when they work together" (26). Their goal is to create what Canetti calls a "Prohibition Crowd." Canetti defines such crowds as a type of crowd that emerges when a group obeys "a prohibition, and this prohibition is sudden and self-imposed" (55). The fruit pickers are a mismatched bunch of laborers with little leadership or organization, and they are easily taken advantage of by the Growers Association, the small but powerful group of California orchard owners. Rather than producing fear in regards to mob forces as many earlier Modernist-era writers did, Steinbeck focuses *In Dubious Battle* on an attempt by Mac and Jim to make "the men work for themselves, in their own defense, as a group," to "teach them to fight in a bunch" (48). Jim and Mac believe that mob action is natural, as Mac argues, "Men always like to work together. There's a hunger in men to work together" (49). Likewise, Canetti notes that "stopping work makes the workers equals," yet "by itself it is not sufficient to make a crowd out of them" (56). The task of making a crowd out of the striking fruit pickers is taken up by Mac and Jim.

Mac and Jim find that mobs often form naturally, without urging from organizers like themselves. When Dan, an old fruit picker, falls from his ladder and breaks his back, a mob immediately gathers, and men "on the outskirts of the mob" began to shout about the faulty ladders provided for the pickers (79). Jim and Mac plan on creating a mob, but they quickly witness a mob forming naturally in response to social injustice. The novel continually refers to the group of pickers as a mob, and Jim and Mac realize that forming a mob will be easy, but that controlling and organizing the mob into unified collective action poses the real challenge in a successful strike. Mobs form naturally, but in order to work toward a common goal for longer than a brief moment, they need organization and structure. Circumstances such as Dan's accident quickly anger the pickers, and this anger unites them against the Growers Association. This mob, however, proves difficult for Jim and Mac to control. Controlling and organizing the mob becomes a matter of keeping them from committing acts of mere mob violence, as part of Mac and Jim's job becomes an effort to "keep the guys from lynchin'" individuals like the farm superintendent (102).

Jim and Mac's ultimate goal is to start a strike with the apple pickers in hopes that "it will just naturally spread over into the cotton," the next big crop that is harvested by migrant workers (25). To achieve this goal, they realize the importance of organizing the crowd, not just inciting it into a mob. Mac tells Jim that "a strike that's settled too quickly won't teach the men how to organize, how to work together. A tough strike is good. We want the men to find out how strong they are when they work together" (26). Mac later tells London, the picker they have identified as a leader, that "most strikes break down because they got no discipline. Suppose we divide the men in squads, let each squad elect a leader, and then he's responsible for his squad. We can work 'em in groups, then" (105). These attempts at organization, as Canetti notes, create "an organization with the functions of a state" (57) as Mac and Jim, through Dakin and London, try to organize the crowd into different groups with different roles.

Without much effort on Jim and Mac's behalf, however, the fruit pickers become a mob of angry workers demanding better conditions through the sheer threat of violence. Doc Burton, Steinbeck's representative of objective scientific examination, questions Mac and Jim's ability to control this mob in a way that will bring about actual social change, rather than simply escalating violence. Doc Burton tells Mac,

> I want to watch these group-men, for they seem to me to be a new individual, not at all like single men. A man in a group isn't himself at all; he's a cell in an organism that isn't like him any more than the cells in your body are like you. I want to watch the group, and see what it's like. People have said, "mobs are crazy, you can't tell what they'll do." Why don't people look at mobs not as men, but as mobs? A mob nearly always seems to act reasonably, for a mob [113–4].

Burton's curiosity, his desire to work with the strikers, not because he believes in Communist Party politics, but rather because he wants to witness mob action, seems to represent Steinbeck's own curiosity with what Burton calls "group-men" (113). Burton brings up the notion that mobs act rationally, arguing that mobs may appear to act irrationally when studied through the standards applied to individuals, but with patterned, rationalized violence when studied as a group. Canetti, through his various studies of crowd behavior a couple decades later, seems to provide a similar argument. Steinbeck, like Wright, Faulkner, Hemingway, and other Modernist-era writers, does not view the mob as a purely irrational body of crazed individuals, but rather as a new organism whose actions make sense when mob behavior is theorized separately from individual behavior. As seen in these writers' depictions, mobs do not act randomly, but rather with a collective and often ritual purpose. Doc Burton adds that mobs are predictable in that they might "get pleasure when individual men are wiped out," noting that "the group simply wants to move, to fight"; the group uses words such as the Communist principles preached by Mac "simply to reassure the brains of individual men" (114). The mob does not care as much for Mac's Communistic values as it does for gaining some concessions they currently lack.

Burton's objective stance often mirrors the stance taken by Steinbeck. Burton states "I want to see the whole picture—as nearly as I can. I don't want to put on the blinders of 'good' and 'bad,' and limit my vision" (113). Burton tries to convince Mac that "it might be worthwhile to know more about group-man, to know his nature, his ends, his desires. They're not the same as ours" (114). When Mac insists to Burton that "we've got no time to mess around with high-falutin' ideas" Burton wisely responds, "Yes, and so you start your work not knowing your medium. And your ignorance trips you up every time" (115). Mac does realize, however, that his lack of understanding is a weakness. He tells Jim and London that "if I could tell in advance what a bunch of guys'd do, I'd be president" (239).

Through Doc Burton, Steinbeck seems to express his concerns with Mac and Jim's insistence on annihilating any sense of individual identity and the potentially dangerous consequences of invoking crowd action. Perhaps because of his focus here on Communist Party politics, Steinbeck is often dismissed by literary critics as a purely proletarian writer, and while Parini notes that Steinbeck himself "learned that the Associated Farmers intended to 'get him' in any manner they could" (*John Steinbeck* 219), in *In Dubious Battle*, as Rick Wartzman argues, "Steinbeck did his utmost to make this story completely apolitical" (77). As the novel follows Jim and Mac's efforts, Steinbeck certainly avoids siding with the corrupt and violent tactics of the Fruit Growers Association, but he also comments on Jim and Mac's ignorance in regard to the ways in which mobs work, as they continually fail to organize the crowd of strikers without reverting to mere violence. In this way, Steinbeck criticizes not only organizations like the Fruit Growers Association, but also the Communist Party's failure to understand group dynamics in a way that would lead to more useful structure and organization.

As the strike carries on, the individual orchard owners, through their anti-strike smear campaign, are able to convince vigilantes to attack the farmers' camp. According to Mac, these vigilantes are

> the dirtiest guys in any town. They're the same ones that burned the houses of old German people during the war. They're the same ones that lynch Negroes. They like to be cruel. They like to hurt people, and they always give it a nice name, patriotism or protecting the constitution. But they're just the old nigger torturers working. The owners use 'em, tell 'em we have to protect people against reds [131].

Mac is able to recognize the rationalized mob mentality of the vigilantes, but he fails to recognize the economic dependence of the vigilantes on the orchard owners and the likely political ignorance of the vigilantes, instead describing them as naturally violent and irrational. The mob of vigilantes, like the mob Mac is trying to manipulate, is acting out of its own economic and political interests, and as the violence of the novel escalates, Mac fails to realize that the vigilantes, like his own mob, are acting irrationally for individuals, but rationally for a crowd. Interestingly, each side of the conflict is continually defined by crowd labels. Mac and Jim align themselves with the "the guys," and the "working stiffs" and proudly identify themselves with labels such as "Reds" and "radicals," labels the opposition would also use to define them. Meanwhile, their opponents are defined as the Growers Association, an association that also works with crowds identified as "vigilantes," "scabs," and "cops." While the conflict begins with the workers retaliating against a select few landowners who control wages and prices, the conflict eventually becomes an all out war between two opposing crowd forces, and a seemingly endless pattern of violence and recrimination takes hold. As Georges Sorel notes, "The *normal development* of strikes is accompanied by an important series of acts of violence" (43). The mob Mac intends to incite functions with the same kind of patterned violence as the vigilantes. Mac's misunderstanding of his own crowd, and the crowd of vigilantes, only leads to escalated violence that moves towards no unified purpose. Thus, as Parini observes, "An orgy of recrimination and mob action occurs as the phalanx spins out of control on both sides" (*John Steinbeck* 166).

As the novel progresses, Mac begins to realize, albeit too late, that he lacks a complete understanding of how a mob might operate, and this failure will ultimately undermine the strike's chances at success. Mac's lack of understanding seems to stem from his notion that individuals must be sacrificed for the good of the crowd, and that the crowd itself might serve as a sacrifice for an even larger group of disenfranchised American workers. Mac always readily admits that he is willing to sacrifice individuals for the good of the crowd of apple pickers. After he helps Lisa deliver her baby, he tells Jim "'course it was nice to help the girl, but hell, even if it killed her—we've got to use anything" (48). Mac's strong commitment to Communist Party ideals in the end makes him a kind of monster, and an ineffective leader of men. When he beats up a high school kid that invades the camp, he tells Jim, "No, he's not a kid, he's an example" (213). Jim seconds such statements, arguing that "sympathy is as bad as fear" (214). Mac argues that "it doesn't make any difference if we lose" (222) because he thinks the strike itself will inspire others. To the men he is trying to lead through London, however, matters of winning and losing *do matter*, and Mac's inability to relate to the men he aligns himself with leads to his failure as a leader and the failure of the strike.

Mac and Jim fail to see the crowd as a collection of individuals, yet Mac and Jim, try as they may to be otherwise, are never able to become part of the crowd themselves. Warren French observes that Mac and Jim "must continually devise further means for maintaining the group's commitment and preventing defections ... suggesting that mob action is the creation of the manipulators rather than the participants" (xv). Mac and Jim never see themselves as equals with the men they are attempting to incite into a crowd—they are not part of the crowd, but attempt to be manipulators of it. While they encourage individual members of the crowd to sacrifice, as they do with Dakin and his beloved truck, Mac and Jim always have a position separate from the crowd. They are not laborers like the rest of the strikers, and when the strike appears to be falling apart, they are willing to send the crowd of strikers into a bloody conflict they cannot possibly win while they make their own separate plans for escape. Jim and Mac insist on self-fashioning identities that separate them from the crowd, and because of this distinctly separate identity, the crowd of strikers can never fully trust them, and this lack of trust stemming from Mac and Jim's individuality apart from the crowd places them in a position where the crowd may turn against them at any moment.

Often mistakenly read as a pure strike novel, *In Dubious Battle* is an example of Steinbeck's own interest in groups as potential agents for social change, and Steinbeck seems to reach the conclusion in the novel that further study is necessary if the crowd's potential is to be understood. Still, Steinbeck provides a wealth of information regarding crowd dynamics, doubtless stemming from his own lengthy observations of crowds, making the novel, like Canetti's *Crowds and Power*, a hugely important work in the study of crowd dynamics. Mac argues, for example, that a crowd is "like blowing up a balloon. You can't tell when it's going to bust. No two of 'em bust just the same" (74). This unpredictability is one of the main problems facing Mac and Jim in their attempt to create a mob, and one of the most confounding aspects of crowds. Mac later states that "a smell of blood seems to steam 'em up. Let 'em kill somethin', even a cat, an' they'll want to go right on killin'. If there's a fight, an' our guys get first blood, they'll put up a hell of a battle. But if we lose a man first, I wouldn't be surprised to see them hit for the trees" (239). The violence of crowds, and the seemingly spontaneous swelling and receding of crowds, seems to confound Steinbeck and his characters.

Crowds in the novel are viewed as potential agents of social change, but at the end of the novel, little positive change has been achieved. French states that "*In Dubious Battle* acknowledges the power of the Establishment that they supported. The novel can be read as a warning to those foolish enough to challenge the status quo" (xix). At the end of the novel, Steinbeck's message becomes clear—the establishment will always win against an uninformed and unorganized opponent. The solution is not mob violence, a tactic Mac and Jim all too often rely upon. Rather, organization of the crowd, as Steinbeck seems to suggest, needs to come from individuals wholly invested in the crowd, and members of the crowd likewise need to be educated regarding what it is they are fighting for. French adds that Steinbeck "aimed to promote an understanding of the necessity for orderly, rational change and the use of the talents of the gifted in facilitating the effort" (xxiv). Mac and Jim, in spite of Mac's previous field experience, are not able to create this atmosphere of orderly or rational change, and thus, little has changed for the workers at the conclusion of Steinbeck's novel. When Jim's face is erased by a shotgun blast at the end of the novel,[3] and when the striking pickers witness his corpse, his facelessness becomes the ultimate symbol of a mob's need to erase individual identity in order to achieve a common goal. At the same time, Steinbeck shows Mac using Jim's death as a way to further incite the mob, a mob that he might be able to get to act, but a mob that he will be unable to understand and use for actual change because he is still an outsider. In the novel, Steinbeck seems to be noting the lack of theoretical approaches to crowds and mob violence, and the novel cites this lack of understanding as a reason for the numerous failings of strikes and other communist-supported activities in the U.S.

In his most famous work, *The Grapes of Wrath*, Steinbeck continues his analysis of mob behavior and mob potential for social change while also furthering his argument that community action is necessary for change to occur. The "Okies" of *The Grapes of Wrath*, like those branded as "working stiffs" in *In Dubious Battle*, have their identities forced on them by a powerful few, and Steinbeck argues that the only way to combat these identities, and survive the economic injustice enforced by such identities, is through the creation of a nurturing community, a crowd of migrant workers working together towards a common goal. This community, then, is for Steinbeck a sign of evolution away from the often aimless and violent behaviors of the crowds witnessed in *In Dubious Battle*. Steinbeck's argument is best symbolized through the character of Rose of Sharon, who after being abandoned by her husband, Connie, gives up her individual economic goals to literally nourish a fellow human being in order to collectively survive Depression-era hardships. Again, Steinbeck reiterates the necessity of organized collective action led by those who are a part of, and therefore better understand, the crowd.

Steinbeck clearly depicts the Joads as members of a larger group, a crowd made up of families displaced by the Dust Bowl, forced to migrate west to California and the promise of economic sustenance found there. This type of crowd is defined by Canetti as a "flight crowd," and Canetti defines such crowds as being "created by a threat. Everyone flees; everyone is drawn along" (53). Suffering economically from being displaced from the land they worked and that fed them, the crowd of *The Grapes of Wrath* is threatened by starvation. Wartzman notes that "the exodus had been underway for nearly a decade, with as many as four hundred thousand folks from Oklahoma, Arkansas, Texas, Missouri, and other states flocking to California in search of a better life" (3). These families, like generations of Americans before them, are heading westward in hopes of finding a new life, a new place that will provide sustenance, but Steinbeck's migrants are continually frustrated, as their arrival in California brings them up against what Wartzman describes as "the state's giant landowners," who "had made a travesty of the Jeffersonian ideal of 160 acres, assembling dominions that ballooned to one thousand times or more that size" (5). Here, the American progress myths of westward migration and capitalism previously explored by writers like Willa Cather come into question. Steinbeck consistently switches his focus from chapter to chapter, concentrating specifically on the Joads while at the same time showing that there are thousands of families facing similar conditions. These families form the group that becomes identified by the few rich landowners as a threatening mob.

The opposition between the migrants and the powerful group of California landowners allows Steinbeck the opportunity to continue to study human beings as a group, to further his theoretical analysis of crowd behavior. Human beings in the novel are consistently seen as a group, as is represented by Jim Casy's thinking of the "Holy Sperit" as "the human sperit" and his notion that "maybe all men got one big soul ever'body's a part of" (24). Casy's comments exemplify a broader social movement, a movement that, as Michael D. Hansen observes, advances "a belief in the unification of peoples, something that Carpenter identifies with Whitman's idealized mass democracy. The ideals of the mass soul and mass democracy take the place of the Christian emphasis on the individual soul" (117). In Steinbeck's work, especially *The Grapes of Wrath*, cultural notions regarding crowds and individual identity are being explored in new ways, as Steinbeck strays from the literary trope that depicts crowds as always persecuting individuals. Simultaneously, American political and cultural views of the crowd would change as well, as evidenced by New Deal politics and the later counterculture movements of the 1960s.

Tom Joad, returning home from prison and thinking about his large family all living in one cramped sharecropper's house, thinks there "must be a mob there now" (68). The Joad family and all of the displaced farmers are indeed a mob, a group moving westward in hopes of escaping their economic problems. Again, as in *In Dubious Battle*, the purpose of the novel seems to be an examination of a mob's ability to work together towards a common goal, to become "the armies of bitterness ... all going the same way," walking "together" (88). This mob streams "out on 66, sometimes a single car, sometimes a little caravan" (119), forming a mob of "two hundred and fifty thousand people over the road" (122). *The Grapes of Wrath* provides a sense of mass migration taking place within the United States that is unmatched even by Cather's prairie novels.

Steinbeck's group in *The Grapes of Wrath* becomes "Manself," a group that changes "I lost my land" to "We lost *our* land" (151). The crowd must come together in the change from "I" to "we," a transformation from being individuals to becoming a group made up of "a half-million people moving over the country" (152). As Foley and others have noted, Steinbeck injects theoretical chapters into the novel to illustrate the social contexts within which the Joads are migrating. As the Joads travel, they join with families such as the Wilsons, representing a larger movement where "twenty families became one family, the children were the children of all. The loss of home became one loss, and the golden time in the West was one dream" (192). As they move westward, the families not only become a larger family, but they come to share responsibilities and goals. Jim and Mac struggle to get their mob of fruit pickers in *In Dubious Battle* to organize towards a common goal, while the migrant workers of *The Grapes of Wrath* are forced into this realization, and as a group, they respond accordingly.

Part of Steinbeck's own response to the migrants' dilemma is to champion New Deal political solutions to the economic crisis of the Great Depression. The "moving, questing" migrants described by Steinbeck become changed by "hostility," and this hostility "made the little towns group and arm as though to repel an invader" (282). Fighting against the identity that individual landowners tried to assign to the migrant workers, identities summarized by rich landowners as "goddamned Okies," "dirty and ignorant," "sexual maniacs," "thieves," and individuals with "no sense of property rights" (283), the only solution seems to be the New Deal–created camps such as Weedpatch. There, a "depity can't pick on one fella" because "he's pickin' on the whole darn camp" (357). The Weedpatch camp is the only place in the novel where the Joads, and those like them, are able to find any degree of comfort, as the camp provides not only a sense of community but adequate shelter, cooking space, and waste removal. The camp and its sense of community provide safety from harassment from private landowners, and community activities such as dances give the Joads and the other families a chance to enjoy some of the pleasures of home and community. For Steinbeck, the camps represent a solution to the economic crisis, a solution that is based on community and collectivity backed by strong leadership and government support. The only problem with the camps is that they lack the money and space to take in all of the migrants, and attempting to find work often forces families such as the Joads to move on to less humane conditions so that the men of the family can find work.

As many critics have noted, much of Steinbeck's focus in *The Grapes of Wrath* is on issues of gender identity during economic hardship. As Michael Szalay argues,

> The only trouble with this federal utopia is that the preponderance of the men in the camp cannot find work. Men want wage labor in *The Grapes of Wrath*, but almost never get it. Instead, they stay at home, which profoundly alters the divisions of labor at the heart of the traditional nuclear family. Inhabiting spaces at once public and private—campsites and rest stops that seem to blur the boundaries between families, as well as between work and leisure—Steinbeck's men amble aimlessly about. In the process, Steinbeck reinvents the family as much as he does the polity to which, in sentimental fiction, it usually corresponds. Conflating the private and the public, the political and the biological, Steinbeck's families grow inexorably larger [175].

From the glimpse Steinbeck provides of such New Deal–inspired camps, it is clear that such camps, if given more federal financial support, could counter the economic hardships facing many Americans. However, the success of such camps relies on government support of such collective enterprises, and as Steinbeck specifically examines, a reevaluation of masculinity, an approach to male social responsibility that focuses on working together as a community rather than pursuing individual family goals. As families combine in order to work together and survive, Steinbeck's men must learn new roles, not as the heads of a household, but as members of a collective unit that is larger than the traditional family unit. In other words, they must give up their roles as leaders in the small units of the home in order to serve a larger purpose in the community. At the same time, Steinbeck's men are branded by individual landowners as lazy, ignorant, and deserving of their economic fate. Like Hemingway and Fitzgerald before him, Steinbeck thus considers transforming gender roles within the context of social change and crowd dynamics.

Because such New Deal camps are overcrowded and because work is scarce, the Joads are forced out of the comforts of the Weedpatch Camp in search of employment, continuing the cycle of abuse facing them and the crowd of migrant workers they belong to. The novel ends with a final glimpse of collective hope, as Rose of Sharon, by offering her breast to suckle a starving man, shows that human kindness and an effort to nurture others are the only true solutions to the difficulties facing the impoverished farm workers. Fittingly, Rose of Sharon participates in this act after giving up on her own individualized bourgeois dreams. She and her husband Connie had planned, at the outset of the Joads' journey west, for Connie to take correspondence courses so that he could leave farm life for a more stable, less labor intensive, middle-class position. Connie, however, abandons Rose of Sharon without explanation, perhaps to chase his own dream, leaving Rose of Sharon pregnant and alone. Through the course of the novel, several others have been witnessed abandoning the group and striking out as individuals. Noah Joad, the oldest Joad son, decides to leave the family and support only himself through hunting and fishing. As Hansen notes in regards to individual action in *The Grapes of Wrath*, "All members are part of an organism—'manself,' or the 'big soul'" in the novel (118), and thus individual action is usually futile. *The Grapes of Wrath* portrays a consistent struggle between individuals and their role in a group of community, and Steinbeck seems to argue with the parting image of Rose of Sharon that community is necessary for survival and that these individual goals only fragment and weaken the community. The novel's ending scene shows that when selfish, individual efforts are put aside, the human mob can help itself by helping each other. Steinbeck's conclusion in *The Grapes of Wrath* shows that he still believes in the power of the crowd to achieve social change by working together, rather than pursuing individualized goals, and his theorizing finds a potential solution in the model of the family seen in the government camps and Rose of Sharon's concluding act. Parini argues that "every man is out for himself at the beginning of the novel, but the spiritual progress of the Joads moves from personal to collective awareness as the sparks of human connection go off, one by one, in each of the characters' hearts" (*John Steinbeck* 107). Likewise, Rose of Sharon gives up her individual, bourgeois goals of easy town living for herself, her spouse, and their child, committing herself to an act that, in the context of the Great Depression and New Deal political reaction, affirms collective action through the unification of individual families as the only alternative to the ills of capitalism. Notably, Rose of Sharon and the crowd she represents come to their conclusions themselves, through their shared experience. They do not need outsiders, like Mac and Jim in *In Dubious Battle*, to unite them.

Much like *The Grapes of Wrath*, Faulkner's Snopes trilogy traces the social and economic changes taking place in the United States prior to, during, and after the Great Depression, alternating between serious and comic examinations of the situation. Additionally, Faulkner continues his theorization of the relationship between crowds and individuals by depicting the events that preface the Great Depression.[4] Faulkner's Snopeses are not heroic, nor do they represent an entirely positive alternative to individualistic, bourgeois values. Rather, Faulkner uses his Snopeses as an ethnographer would, tracing their migration from hamlet to town and examining the opposition they face from individuals who aim to keep them in their subjugated, sharecropping, lower class social position.

Readers of Joseph Blotner's *Faulkner: A Biography* and Blotner's *Selected Letters of William Faulkner* cannot help noticing that Faulkner spent much of his life worrying about his finances. Faulkner's financial hardships are hard to imagine for modern visitors of Faulkner's Rowan Oak estate, currently owned, renovated, and maintained by the University of Mississippi, but it is important to note that Faulkner spent most of his writing life profiting very little from his literary work, struggling as a Hollywood writer, and sharing the responsibility of supporting, as Parini notes "willingly," his mother, a brother, several in-laws, and his own wife and children (*One Matchless Time* 279). It is only later in his life that Faulkner, having gained literary fame thanks to efforts by individuals such as Malcolm Cowley, seems to turn his literary attention to financial issues outside of his own. Cowley's *The Portable Faulkner* appeared in 1946 at a time when, for a few years anyway, Faulkner's financial life had begun to stabilize. Fittingly, Faulkner published *The Hamlet* in 1940, and the novel served as the opening for his economics-focused Snopes trilogy. Over the next two decades, through the completion of *The Mansion* in 1959, Faulkner focused much of his literary output on an extended examination of the economic issues taking place in his apocryphal Yoknapatawpha County.

Still, it is only recently that Faulkner's relationship with the Great Depression has been fully examined. Atkinson posits that

> unlike the Southern Agrarians to his right and Steinbeck, Caldwell, and Wright to his left, Faulkner charted a moderate approach to the plight of rural America in the thirties—a move seemingly out of touch with the times. In retrospect, though, we can understand how this vantage point gave Faulkner a more comprehensive view of the Depression, yielding nuanced, complex, and at times contradictory treatments of social relations [220].

It is in Faulkner's Snopes trilogy specifically that Faulkner provides his most comprehensive view of the economic conditions before, during, and after the Great Depression, and Faulkner uses the character Flem Snopes as a representation of an entire social class that would become known in Yoknapatawpha only as Snopeses, but by extension could represent thousands of Americans throughout the country. As Don H. Doyle observes, one cause of dramatic changes in Depression-era Southern life, represented in Faulkner's Yoknapatawpha County and the city of Jefferson, is that as "rural life decayed," towns such as Jefferson, Faulkner's version of the real-life Oxford, were "vibrant and growing" (349). Doyle adds that beneath this "progress was a slow shift in power and wealth away from the declining old families and toward a new enterprising breed, many of whom were coming in from the county to make their way in town" (349). It is this migration from rural areas to towns, a movement motivated by Depression-era economic conditions, that Faulkner charts through Flem Snopes, who along with his crowd of fellow Snopeses, progresses from the rural backwoods of *The Hamlet* to the more urban confines of *The Town*, where some of the Snopeses are able to comfortably settle down and become part of a new Southern economy in *The Mansion*. Throughout the trilogy, Faulkner attempts to understand this changing economic landscape, and in doing so, he shows that mobs are not only potentially oppressive and violent forces, but also, as Steinbeck suggests throughout his fiction, potential vehicles for dramatic and necessary social change.

Kevin Railey observes that "the materials of Faulkner's fiction thus connect very much to his historical environment" (6), and this observation is certainly true in regard to *The Hamlet*. Here, Faulkner begins his portrayal of what Canetti would later identify as a "Reversal crowd," which Canetti states occur when "those who have been defenceless for so long suddenly find teeth. Their numbers have to make up for the experience in viciousness which they lack" (58). The novel begins the *Snopes* trilogy in Frenchman's Bend, "a section of rich river bottom country lying twenty miles southeast of Jefferson" (7). This rural area is chiefly controlled, economically if not politically as well, by Will Varner, the present owner of the Old Frenchman place," "the chief man of the country," and "the largest landholder" (9). Varner, along with his son Jody, owns, among other enterprises, the only store in the area and several farms worked and occupied by sharecroppers. The Varners are thus the most powerful individuals in the area. When Jody Varner rents one of the farms to Ab Snopes, a man with a barn burning past and the father of young Flem Snopes, the Snopes family gains their first foothold in the economic world of Yoknapatawpha. Although their small sharecropper's farmhouse "aint fitten for hogs" (23), Flem is given the opportunity, thanks chiefly to his father's notoriety, to bargain with Jody Varner for a position in the Varner store, only after turning down Jody's offer to run a farm. As Flem notes, "Aint no benefit in farming. I figure on getting out of it soon as I can" (26). Young Flem's realization represents the realization of many Southern sharecroppers, most of whom inhabit areas such as Faulkner's northeastern Mississippi where sharecropping is an endless, cyclical process of excruciating labor and inevitable debt, a situation similar to that facing Steinbeck's Joads in *The Grapes of Wrath*. As Singal asserts, "Flem emphatically rejects the other key role model dominating southern life during the nineteenth century, the yeoman farmer" (247). Flem represents a crowd of poor white Southerners seeking to give up sharecropping and aiming to adopt bourgeois business values.

Flem uses his position in Varner's store to his advantage in spite of the constant ire of the traditionally middle-class inhabitants of Frenchman's Bend, such as the traveling salesman V.K. Ratliff. These established townsfolk make fun of everything Flem is involved with, from his shirt that clearly "had been cut and stitched by hand and by a stiff and unaccustomed hand too" (52) to his answering "Yes and No to direct questions" without ever looking "directly or long enough at any face to remember the name which went with it" (57). Flem's country ways are consistently made fun of, from the way he talks to the way he dresses, and these traits are part of his economic identity. Flem's economic progress is continually scrutinized by those around him as his clerk position leads to his moving from his father's tenant farm in the rural outskirts to the actual village, and his subsequent addition of "a clean white shirt" and "a necktie" (58) to his wardrobe. This progress by Flem is always followed by sarcastic, if not paranoid, comments from those around him; upon moving into the village, Bookwright comments, "Anyhow, he aint moved into Varner's house yet" (58). For Flem Snopes and those like him, this version of rural Mississippi bourgeois bigotry is a serious obstacle. As Canetti notes, reversal crowds occur in "stratified society. A clear separation of classes, one enjoying more rights than the other, must have lasted for some time, and made itself felt in men's daily life before the need for reversal arises" (58). Such stratified social constructs are evident in Faulkner's Yoknapatawpha and Flem is shown as being one of the first members of the lower classes to challenge these constructs, much to the ire of the individuals who consider themselves to be his superiors.

Flem, although representative of a larger class of Southern sharecroppers slowly trickling in from the country to seek expanded economic opportunities in towns, is not the only Snopes that Frenchman's Bend worries about. As Flem continually moves up in social standing, a new Snopes continually moves in to take his place in what throughout the trilogy becomes a constant pattern of migration from the rural to the town and from the lower class to the middle class. Canetti notes that a reversal crowd "can try to pay back to their superiors themselves what they have suffered and stored up from them," adding that "man alone, weak and helpless as he is, will only rarely be fortunate enough to find an opportunity for this, but, if many men find themselves together in a crowd, they may jointly succeed in what was denied them singly" (58). Flem, who later in the trilogy is shown to care very little for his fellow Snopeses, certainly uses his family to create this reversal and to protect his ever-rising position. As Flem's cousins take over the Frenchman's Bend blacksmith shop and school, Ratliff, a representative of the local middle classes now threatened by the migrant sharecroppers leaving their farms, can only spread defamatory comments about individuals such as Flem, arguing, "Will Varner has caught a bear at last. Flem has grazed up the store and he has grazed up the blacksmith shop and now is starting in on the school. That just leaves Will's house" (70). It becomes clear throughout the trilogy that Ratliff, and in *The Town* and *The Mansion* Gavin Stevens, grows increasingly threatened by the economic progress being made by Flem, the reversal crowd of Snopeses, and the migrating farmers they represent. These middle-class citizens are obviously threatened by the members of the lower class working hard to take their place, and they often resort to bigotry, as in Ratliff's likening of Flem to a grazing animal.

As Bookwright, Ratliff, and other members of the Frenchman's Bend community grow suspicious of the economic progress being made by the Snopeses, they also are shocked by the way the Snopeses, and Flem Snopes specifically, function in a way that differs from the generally accepted codes of honor in the community. The Snopes family comes to represent both economic challenges and social challenges to the old Southern regime. Although new Snopeses continually move into the area on Flem's coattails, Flem does not show any regard for blood relations in his business dealings. Flem's disregard for family when it comes to matters of money catches the Frenchman's Bend community off guard and is emblematic of Faulkner's questioning of Southern codes of honor, codes that Faulkner sees as perhaps heroic and honorable, but also detrimental to the South in an increasingly modernized and capitalistic society. Surprised by Flem's actions, Ratliff realizes "I just never went far enough ... I went as far as one Snopes will set fire to another Snopes's barn and both Snopeses know it, and that was all right. But I stopped there. I never went on to where that first Snopes will turn around and stomp the fire out so he can sue that second Snopes for the reward and both Snopeses know that too" (87). Ratliff and Gavin Stevens continually fail to realize the impossible economic conditions, conditions of desperation, that Flem Snopes was raised in and that the Snopeses are generally striving to escape. Ratliff and others also fail to realize that Flem and his fellow Snopeses are desperate in ways that members of a relatively stable rural middle-class cannot comprehend, and therefore, Flem and his family cannot afford to stick to traditional Southern codes guiding matters of family and business.

Many critics have noted Flem's nontraditional values, as James Gray Watson does when he notes that "Flem lacks even the fundamental human commitment to the blood ties of clan loyalty" (99). When Mink Snopes is arrested for murdering Jack Houston, Bookwright comments that "even Flem Snopes aint going to let his own blood cousin be hung just to save money" (253). What Bookwright and the rest of the community fail to realize is that Flem is not only saving money, but also preserving his only opportunity to rise from his past as a lower class son of a noted barn burner. Sharing what economic advantages he gains would likely keep Flem from progressing any further up the social and economic ladder. Yet, Flem's rise does help the rest of his family as he breaks old barriers that remain broken in his wake. Flem leads by example, rather than philanthropy.

Frenchmen's Bend's criticisms of Flem Snopes and his fellow Snopeses arise not only from their failures to realize the economic conditions facing poor sharecroppers like the Snopeses, but also because Flem is able to continually dupe them in financial matters. Daniel Hoffman notes that "Yoknapatawpha's is not a cash economy but one in which trading looms large, and the man who can hold his own in the trader's agile play of wit, who knows the relative value of every object or creature that comes to hand, who keeps his composure and comes out ahead—such a man is worthy of his neighbor's respect" (80). In Faulkner's world, there is nothing honorable or respectable about wealth, as it is usually only the result of elaborate trickery and scheming, often at the expense of the ignorant.[5] Such trickery is not a sign of Flem's purely evil nature, but rather a sign of Flem's, and those he represents, financial desperation, and their outsiders' attempt to mimic the business practices that have tricked them into being poor farmers in the first place. Likewise, Flem's tricks, and his ability to gain wealth through them, show a flawed financial system that is prone to manipulation by greedy individuals. That this is the only way to financially advance is symptomatic of a corrupt system, not merely a corrupt individual. As Joseph Urgo asserts, "From his father, then, Flem learns that in their economic dealings, men do not respect nor treat other men fairly unless they have some reason to fear them" (153), and Urgo adds that "for Flem, amoral conniving and slick maneuvering resulted in his winning a seat at the pinnacle of the capitalist order, as the community assimilates those who prove victorious and who successfully exploit it" (151). Flem has been taught that there is only one way for him, and the social class he represents, to rise above their poor, sharecropping status. The only path to wealth involves individual manipulation of entire groups and communities. Faulkner is not making fun of Flem, but the economic system that favors Flem's brand of trickery, the same economic system that has oppressed the mob of Snopeses Flem represents. Likewise, Faulkner aligns Flem with an ever-growing capitalist order where the focus is on monetary success rather than clannish values.

In spite of their obvious positions as biased narrators in matters pertaining to Snopeses, and especially Flem Snopes, critics have generally sided with

Ratliff and Stevens, and such critical side choosing has led many critics to misread Faulkner's Snopeses. These critical dialogues are full of references to the Snopeses as subhuman.[6] The Snopeses are obviously threatening, both to the people of Yoknapatawpha and to literary critics, who read their conniving ways only as signs of greed. Too often, the Snopeses are read as greedy individuals, rather than being recognized as the group they are representing, a group that has been oppressed and can only rely on trickery and dishonesty to overthrow this oppression. The Snopeses are not a single family, but representatives of a large part of Yoknapatawpha's population, those who live in its outlying communities, a group who, by extension, represent the nation's changing class structures and migratory patterns from country to town. One need only be familiar with Faulkner's complete literary output to realize the challenges facing Yoknapatawpha's lower classes.

A few critics[7] do see Faulkner's stance towards Flem Snopes as less damning, and it is this understanding of Flem as a politically ambiguous character that I believe Faulkner adopts. Faulkner sees Flem and the Snopeses as representatives of a collective body forcing much needed social change, erasing the dramatic class differences that exist between those like Gavin Stevens and Manfred de Spain, representatives of Yoknapatawpha's upper class, and those like Ab Snopes, individuals who have no steady income or home. Like Steinbeck, however, Faulkner does not take a stance that completely favors the economically disadvantaged crowd; rather, Faulkner views this collective change as positive but dangerous. Railey argues that "the world of the trilogy is indeed a fallen world for Faulkner, a world where the powers of greed have overcome the forces of love and community" (148), but Faulkner's focus on the crowd of Snopeses appears to be, at least equally, a condemnation of the Southern past and its present moral stasis. Faulkner is presenting a fallen world, but a world that was fallen long before Flem Snopes came into town. The Snopeses are not the cause of the ills that have befallen Yoknapatawpha and Jefferson. Hoffman sees the trilogy as Faulkner's lamentation on the "inner decay of Southern society" that is attributed to "the rise of a class of native Southerners, the redneck entrepreneurs" who, according to Hoffman, have no "culture," "religion," or "morals," depicted as swarming "over the South like locusts, insinuating themselves into the operations of society, displacing men of finer character" (72). Such a reading of the trilogy mistakenly assumes Faulkner's allegiance with the cultured, moral, and religious, a group that Faulkner continually found himself at odds with throughout his own public life. Faulkner may indeed be laughing at Flem and his mob of Snopeses,[8] but he is also laughing at Ratliff, Stevens, Will Varner, Manfred de Spain, and other members of Yoknapatawpha bourgeoisie who are caught off guard by the economically motivated, morally nontraditional Snopes clan. Thus, as Parini observes, "Flem's life and times are an implicit critique of the American system and a send-up of the Horatio Alger story that continued to captivate Faulkner's fellow citizens" (*One Matchless Time* 249). Flem's capitalistic motivations are not solely immoral and evil, but rather enabled and even encouraged by the U.S. progress myth and U.S. capitalistic values.[9] Flem merely represents a new group of Americans who must take part in the growing town-centered capitalist economy in order to survive.

Besides, Flem is not the only greedy individual in Yoknapatawpha, as is shown throughout the trilogy. Rather, as Blair Labatt argues, "Flem is surely the most self-effacing villain ever. Almost unsurpassably laconic, he draws to him the indiscretions of all other men. In a sense, Flem never needs to be greedy; he makes use of the pride and greed of others. At crucial moments, he always profits by making his antagonists forget that it is he they are challenging" (77). Adding to the often beast-like qualities attributed to Flem Snopes, this quote makes Flem sound almost devilish. Flem certainly profits from his indirect relationships with Gavin Stevens, a representative of the South's moralizing tradition, a tradition that, as numerous readers have recognized, is often criticized by Faulkner. Likewise, and mostly in *The Hamlet*, Flem profits from Ratliff's financial mistakes and Ratliff's desire to gain an advantage over him. Flem takes advantage of the system that has always taken advantage of him, his family, and their fellow sharecroppers. The capitalistic greed of Yoknapatawpha is easily capitalized on by Flem. He is not the only person to attempt to trick others in the novel—he is just the most consistently successful.

Flem's success allows him to move to Jefferson and allows more Snopeses to invade Frenchmen's Bend in route to Jefferson. As *The Town* begins, it is noted that "there were as many Snopeses in Frenchman's Bend as there were Varners; and five years after that, which was the year Flem moved to Jefferson, there were even more Snopeses than Varners" (355). These poor farming families begin to outnumber the old aristocratic town families of the past. The Snopeses' migration from hamlet to town is particularly threatening to the few most prominent members of the Jefferson community, individuals like Gavin Stevens who are able to take a moralizing position on most issues because of their own histories of economic stability. Stevens fails to see that his own economic status is based on the same system that allows the Snopes migration to appear like a "chain unbroken, every Snopes in Frenchmen's Bend moving up one step, leaving that last slot at the bottom open for the next Snopes to appear from nowhere and fill" (358). Stevens's own financial position was solidified by the generations before him, however, while the Snopeses' economic progress is happening in Stevens's presence, right before his eyes. The crowd of Snopeses represent Jefferson's future rather than its past. Jefferson's stagnation is representative of the Southern economy, as it is noted that "until then, Jefferson was like all the other little Southern towns: nothing had happened in it since the last carpetbagger had given up and gone home or been assimilated into another unregenerate Mississippian" (359). Flem and his clan represent a threatening sense of change to the Southern middle class, and Gavin Stevens is the main representation of the bourgeoisie in *The Town*, joining Ratliff and others in the middle class battle against what they begin to call "Snopesism."

Gavin's own economic relationship to the Snopeses is enough to make him an unreliable narrator; his view of the Snopes clan is clearly a bigoted one. Gavin sees the Snopeses as one nonhuman mass, believing "none of them seemed to bear any specific kinship to another; they were just Snopeses, like colonies of rats or termites are just rats and termites" (385). Gavin, buying into the notion of Flem's immorality, takes it upon himself to try to defend Eula Varner Snopes' reputation, desiring Eula but defending her honor as a married woman against Manfred de Spain and their obvious affair. Blinded by Flem's financial desires, Gavin does not understand that Flem is unaffected by Eula's affair, and is instead interested in using her affair with the mayor to solidify his own position in the Jefferson economy. Concerned with what he sees as a moral issue, Gavin is unable to recognize Flem's financial motivations, which stem from Flem's tenant farmer past. As the Snopes trilogy indicates, these financial factors are replacing belief systems based on morality.

Watson notes that "the weakness of Gavin as a narrator and the humanization of Flem Snopes" are "often cited to demonstrate two major failures of *The Town*" (128), a novel that has faced a good deal of critical disparagement. As referred to above, critics have generally dehumanized Flem Snopes and the Snopes clan; but perhaps Flem, and *The Town* as a work of art, have been criticized in large part by a critical failure to recognize the historical and economic issues Faulkner is examining in the novel and throughout the *Snopes* trilogy. As the trilogy narrows its focus from a large rural county to a small Southern town, Faulkner widens his ethnographic study of Southern life. Gavin Stevens's morality and his position as a member of the stagnant Southern white moderate, makes him an easy victim for Flem Snopes and those like him who are uninterested in the Southern moral traditions that have left the lower classes in a perpetual and impossible struggle as tenant farmers. As Watson argues, "Committed to his own romantically generous view of reality, Gavin is so often and so disastrously wrong in his speculations about Flem that Flem's amorality is revealed by contrast" (129). For Flem and the crowd of migrants like him, capitalist morals, rather than the morals of the traditional religious Southerner, are the belief system that allows for social class advancement. As Urgo rightfully asserts, "Gavin has a fixed idea of Snopes that impedes the further development of his understanding of Flem's behavior and goals. He cannot get past his images of Snopes (and of all Snopeses) as rapacious, greedy, and self-serving" (191), and Parini adds that Faulkner "portrays his hero, Stevens, ironically" (396). Gavin is able to hold to this moral high ground because of his own economic security, but it is this same security that hinders his ability to understand the Snopeses. It appears many have misread the trilogy simply because they have misread the conflict between Flem and Gavin, thinking that Faulkner has fully sided with Gavin Stevens.

Of course, Faulkner is not siding with Flem either, nor is he siding with the mob of Snopeses taking over Jefferson or the capitalist values taking over the South and the country. Like Steinbeck, Faulkner attempts to objectively view this migrant mob, analyzing the social conditions leading to their migration, as well as the changing economic and moral landscape this migration produces. The society Faulkner depicts in the *Snopes* trilogy is an increasingly greedy one, but the Snopeses are not the only greedy members of Faulkner's Yoknapatawpha.[10] Everyone in the trilogy seems out to trick someone else, either economically or through cuckoldry. What shocks the community of Jefferson in its reaction to the Snopeses is that the Snopeses actually stand up for themselves, challenging the economic elite that have traditionally been above them. The Snopeses challenge these economic elites in ways that can surely be judged as immoral, but that does not mean that Faulkner fails to see the necessity of this challenge. As Urgo notes, "If Faulkner admired the Snopes clan, it was for their refusal to allow anyone to treat them like the dirt they sprang from" (149). Faulkner, it appears, does admire the Snopes clan for their ability to overcome economic hardship, for Flem's ability to rise to prominence in spite of the opposition he faces. As usual, Faulkner's moral message is left unclear, but the political message, although often easy to overlook in Faulkner, is rather clear in the Snopes trilogy. Faulkner shows that dramatic economic changes are needed, and the capitalistic values that have favored wealthy individuals are going to be challenged by a mob of poor sharecroppers, as well as other members of the forgotten lower classes, who can no longer survive under the old economic models.

As Gavin, Ratliff, Varner, and Manfred de Spain attempt to thwart and even cuckold the Snopeses, the Snopeses, through a variety of business deals and activities, gain an even stronger hold on Jefferson's economy. Flem's machinations allow him to seize control of the Jefferson bank and Eula Varner's inheritance, and *The Town* ends with Flem Snopes and his clan firmly entrenched in Jefferson's middle-class, in spite of the opposition put up by Gavin Stevens and other members of Jefferson's bourgeoisie. The Snopeses' new economic position in Jefferson allows Faulkner to again widen his ethnographic gaze, even as his trilogy narrows to *The Mansion*. *The Mansion* in part focuses on Linda Snopes Kohl, Flem's adopted daughter, and through Linda, Communist ideals are introduced into Yoknapatawpha as Faulkner continues to analyze the South's changing economy and the nation's political responses to economic turmoil.

By *The Mansion*, it is clear in the Snopes trilogy that the almighty dollar rules Southern life. Increased financial opportunities in towns, not to mention depleted soil in farming areas, motivated a large number of formerly sharecropping and tenant farming families to abandon the farm and migrate from rural areas into towns. Here, like Flem Snopes, they can seek employment as store clerks, security guards, and bankers. Although such farmers are essentially forced to leave these farms due to dire economic conditions, their assimilation into capitalistic town life produces a new collection of social problems. For example, a new age of materialism is seen in the trilogy, one that can be noticed in the names of the various Snopeses who have settled into Jefferson's middle-class. Names such as Montgomery Ward Snopes and Wallstreet Panic Snopes proclaim that now that the Snopeses have gained a position in the middle-class, they are completely dedicated to capitalistic pursuits as capitalism becomes the country's new religion. Likewise, traditional family names have been replaced by names of financial crises and department stores, and as Ted Ownby ironically notes, Montgomery Ward Snopes's pornographic picture business "comes to represent the principle that anything—especially immediate gratification—is available through purchase" (117).

The Mansion also examines the arrival of communist ideology to remote areas such as Faulkner's Yoknapatawpha, and as usual, Faulkner's examination of this local context has national implications. Ironically, Flem Snopes, a man who has manipulated capitalist systems in order to rise in social class, is the man indirectly responsible for bringing Communism to Jefferson. Flem's cutthroat practices allow him to marry the pregnant Eula Varner, and by moving with her to Jefferson, Flem introduces his adopted daughter, the future Communist Linda Snopes, to Jefferson society. Through Flem, Faulkner critiques not only the old traditions and caste-like systems that have kept poor farming families poor, but also the system of U.S. capitalism that allows immoral individuals like Flem to amass great wealth. Doyle argues that Faulkner "was very conscious of the massive forces of change that had swept through his part of the world, and that is what his Yoknapatawpha saga chronicles" (373), and *The Mansion*'s depiction of the spread of Communism as a reaction to rampant capitalism is an example of Doyle's point. Flem does not father Linda, but he does bring her to Jefferson, and in doing so, Communist ideology is introduced to the town's inhabitants.

Although Jefferson generally sees Linda sympathetically since she is the adopted daughter of the detested Flem, her return to Jefferson, with the accompanying information that she has been living with a Communist Jewish sculptor named Barton Kohl, places her in opposition to the traditional social norms of Jefferson. Linda has indeed withdrawn from all of Jefferson's accepted practices; she questions, at various times, myths of patriarchy, race, and class through her actions. In small town Jefferson, Communists are only viewed as

"Negro lovers: consorters, political affiliators with Negroes" who dare question the "native born Jefferson right to buy or raise or dig or find anything as cheaply as cajolery or trickery or threat or force could do it, and then sell it as dear as the necessity or ignorance or timidity of the buyer would stand" (870).

Linda's Communist beliefs stand in ironic opposition to Flem's position in Jefferson society as a wealthy, self-made banker, but Flem has provided a success story for fellow individuals from poor farming backgrounds, and Linda extends this notion of economic inclusivity to Jefferson's black population. Linda's work with local African Americans leads to "the words *Nigger Lover* scrawled huge in chalk on the sidewalk in front of the mansion the next morning for her father to walk steadily through" (880), and "one night ... a crude cross soaked in gasoline blazed suddenly on the lawn in front of the mansion" (882). Like Steinbeck's strike organizers, Linda Snopes Kohl is faced with opposition from an entrenched system, and Linda's presence in *The Mansion* is Faulkner's examination of the growing national debate between capitalism and Communism.

Murdered at the end of the novel by Mink Snopes, the cousin he earlier abandoned, Flem Snopes becomes a representation not only of the large number of poor Southern whites abandoning farming, but also of the moral problems that seem to inherently arise within a capitalistic society.[11] Valuing nothing but money, Flem readily abandons his family and the other poor farmers who were unable to escape the farm. Mink, sent off to prison without any protection from Flem, returns to Jefferson to seek vengeance after Linda Snopes Kohl has attempted to free him. In her attempt, the Communist Linda has openly tried to put an end to Flem, a man who, unlike the other migrant Snopeses, has grown to represent only individual wealth. As Urgo argues, "At the end of *The Mansion*, Flem symbolizes the emptiness that individualist success amounts to, and the extreme danger one invites in saying no, or nope, to the cosmos or to the community" (207). Flem's drive towards individual success, often to the detriment of his own family and community, leaves him a target for the other Snopeses, the other members of his former lower class standing. Thus, Mink usually garners readers' sympathies.[12] By the end of the trilogy, the reversal crowd that Flem inspired now reverses and aligns itself against him as he becomes the new figure of economic power.

Faulkner, as Steinbeck does throughout *In Dubious Battle*, never fully chooses a side in the *Snopes* trilogy, and it is perhaps this refusal to pick a side that has caused Faulkner to often be read as a writer unconcerned with political matters.[13] As Gavin, Ratliff, the Varners, Manfred de Spain, and the other Jefferson elites continually try to block Flem and the other Snopeses from full participation in their social, economic, and cultural institutions, it is clear that these upper-class Jefferson citizens see the Snopeses as a challenge to their moral, political, and economic traditions, and this threat often causes them to act irrationally and immorally in their attempts to defeat Flem. But as Watson posits, for Jefferson's middle- and upper-class, "to fight Snopesism ... would involve examining and then changing themselves first, and rather than make the effort, undergo the strain, they will absorb Snopeses and Snopesism, demanding only that it conform to their own pattern of evil and appear respectable" (136).

Flem is representative of not only the Snopeses, but also an entire social class attempting to rise from rural struggles and achieve the comforts of middle-class town living. Flem also represents the moral disintegration of a society obsessed with monetary gain through financial speculation. As Ownby puts it concerning Flem's focus on material gain, "The positive meaning stresses escape from rural poverty and the confining aspects of Southern traditions, while offering a form of democracy that reveals itself in appearances. The negative meaning stresses the indulgence of the self at the expense of responsibility for other people and communication with them" (95). Like Steinbeck, Faulkner explores a wide range of Depression-era issues, never fully siding with either the working class or the traditional bourgeois. As Beck asserts, concerning the *Snopes* trilogy, "There is, however, no oversimplified reduction to absolute extremes. *The Mansion*, like *The Hamlet* and *The Town*, continues to set forth involvement of relative good and evil in their qualifying interactions" (11).

Steinbeck and Faulkner's refusal to ultimately pick a side—individual or crowd—shows that their focus is at least partly on attempting to theorize crowd behavior, the dynamics of group action in their contemporary America. These works parallel a similar change in American thought as Depression-era political turmoil transformed large groups of Americans into sympathetic examples of an economy gone wrong. The refusals to automatically side with the individual in power relations between individuals and collective groups seen in Steinbeck's work and Faulkner's late work are emblematic of a wider social change that, by the time of *East of Eden*'s and *The Mansion*'s appearances in the 1950s, is often referred to as characteristic of postmodern theory. Faulkner's trilogy and Steinbeck's works dealing with "groupman" display a Heideggerian rejection of the differentiation between subjectivity and objectivity through the reversal of the Modernist-era treatment of mobs and their subjects, as well as a Derridian and Foucaultian distrust of language as truth. Furthermore, these works show an opposition to Modernist generality in dealing with crowds and crowd violence, rejecting, like Lyotard, this version of metanarrative.

Indeed, Steinbeck's work has been referred to as postmodern, as Chris Kocela refers to a "postmodern Steinbeck" (248), and several critics have noted, as Parini does, that "Steinbeck's interest in the biosphere, and his efforts to see human beings in their complete context, which includes their absorption into various larger units as well as their place in the environment, in a strange way makes his writing feel remarkably current" (*John Steinbeck* 488). Of course, Faulkner will be forever linked with Modernism, but his writing career spanned nearly five decades, and great differences exist between his early and late work. One such difference is that critics generally celebrate Faulkner's work of the late 1920s and during the decade of the 1930s, while discounting later novels such as the *Snopes* trilogy and *A Fable* (1954). Steinbeck's work with the mob, generally branded as mere "proletarian" writing, and Faulkner's late work, generally branded as "inferior," are best understood as transitional works in canonical figurations and definitions of Modernism and Postmodernism. These novels display a cultural movement away from the Modernist celebration of individuality in the face of mob pressure to a more postmodern understanding, rising out of Depression-era reactions to super-wealthy individuals and economically suffering masses, regarding an objective view of mobs as dangerous, but potentially useful agents, of real social change. Crowds become useful entities for inspiring social change, but only if the crowd can be organized and controlled.

The Road *to a Conclusion*

With the exception of Mary Rowlandson, an example of an early American author who links mob violence and identity, the writers I have analyzed in this book thus far provide examples of the ways in which Modernist American writers persistently used images of crowd violence to explore matters of individual identity. American authors writing in the first half of the twentieth century worked within both a literary atmosphere that predominantly championed Modernist aesthetics and a cultural and social atmosphere rife with mob violence. These writers often used portrayals of this mob violence as a useful trope in exploring matters of identity self-fashioning and the ways in which societies enforce normative identities or punish certain non-normative identities. The fact that these authors do so, often through specific images of lynching violence, shows that their work does in fact explore political and social issues, while also adhering to Modernist aesthetic philosophies that often keep this political and social conscience submerged beneath an artistic veneer of social disengagement and formal experimentation. Using the prevalent imagery of mob violence found in their culture, Modernist-era U.S. writers often interrogate the American progress myth, arguing that a lack of progress in racial relations, gender roles, and class inequality undermines the idea of American progress.

Cormac McCarthy is the best example of a contemporary American author who has continued this, as well as several other, Modernist aesthetic traditions. McCarthy's Modernism has been discussed elsewhere, most notably by David Holloway in his book *The Late Modernism of Cormac McCarthy*, but little has been made of the way in which McCarthy has linked, like several Modernist authors before him, identity self-fashioning with the threat of crowd violence. McCarthy's depictions of the struggle between self-fashioned individualists and dangerous crowd forces are numerous, but McCarthy's novels are also full of dangerous individuals who threaten the larger community, such as the leader of the violent gang in *Outer Dark* (1968), the serial killer and necrophiliac Lester Ballard in *Child of God* (1974), the Judge in *Blood Meridian* (1985), and Anton Chigurh in *No Country for Old Men* (2005). For McCarthy, then, it would seem that individuals are equally dangerous, if not more dangerous, than mob forces. Often, McCarthy even differs from many Modernist writers before him by portraying individual characters who find personal safety or comfort, at least temporarily, when they seek and find the company and protection of a crowd, mob, or gang. Such examples include Rinthy Holme in *Outer Dark*, Cornelius Suttree in *Suttree* (1979), the Kid in *Blood Meridian*, and, at various moments, John Grady Cole and Billy Parham in *The Border Trilogy* (*All the Pretty Horses* [1992], *The Crossing* [1994], and *Cities of the Plain* [1998]). Likewise, individual characters who wish to remain apart from any form of collective society, and the protection such societies usually offer, are often eventually persecuted or even consumed by collective forces. For example, Arthur Ownby is eventually jailed in *The Orchard Keeper* (1965) and Lester Ballard, finally apprehended by the community in *Child of God*, is eventually dissected by medical students. John Grady Cole and Billy Parham both find solace within groups at various times in *The Border Trilogy*, but both are hunted by gangs at various times as well, often persecuted in their attempt to escape their contemporary American society and relive the romanticized days of the American cowboy. McCarthy's most recent and perhaps most important novel, his 2007 Pulitzer Prize–winning novel *The Road*, provides McCarthy's strongest acknowledgment of the need for individuals to connect with some form of community, or face the consequences of death at the hands of an angry mob.

When readers look at the progression of Cormac McCarthy's literary oeuvre even before the publication of *The Road*, it is hard not to notice McCarthy prophesying the impending end of the world as we know it. Of course, since McCarthy's novels are often set in the past, it can also be surmised that McCarthy has felt like we have been on the brink of an apocalyptic moment for a very long time. Critics thus often argue that McCarthy's novels are deterministic, nihilistic, and even cosmocentric.[1] However, it is in McCarthy's most recent and most obviously apocalyptic novel that McCarthy provides a hint at a possible path for sustenance and even survival, at least in the short term. *The Road* shows the necessity of community if humankind is to have any hope of rebuilding a damaged world controlled by mob violence.

Importantly, reading McCarthy in this way helps to bridge one of the major disconnections in McCarthy's writing that critics often focus on—his movement from writing novels set in the American South, especially in Tennessee where McCarthy spent most of his early life, to novels set in the American Southwest and Mexico. The theme of mob violence has been a constant in McCarthy's work, no matter the geographical setting. Generalizing about any author's work, especially an author as complex as McCarthy, can be a dangerous critical game, but it seems safe to note that setting, in the sense of both time and place, has always been an important focus of McCarthy's work. In *The Road*, however, McCarthy removes readers from any specific sense of time and place—we are left only to assume that the novel takes place in the eastern part of the United States, somewhere close to the present day. McCarthy seems to aspire toward a more general message in *The Road*, a message free from the regional confines of his previous work, and in spite of the novel's apocalyptic bleakness and frequent, graphic violence, McCarthy's message suggests that hope still exists in the human world, even as the human world slowly begins to disappear.

The setting of *The Road*, which Carol Juge calls "peculiar" in part because the novel does not take place in the American South or Southwest (24), is also peculiar because, as Juge adds, McCarthy made the "inexplicable" decision to leave his famed, self-imposed seclusion and "promote the novel all the way to Oprah's couch" (24). McCarthy, asked to participate in an interview by Oprah Winfrey after his novel was chosen for her famous book club, surprisingly accepted Winfrey's invitation, signaling that McCarthy's novel may have a message that McCarthy values above any message offered in any of his previous novels. This message centers, as the entire novel does, around the relationship between the man and the boy, and McCarthy notes in another equally unusual interview with *The Wall Street Journal* that the novel took on a special meaning for him as he raised his young son, John Francis McCarthy. Regarding his son, McCarthy explains to *The Wall Street Journal*, "I tell people that he is so morally superior to me that I feel foolish correcting him about things, but I've got to do something—I'm his father" ("Hollywood's Favorite Cowboy"). The child's moral superiority is a major message of *The Road*, as the boy in the novel is shown to be morally superior to the man, while the man's actions and motivations become more and more questionable as the plot progresses. In fact, in a novel that could be said to be lacking plot (the man and boy simply wander from place to place), this conflict between the man and boy, with the threat of mob violence persistently in the background, makes up the main action of the novel. While the man has grown to view all other human beings as potential members of dangerous mobs, the boy realizes that human survival depends on community, and that isolation and individuality are only paths to destruction and death. Perhaps, in leaving seclusion to participate in interviews with Oprah and *The Wall Street Journal* regarding *The Road*, McCarthy is hinting to readers that this message has had a profound effect on him personally, and that we should all consider this message seriously.

The man in *The Road* is of course not wrong in his fears of crowds and mob violence. Indeed, the novel often provides hints at the dangerous mobs roaming the post-world of *The Road*, and in several key scenes, these hints become explicit realities. As numerous readers like Ashley Kunsa have noted, "maiming, killing and the defiling of corpses" are persistent images in

McCarthy's fiction (58), and *The Road* is no exception. McCarthy's novel never explicitly informs readers what exactly caused the apocalyptic event that has destroyed the world of *The Road*, telling us only that "the clocks stopped at 1:17. A long shear of light and a series of low concussions" were followed by "a dull rose glow" (52), but we do learn that shortly after this earth-shattering event, "there were fires on the ridges and deranged chanting" (32). Mobs form quickly after this disaster, and are evident throughout the novel. Indeed, the greatest fear the man and the boy face are the persistent mobs of cannibals scouring the remains of the Earth for food, *any* food, even human flesh. The man and the boy witness several such mobs, including the mob that accompanies a reworked diesel truck, "shuffling through the ash casting their hooded heads from side to side" (61). Later, near the apple orchard where the man finds old apples and a cistern of water, they witness a marching army,

> an army in tennis shoes, tramping.... The phalanx following carried spears or lances tasseled with ribbons.... Behind them came wagons drawn by slaves in harness and piled with goods or war and after that the women, perhaps a dozen in number, some of them pregnant, and lastly a supplementary consort of catamites illclothed against the cold and fitted in dogcollars and yoked each to each [91–92].

Even when the mobs are not physically witnessed by the man and the boy, the effects of mob violence are found everywhere. After the man kills the roadrat traveling with the diesel truck, the man and boy escape and return to the site of their first encounter with the truck to retake possession of the shopping cart containing their few belongings, clothing, blankets, and food, only to find that the dead roadrat has been consumed by the mob of roadrats, "the bones and skin piled together with rocks over them. A pool of guts" (71). Later, the man and boy come across a campsite where an infant has been devoured by an apparent mob, and as Shelly Rambo notes, "the images of a child on a spit and burnt flesh cannot easily be erased as we think of the future of the boy without his father" (100).

One of the most persistent crowd presences in the novel is the existence of the numerous dead that the man and the boy encounter on their journey. In *Crowds and Power*, Canetti identifies crowds of the dead as "invisible crowds," stating "the action of the dead upon the living has been an essential part of life itself" (42). Seemingly everywhere the man and the boy turn in *The Road*, they find dead bodies. Often, as in the example mentioned by Rambo of the burnt child on the spit, the dead are found horribly mutilated and consumed by the violent bands of cannibals now roaming the land. Just as often, the dead appear as a crowd, as they do when the man and boy come across a crowd of dead who were consumed by fire, one of Canetti's symbols of the crowd, leaving the dead bodies in horrifying states, "figures half mired in the blacktop, clutching themselves, mouths howling" (190). These dead still play important parts for the living; the dead provide warnings that cannibals may be nearby, while also warning of dangers such as wildfires. Likewise, these dead serve as a warning of what has passed, what has left the world of *The Road*.

The man and the boy must fashion their own identities against these two prominent crowds in order to make their seemingly purposeless and useless existence meaningful. The man coaches the boy throughout their journey, ensuring the boy that they are "the good guys" (77) and, more importantly, that they are "carrying the fire" (83). As Rambo states, "The father has given their journey purpose. The implication is that someone is waiting to receive the fire that they bear" (104). The man and the boy define themselves morally as the good guys, as completely different from the various cannibals they witness and encounter. As Canetti argues, fire is an important symbol of the crowd, and thus, the man's statement and the boy's understanding of the statement become an important interpretive crux in the novel. Of course, the fire could be understood as the life inside of them, meaning that the man is demanding that he and the boy survive so that life on Earth continues, contrasting their identities with the crowds of dead they witness on their journey. This seems to be the argument the man makes with his wife when he tries to convince her to avoid killing herself by telling her "we're survivors," to which she responds, unconvinced, "We're not survivors. We are the walking dead in a horror film" (55). Likewise, the fire might symbolize something more than the mere survival of the human race—coupled with the man's mantra that he and the boy are "the good guys," the fire might represent some kind of moral code, the goodness within them that must be sustained and eventually passed on through good deeds performed for others.

However these mantras are interpreted, they and their respective interpretations become a point of disagreement between the man and the boy, and this disagreement creates emotional and moral distance between them, the emotional and moral distance that ignites the true conflict of the narrative. The man's actions and thoughts are characterized by his conception of himself and the boy as isolated individuals in a world that is quickly dying. As the man suggests to his wife in the early days of their survival, he values survival only because to be alive is to not be dead. According to Canetti, "The moment of *survival* is the moment of power. Horror at the sight of the dead turns into satisfaction that it is someone else who is dead" (227). The man seems to feel some satisfaction from the fact of this survival alone. He thinks of himself and the boy as "good guys" because they manage to survive without going out of their way to harm others. They survive independently of others, rather than by consuming others. Canetti adds that "the lowest form of survival is killing" (227), and since the man avoids this, at least at the beginning of the novel, he identifies himself as one of the "good guys." To the man, the fire that he and the boy are carrying seems to be nothing more than the fact of the life within them. The boy, on the other hand, finds their survival to be meaningless unless they maintain their stance as "good guys." For the boy, the fire within them does not only represent human life, the fact that they are survivors and thus still alive, but positive human qualities such as charity, forgiveness, love, and perhaps most importantly for continued survival, community. Thus, the man views other human beings as likely bad guys and prefers that he and the boy travel in isolation, while the boy views other people as potential companions in forming a new community. Thus, the novel can be read as a conflict between the individual (the man) and the crowd (the boy), one that reaches its crisis when the man starts performing deeds that the boy cannot reconcile with his understanding of the "good guys."

In many ways, the man in *The Road* can be read as an example of the tortured Modernist hero. He is unable to reconcile his past life with his and the boy's uncertain future, and isolated from any kind of human society or community, he struggles to self-fashion a meaningful personal identity. He tells the boy that they are "good guys" who are "carrying the fire," but through the narrative's access to the man's thoughts, readers see that the man values these mantras as little more than ways to motivate the boy to keep moving. The man's feelings of loss for the past center on what Canetti calls the invisible crowd of dead, while his hopes for any future are perilous in the face of the living crowds of cannibals who seek to destroy and eat anything they can find. The only personal identity the man seems to be capable of maintaining is his self-fashioned identity for both he and the boy—"He knew only that the child was his warrant" and that if the boy was not "the word of God God never spoke" (5). With the old world gone, the man self-fashions an identity for himself as the child's protector, simultaneously identifying the boy as the final sign of either God's existence or non-existence. The man tells the boy they are "good guys" who are "carrying the fire," but the man's only true purpose is the protection of his son. The fire does not reside within the man, a fact he recognizes—it resides only in the boy, whom he protects.

The man's self-fashioned identities for himself and the boy do not involve their finding, helping, or working with other human beings. The man only defines their identities as unlike the crowds they encounter. They are not like the dead of the past or the dead they find in the streets, hence the man's persistent insistence to his son that "we're not going to die" (100), an insistence that perhaps can be traced back to his conversation with his wife, who insists that they are already dead. Likewise, they are not like the cannibals who serve as clear opposition to the "good guys." With self-fashioned identities that set them apart from these crowds, the man physically isolates himself and the boy from other potential "good guys." This makes his self-fashioned identity problematic, as it is hard for anyone to be one of the "good guys" without performing good deeds, deeds which usually involve other people. Thus, as Erik

Wielenberg aptly argues, the man "does possess an important flaw. The man has been damaged by his horrific experiences. He has lost the capacity to trust and make connections with others," and Wielenberg adds, "This flaw has an important implication for the child—the child is unable to connect with other good guys as long as his father is alive" (8).

The man's inability to trust others and connect with other human beings stems from the traumatic loss he has suffered. Unlike the boy, who was born into the post-apocalyptic world of *The Road* and thus knows no other way of life, the man is encumbered with the loss of his past, and his memories continually revisit this relationship with this wife, as well as his uncle and father. His memories also often revolve around memories of pastoral scenes of nature that no longer exist. These feelings of loss, the loss of his loved ones and the loss of his beloved natural world, are compounded by the appearance of the world that he and the boy now face. His loved ones have been replaced by bands of cannibals, and the natural world he so obviously valued has been replaced by a natural world that, through rain, lighting, fire, and cold, seems to be actively trying to kill him and his son. The man has seen a great deal of death and destruction, and it appears that such loss has made him fear making any new connections, because he has been conditioned to accept that love ends with loss. He perceives his objective as *containing* the fire within the boy, rather than allowing the fire to spread, something fire seeks to do naturally.

The man's trauma, specifically the death of his wife, which he feels guilty for, causes him to think "there is no other story to tell" (32). This view conflicts with his ultimate goal of helping his son to survive, to learn skills like swimming (39), skills that hinge upon a future for the boy, with future stories to be told. In this respect, the man is not all that different from the woman. He accepts his own death and leaves the future for the boy to face alone. Thus, the man instills a false sense of progress in the boy, repeatedly prodding him on, telling him that "we have to keep moving. We have to keep heading south" (42). The man tries to convince the boy that the two of them are heading south for warmth while searching out other "good guys," but whenever they reach a sanctuary that might attract other "good guys," the man usually makes them leave, as he does in an early scene at a waterfall where he tells the boy the waterfall "is an attraction. It was for us and it will be for others and we dont know who they will be" (42). It would seem reasonable, if the possibility of connecting with other human beings was imminent, for the man and the boy to wait at a safe distance and watch for "good guys" at such attractions, but their consistent pattern of movement signifies escape rather than a meaningful search for other human beings that still act human.

In the several scenes of encounter between the man, the boy, and other travelers of the road, the man shows that he will likely never be open to the possibility of joining with more companions. The man's protection of the boy is well-intended, but ultimately damning to any possibility of long-term survival for the boy. The man and the boy will live a life of desperate isolation as long as the man is alive, and when he dies, the boy will be left alone. When the man encounters the roadrat, for example, the man assumes the roadrat is looking at the boy because the roadrat is a cannibal and intends to eat him. However, it seems just as likely that the roadrat is in awe of the boy, since few children still exist in the world. Perhaps, the roadrats are indeed simply looking for others to join their community, as the roadrat they encounter suggests (62–66). The man does later find what appears likely to be the skin and bones of the roadrat he guns down, showing that the roadrat was probably eaten by his fellow travelers. However, the fact that the roadrats eat the deceased man's body does not necessarily indicate that they would kill other human beings simply to eat them. The man's paranoia might save them in this situation, but it might cause his and the boy's eventual death if they are never able to reconnect with others like them. The roadrat "was the first human being other than the boy that he'd spoken to in more than a year" (75). The man recognizes the roadrat as "my brother at last," but he doesn't view him as a fellow human, noting that "the reptilian calculations in those cold and shifting eyes" (75). Earlier, from the man's perspective, the roadrat's eyes have been described "like an animal inside a skull looking out the eyeholes" (63).

Soon after the scene with the roadrats, the man and the boy travel through a town where a dog is seen by the boy, and later heard barking by both the man and the boy. They also see signs of human life, humans who are probably not cannibals since they have not yet eaten the dog and since they travel with a child that the boy witnesses (82). Still, the man does not allow them to seek human company in the town. Instead, they leave the town and soon observe the marching army near the orchard, but the existence of the other boy and the dog seem to signal that not *all* of the survivors are threatening, that there is a chance of finding community in the ruins of society.

For many, the most troubling scene in the novel takes place when the man and the boy find the naked prisoners in the house where "Chattel slaves had once trod those boards bearing food and drink on silver trays" (106). The man convinces the boy, who rightfully has a bad feeling about the house, that they must search the house because they are yet again on the brink of starvation. They encounter various signs that signal the presence of cannibalism, including the pile of clothes and shoes (107) and the "forty gallon castiron cauldron of the kind once used for rendering hogs" (109). Still, the man insists they are searching the house for food, and since they have "had no food and little sleep in five days" (105), readers are left to wonder if the self-proclaimed "good guys" are about to give in to their hunger and finally resort to cannibalism. The boy continually insists, "Papa let's not go up there" (106), "I dont think we should go up there," "We should go Papa," and "We could find something somewhere else" (106). Then, he insists, "I'm not hungry" (108). Clearly, the boy senses not only the physical danger of the scene, but the moral and ethical implications as well. At this point, the man might be desperate enough to eat *anything*. Once the man opens the hatch and they encounter the "huddled ... naked people, male and female, all trying to hide," the prisoners cry, "Please help us" (110) and, "Please" (111). They do not react violently, but instead meekly plea for help. The man never considers helping, and as they hurry from the hatch, he even swings the hatch door back over the opening, keeping the obviously weak and delirious prisoners from having any chance of escaping the cannibals who are keeping them hostage. In spite of his persistent claims of being one of the "good guys," the man's only generous acts in the entire novel are his selfish sustaining of himself and his son. He never helps anyone without prodding from the boy.

The man will not admit it to the boy, but he is aware that he has lost his own moral conscience. The man sobs in his sleep "about beauty or about goodness" (129), but he recognizes that these are "things that he'd no longer any way to think about at all" (129–130). The man's change, not only physically but morally, causes him to raise his pistol when he sees himself in the mirror as they search yet another house for food (132). He no longer recognizes himself. The man looks at the troubled boy's face and worries that "something was gone that could not be put right again" (136), as he realizes his own moral loss in comparison with the boy's more innate goodness. This comes after the man and the boy have abandoned the men and women trapped in the cellar, an episode which causes the man to drop the fire in both a literal and a physical sense: the man drops their lighter, and the man refuses to help other people, showing his claim of being one of the "good guys" to be spurious at best. As Donovan Gwinner points out regarding the man's decision to leave the people in the cellar behind, "for good guys on the lookout for other (potential) good guys, the father's response casts a slight ethical shadow, especially since the symbolic fire he carries, the lighter, is left behind with the damned men and women in the larder" (150). Later, as the man opens the second hatch that he and the boy come across (the bunker full of provisions), the boy wonders if they are once again being tempted to become cannibals, telling his father, "Dont open it" (134).

The man and the boy next encounter the only named character in the novel, the old and nearly blind traveler Ely. Ely appears to be safe, a potential "good guy," yet the boy has to convince the man to share food with Ely, and even has to convince the man to let Ely share their communal fire for a night (162–5). Again, it is evident that the man wishes to protect both the literal and the metaphoric fire, rather than sharing it or passing it on to others. The man tells Ely, "You cant go with us, you know," (168), but the man never justifies this position. Instead of engaging Ely in a discussion about their respective plans, or a discussion regarding how the old man has managed to survive this long, the man seems to patronize Ely in conversation, suspicious all along of Ely's intentions. The existence of Ely alone affirms Ely's claim that "there's other people on the road" (170). Given his own apparent weakness, his age and confessed lack of vision, it would seem like the road is not as dangerous as the man makes it out to be. While Ely seems to second the man's desire for isolation by stating that "it's better to be alone" (172), Ely's presence indicates that there is hope for the boy in connecting with new people. Likewise, Ely's presence further signals the differences between the man and the boy: the boy convinces the man to give Ely "some cans of vegetables and of fruit" upon their departure. The man tells Ely that "you should thank him you know" because the man admits he "wouldn't have given you anything." When Ely asks, "Why did he do it?" the man can only respond, "You wouldnt understand" and "I'm not sure I do" (173). As Wielenberg observes, "The man also struggles when it comes to helping others. He is suspicious and distrustful of others. He is reluctant to share what little food they have. The child, by contrast, typically tries to reach out to other people and help them" (5). The boy is different from the man, and the man, in his failure to understand the boy's charity, does understand his own weakness as a moral guide.

The man's weakness as a moral guide is perhaps most evident when he and the boy have their belongings stolen at the beach late in the novel. The man and the boy chase down the culprit and demand the return of their possessions at gunpoint. When the thief gives them their belongings, the man further demands that the thief take off even his own clothing and shoes, virtually leaving the man for dead while the boy cries, "Papa please dont kill the man" (256). The thief tells the man, "I'm starving, man. You'd have done the same" (257). Given the man's desire to simply survive and his prior treatment of other human beings beside the boy, the thief is probably right. As Gwinner notes, "If the father's actual violence in killing the roadrat early in the novel leaves the boy bloodied and traumatized but safe, the father's threats of violence and stripping of the thief leave the boy physically safe but psychologically and morally devastated" (151).

With the man's stance as one of the "good guys" virtually refuted, the man's health worsens near the end of the novel and he begins to recognize "some new distance" between himself and the boy (190). This distance is a moral distance, a distance that is intensified by the man and boy's growing realization that the man will soon join the invisible crowd of the dead. Dying, the man must realize that he should be seeking out new caretakers for the boy, some new community, yet, when the man is open to the idea of others like he and the boy, they are always distant and imagined, like the imagined father and son on the other side of the sea (216–219). Wielenberg states that the man "is broken and knows it" (8). Indeed, the man at times seems to realize his harmful cynicism. At the beach, the boy suggests that they "could write a letter to the good guys" in the sand "so if they came along they'd know we were here" (245). The man suggests they shouldn't because the "bad guys" might see it, but then corrects himself and states in response to the boy's immediate dejectedness, "I shouldnt have said that. We could write them a letter" (245).

Further, the man comes to the subconscious, if not conscious, realization that he has done the boy a disservice in keeping him isolated from others, and his realization is symbolized by his interactions with the sinking sailboat named the *Pajaro de Esperanza* (Bird of Hope). The ship's name implies that hope exists, and the ship does provide some important supplies while also signaling that other such boats might exist, carrying with them supplies that the man and boy might anticipate procuring if they continue their travels near the coast. More importantly, as Canetti notes, ships can symbolize "isolated individuals" since they are "much alone" on the "vast surface" of the sea (171). In *The Road*, the sinking ship represents the man's lost hope in living a life of isolation with the boy. His life, like the solitary sailboat's, is sinking. The man continually swims out to the *Pajaro de Esperanza* in search of supplies and tools, specifically for the flare gun that he eventually finds. The flare gun provides them with another means of defense, which is what the man intends to use it for, but more useful for the boy's survival, the flare gun is a tool intended to signal to other people, a tool usually used to reconnect lost individuals with their community. The man proudly shows the flare gun to the boy, and the boy is fascinated by the flare gun and its intended purpose. When the man shoots the flare gun for their "celebration," the boy considers whether or not the flare might have attracted the "good guys" (246). Later, when the man dies and new people, apparent "good guys," immediately find the boy, we might wonder if the flare shot in celebration played a part in the boy finding this new community.

Dying, the man tells the boy to "find the good guys but you cant take any chances" (278). The man again acknowledges that they really should have been looking for others all along, but still doesn't seem to realize that the risk is necessary—the boy cannot survive alone. Countering the man's dying directions, the boy immediately finds others who are apparently good, and he does so by taking a chance his father would have never allowed them to take. He sees in the road that "someone was coming," and trained by his father, his first reaction is to hide in the woods (281). However, he decides to stand in the road and wait, taking a necessary risk his father would never have taken, a risk that connects him not only with a new man, but a new family, a new community. It is this new community that the boy has been craving all along, a community that suggests that the boy will be able to carry out his dreams of being one of the "good guys" and "carrying the fire." These dreams both rely on the boy's ability to connect with other people, to be good by helping others and to spread the fire that he identifies within himself.

Early in the novel, long before readers learn about the night that effectively ended the world as the man and woman slept, the narrative hints at the idea that the biggest issue in this post-apocalyptic landscape is the fragmented isolation of all life. Throughout the novel, McCarthy seems to assert that human connections are a way to combat this destroyed world. The novel begins with the man reaching out to the boy, signifying McCarthy's ultimate message of the need for community in a world torn asunder by violence. McCarthy writes, "When he woke in the woods in the dark and the cold of the night he'd reach out to touch the child sleeping beside him" (3). McCarthy follows this opening with the man's dream of the creature in the cave, monstrous in its blind solitude (3-4). The man and the boy are "each the other's world entire" (6) because they lack any community apart from each other. Images of coldness and warmth pervade the novel, and the man and the boy spend a great deal of time trying to warm each other up through the physical closeness of their bodies. The absence of the sun and of warmth in general show that humanity is suffering, but that warmth can be provided by other human beings, sustaining life until, perhaps, the sun comes out again. The world itself is described with "everything uncoupled from its shoring" (11) rather than as being united, showing that a lack of unity is affecting both the natural and human world. Readers soon learn that "in those first years the roads were peopled with refugees" but that they were "creedless shells of men," individuals rather than groups working towards a common goal (28). Fragmentation and isolation persist throughout the novel, but McCarthy provides a parallel to this fragmentation and isolation in human relationships centered on love. Indeed, relationships with other humans are all that is keeping the man and boy alive. The man thinks "that the boy was all that stood between him and death" (29). Similarly, the woman advises the man how to best survive. She tells the man "you wont survive for yourself.... A person who had no one would be well advised to cobble together some passable ghost. Breathe it into being and coax it along with the words of love. Offer it each phantom crumb and shield it from harm with your body" (57).

Unpolluted by notions and memories from the world of the past, the boy recognizes that the only way human life can continue is through community. Without the prospect of community, the boy realizes the meaninglessness of existence, as is shown in the scene when the man returns with the flare gun near the end of the novel. When the man finds the flare gun, the boy asks if "there's nobody to signal to" (241). The man responds that there is not. The boy continues to wonder about others though, seeming to realize that soon he will not have his father, who he has already watched with concern while the man coughs (192). The boy asks about the people who were on the ship

(242) and then asks the man how many people he thinks are still alive on the Earth (243). When the man responds and tells the boy, "I don't think there are many" (243), the boy turns away and states, "I dont know what we're doing" (244). All along, the boy has thought that their mission was to find other people. To reassure the boy, the man tells him that "there are people and we'll find them" (244). As Lydia Cooper surmises, "The father's love for his son becomes the boy's longing for his father and for community with others. That longing is depicted as a boy's journey through a physically broken world in a relentless attempt to find that other whose pain and whose joy he can share. In a world poisoned by greed, dissociation, and despair, longing may itself be a form of redemption" (234). The boy longs for community, but the man will not allow them to approach other humans.

While Cooper and Wielenberg both express redemptive readings of the boy and the novel, an alternative interpretation of the boy and his understanding of the "carrying the fire" mantra hinges on Canetti's connection between the crowd and fire. Canetti identifies fire as "the strongest and oldest symbol of the crowd" (26). While Canetti links fire to crowds because of fire's destructive forces and its ability to spread unpredictably, he also argues that "life within a community is normally a protection against physical destruction" (72). Important to the boy's situation in *The Road*, Canetti also discusses the invisible crowds of "*posterity*," which he argues are "perhaps the most important of all" invisible crowds and the most "natural to us today" (46). It is this fire, the fire of community and progeny, that the boy believes lies within himself. His fire is not merely his own life, nor is it *only* a moral or ethical goodness. Rather, his fire is the fire of the crowd or community, and this crowd or community will offer the boy the possibility of protection, as well as the opportunity to produce good deeds and to further the human race through his progeny. In *The Road*, fire is a sign of the crowd and the furthering of a community of goodness, much as it is in Sheriff Ed Tom's dream of his father at the end of McCarthy's previous novel, *No Country for Old Men*:

> He just rode on past and he had this blanket wrapped around him and he had his head down and when he rode past I seen he was carryin fire in a horn the way people used to do and I could see the horn from the light inside of it. About the color of the moon. And in the dream I knew that he was going on ahead and that he was fixin to make a fire somewhere out there in all that dark and cold and I knew that whenever I got there he would be there [309].

The boy struggles for opportunities to carry this crowd fire throughout the novel. He dreams of doing good for others, and his greatest nightmare is to be alone, as is shown in his early dream of the windup penguin toy that marches in his dream even though "nobody had wound it up" (36). The boy has "fantasies" of "other children" (54), showing his desire not only for community, but for posterity. He desires a community that includes people like him in age and experience. When he thinks he sees another boy like himself, the boy is willing to risk death to seek out the human companionship with someone his own age, someone raised only in the new world like himself (84–85). The man coldly rejects the notion that another boy exists and shows no care for the other boy that his son claims to exist, and the man's position as one of the "good guys" is severely weakened in such instances. If the man carries the fire, it is a different fire than that carried by the boy. Thus, the boy grows to realize that the man has no intention of uniting them with other "good guys." He asks, "What if some good guys came?," and the man tells him, "Well, I dont think we're likely to meet any good guys on the road." The boy responds, "We're on the road," implying that he thinks others like themselves must exist, a belief the man seems to have given up. The man says they "should always be on the lookout. If trouble comes when you least expect it then maybe the thing to do is to always expect it" (151). It is this kind of thinking that makes the boy wonder what their "long term goals" (161) are once they leave the bunker where he has already prayed to the people who created the bunker and stocked it with food, showing his humanist ways (145–6).

The boy is open to the possibility of other good guys while the man is not. However, this does not mean that the boy is blind to the dangerous powers of the violent cannibal mobs. Indeed, he is in awe of their multitude, telling his father that "there's a lot of them, those bad guys" (92) when they witness the marching army. When they emerge from the snow storm and the man tells the boy, "Someone's coming," the boy asks, "They could be good guys. Couldnt they" (103). Even after witnessing the horrifying mob of cannibals the boy still has hope, and this hope is a significant part of the fire within him. Daniel Luttrull states that

> the boy now realizes that he and the man are part of a community of fire carriers, a community of people who refuse to live off others. At the same time, though, he realizes that many people do not belong to the community. And this realization requires vigilance, not only in the form of self-defense against those who do not carry the fire but also in the form of defense for those who cannot protect themselves [23].

Unlike the man, the boy recognizes that the existence of bad guys does not negate the existence of good guys. In fact, as Cooper puts it, "the boy's generosity in the face of terror suggests that if there is any value to human life, it lies in a categorical rejection of fear-based behavior" (234).

Indeed, the boy's most noble conception of the fire is his belief that "carrying the fire" involves doing good for others, which is the only way to be one of the "good guys." Wielenberg argues that "this is what provides human lives—both in the world of *The Road* and in our world—with meaning: connections with other people. In a word, the point of it all is love" (10). Indeed, the boy shows his love for others throughout the novel by attempting to share his communal fire. The boy always wants to help others, even those who appear beyond hope, as is the case with the man struck by lightning who inspires the boy to ask, "Cant we help him Papa?" (50). The man and the boy play out the continual struggle between community and self-reliance in their dialogues. Later, when the man is angry at the boy for giving Ely some of their food, he tells the boy, "When we're out of food you'll have more time to think about it" (174). The boy wisely responds, "I know. But I wont remember it the way you do" (174). Once they leave the thief who steals their cart and their belongings naked in the road, the boy is once again left to demand that his father help someone. The man seems unconcerned at first, brutally responding, "He's going to die anyway" (259). Yet the boy smartly corrects his father. When the man tells the boy, "You're not the one who has to worry about everything," the boy wisely replies, "Yes I am ... I am the one" (259). The boy realizes that any future relies on him, and others like him. He is the "one" who will produce more "good guys" like himself through his descendants. Likewise, he realizes his father will not be around forever, perhaps even senses that his father will soon die, meaning that when it comes to thinking about the future, the boy is the one that should be most concerned. When the man states that "I wasnt going to kill him" in reference to the thief, the boy corrects him by telling him, "But we did kill him" (260). By the end of the novel, the boy has assumed moral authority over the man.

The man dies at the end of the novel, separating the boy, at least momentarily, from all human connections. However, the boy has shown that he has already outlived the man's influence. In one of their final conversations, the man offers to tell the boy a story, but the boy responds that "those stories are not true" because "in the stories we're always helping people and we dont help people" (268). For the stories to be true, for them to be meaningful, the boy realizes that he needs to work with others. Thus, the new man that the boy finds at the end of the novel challenges the boy with the same dilemma that he has faced all along: "You can stay here with your papa and die," or he can join with new people (283). The boy is clearly distraught over the death of his father, but he realizes that he has meaningful work to do apart from his father, work that could not be carried out while his father was alive. The boy joins a new family, and this new family will provide him with the community he has been longing for, the opportunity not just to carry the fire, but to spread it. Since the new family has a little boy and a little girl, the boy is provided the hope that the invisible crowd of his progeny will one day walk the Earth as his fire is passed on. For readers of McCarthy, this ending has proven to be especially hopeful in comparison with his other works. Regarding the novel's seemingly hopeful ending, Rune Graulund posits that "contrary to all former expectations, it turns out that good guys *do exist*, in essence as in presence. Not only is the boy rewarded for his persistence in trying to be good, confirmed in the belief that *it does matter* to be good. He is also shown that goodness is able to exist outside the knit union of father and son" (72). For Graulund, "Hope, otherwise in short supply in McCarthy's authorship and never before living under tougher conditions that in *The Road*, is suddenly present in abundance" (72). Sara Spurgeon adds that the boy's "genuine belief in the potential for human goodness" is validated at the end of the novel, and this validation "is a startling claim in the face of the frequent accusations of nihilism directed at McCarthy" (17).

As Vereen Bell noted long before *The Road* was ever published, "For McCarthy a belief in the reality of other people is the first principle of responsible existence" (114). In *The Road*, McCarthy offers a message that conflicts with the typical Modernist-era narrative that often portrayed an isolated hero subjected to persecution from a violent crowd, a mob-like force. McCarthy, through the man/boy dichotomy of *The Road*, shows that violent crowds do exist, but that human beings cannot survive without seeking the sanctuary of community, and that such survival is only meaningful if one is able to perform good deeds within that community. McCarthy dedicates *The Road* to his then eight-year-old son John Francis McCarthy, and McCarthy might be providing his son with some fatherly advice, advice that dictates that the boy should not follow in the reclusive footsteps of the man. Regarding *The Road*, Graulund has argued, "In a world in which nature has been so decimated that it cannot rightly be said to exist anymore, it is of course appropriate to question whether the author has meant his book as a warning to a humanity run rampant" (68). More pointedly, McCarthy's novel, through its critique of the man's behavior in this apocalyptic scenario, portrays isolated individualism run rampant, and demands that readers avoid allowing their fear of the crowd to keep them from forming meaningful identities within a shared community.

Historically, the study of Modernist American literature has not explored this relationship between crowd violence and identity self-fashioning. Furthermore, this Modernist focus on social and political issues of mob violence and individual identities (racial identity, gender identity, national identity, and class identity) demands further exploration. McCarthy, for example, is often considered to be a late American Modernist, in part because his writing often seems to avoid explicit treatment of modern political issues. Because of this indirect approach to political and social issues, readers have overlooked this political engagement. Some readers of *The Road* have connected the novel with sensibilities arising in post–9/11 America, and as Cooper asserts, "The apocalypticism of *The Road* seems to be a response to an immediate and visceral fear of cataclysmic doom in the United States after the terrorist attacks on 9/11" (221). The fear Cooper mentions in McCarthy's novel might represent a general ideological shift in American society since the era traditionally identified as the Modernist era. After the events of 9/11, and perhaps even before those events, it seems that the fear many Americans struggle with is not a fear of mobs or crowds, but rather, a fear of a single individual who might attempt to destroy the constructs of the community. Terrorist acts and maniacal dictators with nuclear weapons strike fear in Americans, and more locally, fear is often produced by deranged serial murderers and increasingly publicized mass shootings.

There is also a general lack in theorization of mobs and mob violence, and such theorization will become important in studies of American literature, especially early American literature and Modernist American literature. American literature has long been fascinated with the obvious contradictions of American political philosophy. Americans celebrate their individualism while also functioning within a democratic political system, the rules of the masses. Aside from Le Bon's flawed but seminal work and Canetti's later studies of crowds, neither of which take into account the specific contradictory nature of American politics, Modernist American authors provide some of the few extended examinations of mob behavior, especially the effects mob behavior can have on individuals who are apart from, and in opposition to, the mob itself. Further studies of Modernist-era American writers' engagement with issues of crowd violence and identity can provide important close reading of Modernist writers and texts, while also providing important theoretical exposition in regards to mob violence. Crowd violence is likewise a particularly strong force in Modernist-era America, and examinations of mob violence in this time period can further our understanding of this period of U.S. history.

Le Bon and Canetti never make a clear connection between mob violence and identity formation and enforcement, yet this is the aspect of mob violence that American writers often focus on in their work. Identity self-fashioning in the face of massive political, social, and economic systems, systems that are growing rapidly during the Modernist era, are already recognized as a central concern of Modernist literature. The focus on identity, as it is shaped and controlled by mobs, mob violence, and other crowd forces, has gone unnoticed, and surely exists in Modernist-era works outside of the canonical authors this particular study examines. Indeed, Le Bon's declaration that the Modernist era would be an era of crowds holds true in Modernist-era society and the literature that documents this society. Surprisingly, given their consistent presence throughout the era, and indeed beyond and into the new millennium, mobs and crowds remain hauntingly un-theorized. It would seem that now is the time for the dynamics of mobs and crowds, and especially their relations to individuals, to receive this overdue attention. Modernist-era American literature, composed in a time that saw lynchings, labor riots, strict gender roles, and rampant westward expansion, is an ideal place to begin such examinations.

Chapter Notes

Introduction

1. For an extended definition, see Peter Faulkner's *Modernism*. While Faulkner notes that the term "Modernism" has been applied to an "immense variety of works in all the arts," he also notes that the term has been a commonplace of literary criticism since 1971 (ix).

Chapter I

1. See Pfeiffer's article, "Individualism, Success, and American Identity in *The Autobiography of an Ex-Colored Man*," *African American Review* 30 (1996): 403–19.

2. "Bright and Morning Star" did not appear in the original version of *Uncle Tom's Children*, and was later added in place of "The Ethics of Living Jim Crow." The edition used here includes both "The Ethics of Living Jim Crow" and "Bright and Morning Star."

Chapter II

1. In his book, *The Many Faces of Judge Lynch: Extralegal Violence and Punishment in America*, Waldrep uses the adjective "high-tech" to describe lynching-like activities that take place in the press and in the U.S. court system, representing a kind of legalized lynching.

2. I read Faulkner's first three novels, *Soldier's Pay* (1926), *Mosquitoes* (1927), and *Flags in the Dust* (1929), as a kind of writing apprenticeship for Faulkner, a period of experimentation during which he was trying to discover the kind of novel he would like to write. These novels lack a unified theme, but certainly deal with issues of identity, especially gender (*Mosquitoes*) and racial identity (*Flags in the Dust*).

3. Tuhkanen also links the lack of racial progress in *Native Son* with Foucault's *Discipline and Punish*, observing that Bigger's trial shows that "the historical shift from spectacle to discipline which Foucault argues to have taken place in European societies within the past 400 years does not seem completely applicable to the African-American context" (131).

4. Importantly, Bigger's ancestry clearly references both the crowd violence of the South and the Great Migration, as he relates that his father was killed "'in a riot'" in Mississippi (515).

Chapter III

1. It is surprising that Roberts refers to *Mrs.* Compson here, rather than Mr. Compson. Mr. Compson certainly seems to be more interested in his daughter's virginity than her mother does.

2. Caddy's daughter Quentin seems to be facing the same struggle her mother faced growing up in the Compson household. While the Compson family is in obvious decline, the women in the family are apparently repeating a cycle that continually denies them the

ability to define their own identity. It is easy to envision Quentin living the same kind of damned and outcast life her mother lives.

3. Roberts, regarding the male-centric narrating in the novel, notes, "Men compose most of the speakers of the novel" (198).

Chapter IV

1. Sarah Beebe Frye's *Fitzgerald's New Women: Harbinger's of Change* consistently notes the kinds of criticisms Fitzgerald's women have faced. For an interesting defense of one of Fitzgerald's most often attacked women, Daisy Buchanan, see Frye's fourth chapter, "Beneath the Mask: The Plight of Daisy Buchanan."

2. The second chapter of Nancy R. Comley and Robert Scholes' *Hemingway's Genders: Rereading the Hemingway Text* discusses the ways that Hemingway's women often fit into the simplistic and stereotypical categories of "Mothers, Nurses, Bitches, Girls, and Devils."

3. Stephen Cooper breaks down the violence of *In Our Time*'s prefaces as follows: "In this collection of stories, Hemingway shows us a world filled with violence.... Of the fifteen short chapters which alternate with the longer stories of *In Our Time*, six deal with war, six with bullfighting, two with executions, and one with a police shooting" (22).

4. As Fitzgerald biographer Matthew J. Bruccoli adds in the notes to the version of *The Great Gatsby* found in the Works Cited, Fitzgerald is actually referencing Lothrop Stoddard's *The Rising Tide of Color* (1920). While Bruccoli asserts that "it seems clear that Fitzgerald did not want to provide the correct title and author" (208n), I would argue that Tom Buchanan has misremembered the work's title and author, just as he has misinterpreted much of Stoddard's meaning.

5. Michael Soto argues that the novel is not only representative of 1920s culture, but also notes its influence, stating, "It is easy to overestimate Hemingway's influence on the shape of his generation's critique of American culture; after all, older figures such as Mencken and Sinclair Lewis had already paved the way for lost generation rhetoric by belittling puritan bogeys and denigrating holdovers from the pioneer days. Still, while the early critical fanfare for *The Sun Also Rises* was drowned by raves for more established writers, the novel soon became a life handbook for young Americans at home and abroad" (38–9). Malcolm Cowley also refers to the novel's popular culture significance, observing, "girls in New York were modeling themselves after Lady Brett in *The Sun Also Rises*. Hundreds of bright young men from the Middle West were trying to be Hemingway heroes" (225).

6. Messent disagrees at least partly with the danger Brett poses to traditional masculinity, arguing that she "is inconsistent in the challenge she poses to gender conventions" (*New Readings* 115).

7. As Gajdusek observes, "Jake, Cohn, and Romero are all defeated or injured in actual fights or in moral encounters or humiliations" (74) after becoming romantically involved with Brett.

8. Fittingly, Berman states that "*A Farewell to Arms* is not entirely a war book but a postwar book" (*Fitzgerald, Hemingway, and the Twenties* 115).

9. Gajdusek comments that "in Pablo's town Hemingway has, in almost pure Jungian dialectical terms, illustrated the psychic meaning of revolution, and in Ohio he has demonstrated the metaphoric meaning of patriarchal fascist control" (144).

10. Joseph describes Dick as suffering from "noncombatant's shell-shock," but notes that "we might think of Dick, then, as not just shell shocked, but shocked—shocked by his own fading career, shocked by the suddenly untenable ideal of masculinity, shocked by the postwar world itself" (71).

Chapter V

1. See Schwartz's *Creating Faulkner's Reputation: The Politics of Modern Literary Criticism*. While Faulkner's work with the U.S. State Department and Nobel Prize speech can be used to support Schwartz's claim, it is important to note that many of Faulkner's novels (*The Sound and the Fury*, *As I Lay Dying*, *Light in August*, for example) lack a main character, and there is

certainly a shortage of individual heroes or heroines in his work. I would argue that Faulkner's public comments, often made spontaneously while he was drunk and uncomfortable, as Blotner, Parini, and others have noted, should be treated separately from his carefully thought out, constantly revised literary output.

2. It is important to note Steinbeck's own relationship with the Communist Party. As Barbara Foley states, "Steinbeck was a Popular Frontist when he wrote *The Grapes of Wrath*: he railed against the 'fascist utilities and banks' running California and was loosely affiliated with the CP through the League of American Writers" (417).

3. Owens similarly reads Jim Nolan's death, while also recognizing a similar occurrence with Pepé's death in "Flight," arguing, "In spite of the faint traces of human warmth left in Jim, it is appropriate that when he is killed his face is erased by the shotgun. Jim has lost his individual identity in his absolute commitment to the cause at the same time that he has increasingly lost his ties to humanity.... In 'Flight'—a story of Everyman's flight from and toward death—Pepé became faceless when an avalanche delicately covered his face at the moment of death" (93).

4. As Abby H.P. Werlock posits, "Steinbeck places a number of his writings" during the "era of the Great Depression. Faulkner writes not only of those years but of the hungry ones leading up to them" (172).

5. According to Hoffman, Flem's focus on trade means that he "has no other ambition, no other emotion, but to get the better of everyone else by outsharping them in his deals, thereby moving upward in society himself and bringing in his train his tribe of nasty cousins" (73).

6. Watson states, "Flem is a character so completely resistant to moral definition as to be literally inhuman" (12), adding that Flem is "figuratively a creation of the devil" who "demands not paradise, but hell, and gets it" (43). Warren Beck argues that Flem's "steadfastness ... is of its own kind and in no way admirable" (78), and Doyle notes, "the sinister image some have of subhuman Snopeses who are seen crawling in from the country like locusts to invade the town and topple its traditional leaders" (369).

7. Singal, for example, sees "Flem and his tribe in conventional moral terms as parasitic opportunists," while also recognizing "their role as inevitable and even desirable agents of change" (245).

8. As Urgo puts it, "Faulkner may have laughed at the Snopes clan and their ridiculous given names, their lack of sophistication, and their mulish stubbornness, but he held a great respect for their spirit" (149).

9. Urgo posits, "Flem's method of revenge on the community is the most threatening because it is legal and is actually encouraged by the American rags-to-riches mythology" (180).

10. Parini observes, "People are out for themselves here—an indictment of the South that becomes an indictment of American society as a whole" (396).

11. As Singal observes, "Flem's real secret ... is his willingness to detach himself radically from the reigning culture. He thinks nothing, for example, of violating traditional mores by dissociating himself from his family if that can work to his advantage" (246).

12. For example, Railey asserts that "Mink's value as a character stems from his recognition of other values besides those of money as well as his recognition of the natural ties and responsibilities between people" (163).

13. Charles Hannon aptly puts it, however, "Faulkner produced a literary discourse remarkably contiguous with other discourses of his culture. Whether these emanated from academic disciplines (such as history, anthropology, or sociology), from professions (such as the law), from labor history, national politics, or national or regional economics, the discourses that shaped America from the 1920s through the 1950s are represented in the discursive architecture of Faulkner's novels" (157).

The Road to a Conclusion

1. In his article "'Do you see?': Levels of Ellipsis in *No Country for Old Men*," Jay Ellis describes McCarthy as "a cosmocentric artist" rather than an "anthropocentric" artist (97).

Works Cited

Atkinson, Ted. *Faulkner and the Great Depression: Aesthetics, Ideology, and Cultural Politics.* Athens: University of Georgia Press, 2006.
Baker, Houston A., Jr. "Racial Wisdom and Richard Wright's *Native Son.*" *Long Black Song.* Charlottesville: University Press of Virginia, 1972. 122–41. Rpt. in *Critical Essays on Richard Wright.* Ed. Yoshinobu Hakutani. Boston: G.K. Hall, 1982. 66–81.
Beck, Warren. *Man in Motion: Faulkner's Trilogy.* Madison: University of Wisconsin Press, 1961.
Bell, Millicent. "*A Farewell to Arms:* Pseudoautobiography and Personal Metaphor." *Ernest Hemingway: The Writer in Context.* Ed. James Nagel. Madison: University of Wisconsin Press, 1984. 107–28.
Bell, Vereen M. *The Achievement of Cormac McCarthy.* Baton Rouge: Louisiana State University Press, 1988.
Berman, Ronald. *Fitzgerald, Hemingway, and the Twenties.* Tuscaloosa: University of Alabama Press, 2001.
———. *Modernity and Progress: Fitzgerald, Hemingway, Orwell.* Tuscaloosa: University of Alabama Press, 2005.
Blotner, Joseph. *Faulkner: A Biography.* 1974. Jackson: University Press of Mississippi, 2005.
Brannigan, John. *New Historicism and Cultural Materialism.* New York: St. Martin's, 1998.
Bruccoli, Matthew J. *Some Sort of Epic Grandeur: The Life of F. Scott Fitzgerald,* 2d ed. Columbia: University of South Carolina Press, 2002.
Burnham, Michelle. *Captivity & Sentiment: Cultural Exchange in American Literature, 1682–1861.* Dartmouth: University Press of New England, 1997. Print.
Butler, Robert. *Native Son: The Emergence of a New Black Hero.* Boston: Twayne, 1991.
Canetti, Elias. *Crowds and Power.* 1960. Trans. Carol Stewart. New York: Farrar, 1984.
Castiglia, Christopher. *Bound and Determined: Captivity, Culture-Crossing, and White Womanhood from Mary Rowlandson to Patty Hearst.* Chicago: University of Chicago Press, 1996. Print.
Certeau, Michel de. *The Practice of Everyday Life.* Berkeley: University of California Press, 1984.

———. *The Writing of History*. Trans. Tom Conley. New York: Columbia University Press, 1988.
Cokal, Susann. "Caught in the Wrong Story: Psychoanalysis and Narrative Structure in *Tender Is the Night*." *Texas Studies in Literature and Language* 47 (2005): 75–100.
Comley, Nancy R., and Robert Scholes. *Hemingway's Genders: Rereading the Hemingway Text*. New Haven: Yale University Press, 1994.
Cooper, Lydia. "Cormac McCarthy's *The Road* as Apocalyptic Grail Narrative." *Studies in the Novel* 43.2 (2011): 218–236.
Cooper, Stephen. *The Politics of Ernest Hemingway*. Studies in Mod. Lit. 71. Ann Arbor: UMI Research Press, 1987.
Davis, Margaret H. "Mary White Rowlandson's Self-Fashioning as Puritan Goodwife." *Early American Literature* 27.1 (1992): 49–60.
Ditsky, John. "Steinbeck, Bourne, and the Human Herd: A New/Old Gloss on *The Moon Is Down*." *Rediscovering Steinbeck: Revisionist Views of his Art, Politics, and Intellect*. Ed. Cliff Lewis and Carroll Britch. Lewiston, NY: Edwin Mellen, 1989. 177–90.
Doyle, Don H. *Faulkner's County: The Historical Roots of Yoknapatawpha*. Chapel Hill: University of North Carolina Press, 2001.
Ellis, Jay. "'Do you see?': Levels of Ellipsis in *No Country for Old Men*." *Cormac McCarthy: All the Pretty Horses, No Country for Old Men, and The Road*. Ed. Sara L. Spurgeon. London: Continuum, 2011. 94–116.
Faery, Rebecca Blevins. *Cartographies of Desire: Captivity, Race, and Sex in the Shaping of an American Nation*. Norman: University of Oklahoma Press, 1999.
Faulkner, Peter. *Modernism*. London: Methuen, 1977.
Faulkner, William. *As I Lay Dying*. 1930. New York: Vintage, 1990.
———. "Introduction to the Modern Library Edition of *Sanctuary*." 1932. *William Faulkner: Essays, Speeches, Public Letters*. Ed. James B. Meriwether. New York: Modern Library, 2004. 176–82.
———. *Light in August*. 1932. New York: Vintage, 1990.
———. *Sanctuary*. 1931. New York: Vintage, 1993.
———. *Selected Letters of William Faulkner*. Ed. Joseph Blotner. New York: Vintage, 1977.
———. *Snopes*: The Hamlet, The Town, *and* The Mansion. New York: Modern Library, 1994.
———. *The Sound and the Fury*. 1929. New York: Vintage, 1990.
———. "Two Introductions to *The Sound and the Fury*." *William Faulkner: Essays, Speeches, Public Letters*. Ed. James B. Meriwether. New York: Modern Library, 2004. 289–300.
Fitzgerald, F. Scott. *The Great Gatsby*. 1925. New York: Scribner, 1999.
———. *Tender Is the Night*. 1934. New York: Scribner, 1995.
Fleming, Robert E. *James Weldon Johnson*. Boston: Twayne, 1987.
Foley, Barbara. *Radical Representations: Politics and Form in U.S. Proletarian Fiction, 1929–1941*. Durham: Duke University Press, 1993.
Fowler, Doreen. *Faulkner: The Return of the Repressed*. Charlottesville: University Press of Virginia, 1997.
French, Warren. "Introduction." *In Dubious Battle*. New York: Penguin, 2006. vii–xxiv.
Frye, Sarah Beebe. *Fitzgerald's New Women: Harbingers of Change*. Studies in Mod. Lit. 86. Ann Arbor: UMI Research Press, 1988.

Gajdusek, Robert E. *Hemingway in His Own Country*. South Bend, IN: University of Notre Dame Press, 2002.

Gallagher, Catherine, and Stephen Greenblatt. *Practicing New Historicism*. Chicago: Chicago University Press, 2000.

Geertz, Clifford. "From the Native's Point of View: On the Nature of Anthropological Understanding." *Culture Theory: Essays on Mind, Self, and Emotion*. Ed. Richard A. Shweder and Robert A. Levine. New York: Cambridge University Press, 1984. 123–36.

———. *Local Knowledge: Further Essays in Interpretive Anthropology*. 1983. New York: Basic, 2000.

Goldsby, Jacqueline. *A Spectacular Secret: Lynching in American Life and Literature*. Chicago: University of Chicago Press, 2006.

Greenblatt, Stephen. *Renaissance Self-Fashioning: From More to Shakespeare*. Chicago: University of Chicago Press, 1980. Print.

———. *Shakespearean Negotiations*. Berkeley: University of California Press, 1988.

Graulund, Rune. "Fulcrums and Borderlands: A Desert Reading of Cormac McCarthy's *The Road*." *Orbis Litterarum* 65.1 (2010): 57–78.

Gwinner, Donovan. "'Everything uncoupled from its shoring': Quandaries of Epistemology and Ethics in *The Road*." *Cormac McCarthy: All the Pretty Horses, No Country for Old Men, and The Road*. Ed. Sara L. Spurgeon. London: Continuum, 2011. 137–156.

Hannon, Charles. *Faulkner and the Discourses of Culture*. Baton Rouge: Louisiana State University Press, 2005.

Hansen, Michael D. "The Power of Strange Faces: Revisiting *The Grapes of Wrath* with the Postmodern Ethics of Emmanuel Levinas." *The Moral Philosophy of John Steinbeck*. Ed. Stephen K. George. Lanham, MD: Scarecrow, 2005. 107–129.

Harris, Trudier. "Native Sons and Foreign Daughters." *New Essays on* Native Son. Ed. Keneth Kinnamon. New York: Cambridge University Press, 1990. 63–84.

———. "White Men as Performers in the Lynching Ritual." *Black on White: Black Writers on What It Means to Be White*. Ed. David R. Roediger. New York: Schocken, 1998. 299–304.

Hemingway, Ernest. *A Farewell to Arms*. 1929. New York: Scribner, 1995.

———. *For Whom the Bell Tolls*. 1940. New York: Scribner, 1995.

———. *The Sun Also Rises*. 1926. New York: Scribner, 2003.

Hoffman, Daniel. *Faulkner's Country Matters: Folklore and Fable in Yoknapatawpha*. Baton Rouge: Louisiana State University Press, 1989.

Holloway, David. *The Late Modernism of Cormac McCarthy*. Westport, CT: Greenwood, 2002.

Japtok, Martin. "Between 'Race' as Construct and 'Race' as Essence: *The Autobiography of an Ex-Colored Man*." *Southern Literary Journal* 28.2 (1996): 32–47.

Johnson, James Weldon. *Along this Way: The Autobiography of James Weldon Johnson*. 1933. New York: Viking, 1968.

———. *The Autobiography of an Ex-Colored Man*. 1912. New York: Dover, 1995.

———. *The Selected Writings of James Weldon Johnson*. 2 vols. Ed. Sondra Kathryn Wilson. New York: Oxford University Press, 1995.

Joseph, Tiffany. "'Non-Combatant's Shell-Shock': Trauma and Gender in F. Scott Fitzgerald's *Tender is the Night*." *National Women's Studies Association Journal* 15.3 (2003): 64–81.

Juge, Carole. "The Road to the Sun They Cannot See: Plato's Allegory of the Cave, Oblivion, and Guidance in Cormac McCarthy's *The Road.*" *Cormac McCarthy Journal* 7.1 (2009): 16–30.
Jurgensen, John. "Hollywood's Favorite Cowboy." *The Wall Street Journal.* May 2012. 29 Nov. 2009. http//:online.wsj.com.
Kestler, Frances Roe. *The Indian Captivity Narrative: A Woman's View.* New York: Garland, 1990.
Kocela, Chris. "A Postmodern Steinbeck, or Rose of Sharon Meets Oedipa Maas." *The Critical Response to John Steinbeck's* The Grapes of Wrath. Ed. Barbara A. Heavilin. Westport, CT: Greenwood, 2000. 247–266.
Kostelanetz, Richard. *Politics in the African-American Novel: James Weldon Johnson, W.E.B. Du Bois, Richard Wright, and Ralph Ellison.* New York: Greenwood, 1991.
Kunsa, Ashley. "'Maps of the World in Its Becoming': Post-Apocalyptic Naming in Cormac McCarthy's *The Road.*" *Journal of Modern Literature* 33.1 (2009): 57–74.
Labatt, Blair. *Faulkner the Storyteller.* Tuscaloosa: University of Alabama Press, 2005.
LaCapra, Dominick. *History and Criticism.* Ithaca: Cornell University Press, 1985.
Le Bon, Gustave. *The Crowd: A Study of the Popular Mind.* 1896. London: T. Fisher Unwin, 1914.
____. *The Psychology of Revolution.* 1913. Wells, VT: Fraser, 1968.
Levy, Eugene. *James Weldon Johnson: Black Leader, Black Voice.* Chicago: University of Chicago Press, 1973.
Light, James F. "Political Conscience in the Novels of F. Scott Fitzgerald." *Ball State Teacher's College Forum* 4 (1963): 13–25. Rpt. in *Critical Essays on F. Scott Fitzgerald's* Tender Is the Night. Ed. Milton R. Stern. Boston: G.K. Hall, 1986. 132–7.
Logan, Lisa. "Mary Rowlandson's Captivity and the 'Place' of the Woman Subject." *Early American Literature* 28.3 (1993): 255–77. Print.
Luttrull, Daniel. "Prometheus Hits *The Road*: Revising the Myth." *Cormac McCarthy Journal* 8.1 (2010): 17–28.
Lyotard, Jean-François. *The Postmodern Condition: A Report on Knowledge.* 1979. Trans. Geoff Bennington and Brian Massumi. Minneapolis: University of Minnesota Press, 1984.
Marcell, David W. *Progress and Pragmatism: James, Dewey, Beard, and the American Idea of Progress.* Contributions in Amer. Studies 9. Westport, CT: Greenwood, 1974.
Matthews, John T. *The Sound and the Fury: Faulkner and the Lost Cause.* Boston: Twayne, 1991.
McCarthy, Cormac. *All the Pretty Horses.* New York: Vintage, 1992.
____. *Blood Meridian.* 1985. New York: Vintage, 1992.
____. *Child of God.* 1973. New York: Vintage, 1993.
____. *Cities of the Plain.* 1998. New York: Vintage, 1999.
____. *The Crossing.* 1994. New York: Vintage, 1995.
____. *No Country for Old Men.* New York: Vintage, 2005.
____. *The Orchard Keeper.* 1965. New York: Vintage, 1993.
____. *Outer Dark.* 1968. New York: Vintage, 1993.
____. *The Road.* 2006. New York: Vintage, 2007.
____. *Suttree.* 1979. New York: Vintage, 1992.
McClelland, J.S. *The Crowd and the Mob: From Plato to Canetti.* London: Unwin, 1989.
Messent, Peter B. *Ernest Hemingway.* New York: St. Martin's, 1992.

———. *New Readings of the American Novel: Narrative Theory and Its Application.* New York: St. Martin's, 1990.
Michaels, Walter Benn. *Our America: Nativism, Modernism, and Pluralism.* Durham: Duke University Press, 1995.
Minter, David. *Faulkner's Questioning Narratives: Fictions of His Major Phase, 1929–42.* Urbana: University of Illinois Press, 2001.
Morrison, Toni. *Playing in the Dark: Whiteness and the Literary Imagination.* New York: Vintage, 1992.
Mortimer, Gail L. *Faulkner's Rhetoric of Loss: A Study in Perception and Meaning.* Austin: University of Texas Press, 1983.
Owens, Louis. *John Steinbeck's Re-Vision of America.* Athens: University of Georgia Press, 1985.
Ownby, Ted. "The Snopes Trilogy and the Emergence of Consumer Culture." *Faulkner and Ideology: Faulkner and Yoknapatawpha 1992.* Ed. Donald M. Kartiganer and Ann J. Abadie. Jackson: University of Mississippi Press, 1992. 95–128.
Parini, Jay. *John Steinbeck: A Biography.* New York: Henry Holt, 1995.
———. *One Matchless Time: A Life of William Faulkner.* New York: HarperCollins, 2004.
Pearce, Roy Harvey. "The Significance of the Captivity Narrative." *American Literature* 29 (1947): 1–20.
Polk, Noel. *Children of the Dark House: Text and Context in Faulkner.* Jackson: University Press of Mississippi, 1996.
Railey, Kevin. *Natural Aristocracy: History, Ideology, and the Production of William Faulkner.* Tuscaloosa: University of Alabama Press, 1999.
Railsback, Brian E. *Parallel Expeditions: Charles Darwin and the Art of John Steinbeck.* Moscow: University of Idaho Press, 1995.
Rambo, Shelly L. "Beyond Redemption? Reading Cormac McCarthy's *The Road* after the End of the World." *Studies in the Literary Imagination* 41.2 (2008): 99–120.
Rhodes, Chip. *Structures of the Jazz Age: Mass Culture, Progressive Education, and Racial Discourse in American Modernism.* London: Verso, 1998.
Roberts, Diane. *Faulkner and Southern Womanhood.* Athens: University of Georgia Press, 1994.
Rowlandson, Mary. *The Sovereignty and Goodness of God.* 1682. *American Captivity Narratives: Olaudah Equiano, Mary Rowlandson, and Others.* Ed. Gordon M. Sayre. Boston: Wadsworth, 2000. 132–176. Print.
Sayre, Gordon M. "The Foundational Narrative of Mary Rowlandson." *American Captivity Narratives: Olaudah Equiano, Mary Rowlandson, and Others.* Ed. Gordon M. Sayre. Boston: Wadsworth, 2000. 127–131.
———. "Introduction." *American Captivity Narratives: Olaudah Equiano, Mary Rowlandson, and Others.* Ed. Gordon M. Sayre. Boston: Wadsworth, 2000. 1–17. Print.
Scheick, William J. *Authority and Female Authorship in Colonial America.* Lexington: University Press of Kentucky, 1998. Print.
Schwartz, Lawrence H. *Creating Faulkner's Reputation: The Politics of Modern Literary Criticism.* Knoxville: University of Tennessee Press, 1988.
Sheehy, John. "The Mirror and the Veil: The Passing Novel and the Quest for American Racial Identity." *African American Review* 33 (1999): 401–15.
Singal, Daniel J. *William Faulkner: The Making of a Modernist.* Chapel Hill: University of North Carolina Press, 1997.

Slotkin, Richard. *Regeneration through Violence: The Mythology of the American Frontier, 1600–1860.* 1973. Norman: University of Oklahoma Press, 2000. Print.

Smelser, Neil J. *Theory of Collective Behavior.* New York: Free Press, 1962.

Smith, Carol H. "Women and the Loss of Eden in Hemingway's Mythology." *Ernest Hemingway: The Writer in Context.* Ed. James Nagel. Madison: University of Wisconsin Press, 1984. 129–44.

Smith, Valerie. "Privilege and Evasion in *The Autobiography of an Ex-Colored Man.*" *Self-Discovery and Authority in Afro-American Narrative.* Cambridge: Harvard University Press, 1987. 44–64. Rpt. in *Critical Essays on James Weldon Johnson.* Ed. Kenneth M. Price and Lawrence J. Oliver. New York: G.K. Hall, 1997. 88–101.

Sorel, Georges. *Reflections on Violence.* 1915. Trans. T.E. Hulme. New York: Peter Smith, 1941.

Soto, Michael. *The Modernist Nation: Generation, Renaissance, and Twentieth-Century American Literature.* Tuscaloosa: University of Alabama Press, 2004.

Spurgeon, Sara L. "Introduction." *Cormac McCarthy: All the Pretty Horses, No Country for Old Men, and The Road.* Ed. Sara L. Spurgeon. London: Continuum, 2011. 1–22.

Steinbeck, John. *East of Eden.* 1952. New York: Penguin, 2002.

———. *The Grapes of Wrath.* 1939. New York: Penguin, 2006.

———. *In Dubious Battle.* 1936. New York: Penguin, 1992.

———. *The Long Valley.* 1938. New York: Penguin, 1995.

———. *Tortilla Flat.* 1935. New York: Penguin, 1997.

Stern, Milton R. *Tender Is the Night: The Broken Universe.* New York: Twayne, 1994.

Strychacz, Thomas F. *Hemingway's Theaters of Masculinity.* Baton Rouge: Louisiana State University Press, 2003.

Szalay, Michael. *New Deal Modernism: American Literature and the Invention of the Welfare State.* Durham: Duke University Press, 2000.

Tratner, Michael. *Modernism and Mass Politics: Joyce, Woolf, Eliot, Yeats.* Stanford: Stanford University Press, 1995.

Tuhkanen, Mikko Juhani. "'A [B]igger's Place': Lynching and Specularity in Richard Wright's 'Fire and Cloud' and *Native Son.*" *African American Review* 33.1 (1999): 125–33.

Urgo, Joseph R. *Faulkner's Apocrypha: A Fable, Snopes, and the Spirit of Human Rebellion.* Jackson: University of Mississippi Press, 1989.

Vernon, Alex. *Soldiers Once and Still: Ernest Hemingway, James Salter, and Tim O'Brien.* Iowa City: University of Iowa Press, 2004.

VanDerBeets, Richard. "The Indian Captivity Narrative as Ritual." *American Literature* 43 (1972): 548–62.

Waldrep, Christopher. *The Many Faces of Judge Lynch: Extralegal Violence and Punishment in America.* New York: Palgrave, 2002.

Wang, Maria Su. "'Mob': English." *Crowds.* Ed. Jeffrey T. Schnapp and Matthew Tiews. Stanford: Stanford University Press, 2006. 186–90.

Wartzman, Rick. *Obscene in the Extreme: The Burning and Banning of John Steinbeck's The Grapes of Wrath.* New York: PublicAffairs, 2008.

Watson, James Gray. *The Snopes Dilemma: Faulkner's Trilogy.* Coral Gables: University of Miami Press, 1968.

Werlock, Abby H.P. "Poor Whites: Joads and Snopeses." *San Jose Studies* 18.1 (1992): 61–71. Rpt. in *The Critical Response to John Steinbeck's The Grapes of Wrath.* Ed. Barbara A. Heavilin. Westport, CT: Greenwood, 2000. 171–182.

Werner, Craig. "Bigger's Blues: *Native Son* and the Articulation of Afro-American Modernism." *New Essays on* Native Son. Ed. Keneth Kinnamon. New York: Cambridge University Press, 1990. 117–152.

Wielenberg, Erik J. "God, Morality, and Meaning in Cormac McCarthy's *The Road*." *Cormac McCarthy Journal* 8.1 (2010): 1–16.

Williams, David. *Faulkner's Women: The Myth and the Muse*. Montreal: McGill-Queen's University Press, 1977.

Williamson, Joel. *William Faulkner and Southern History*. New York: Oxford University Press, 1993.

Wood, Amy Louise. *Lynching and Spectacle: Witnessing Racial Violence in America, 1890-1940*. Chapel Hill: University of North Carolina Press, 2009.

Woodard, Maureen L. "Female Captivity and the Deployment of Race in Three Early American Texts." *Papers on Language and Literature* 32.2 (1996): 115–46. Print.

Wright, Richard. *Early Works: Lawd Today!, Uncle Tom's Children, and Native Son*. New York: Library of America, 1991.

Zender, Karl F. *Faulkner and the Politics of Reading*. Baton Rouge: Louisiana State University Press, 2002.

Index

Abolitionism 26, 68
Absalom, Absalom! 59, 101, 130
Africanist presence 39–40, 106
Alger myth 76–77, 150
All the Pretty Horses 158
Allen, James 24
Along This Way 42–43
American Civil War 12, 26–27, 86, 119
American Communist Party 134, 136–138, 177ch5n2
American Dream 77, 118, 120, 123
American Indians 1, 3–20, 26, 42
American Renaissance 26
American South 12, 15, 26–27, 46–48, 55, 57–60, 62–65, 68–69, 78, 80–102, 117–120, 144–147, 149–155, 158–159, 175ch2n4, 177ch5n9
American Southwest 158–159
Ames, Dalton 88, 90
Armstrong, Nancy 11
As I Lay Dying 59, 83–84, 94–102, 130, 176–177ch5n1
Ashley, Lady Brett 104–106, 108–111, 176ch4n5, 176ch4n6, 176ch4n7
Atkinson, Ted 80–81, 94, 129–130, 144
Atlanta Constitution 42
Autobiography of an Ex-Colored Man 24, 41–51, 53, 77–78, 113, 175ch1n1
Aymo 112, 114

Baker, Houston, Jr. 51
Baker, Jordan 120
Baldwin, James 66
Ballard, Lester 157–158
Barban, Tommy 126–127
Barkley, Catherine 104, 112–113, 115
Barnes, Jake 104, 106–113, 118, 126, 176ch4n7
Beck, Warren 177ch5n6
Beebe, Sarah Frye 105, 176ch4n1
Bell, Millicent 111, 113
Bell, Vereen 172

Berman, Ronald 111, 115, 117, 121, 176ch4n8
Bible 2, 6–10, 13, 16
Big Boy 53–57, 69
Blood Meridian 158
Blotner, Joseph 86, 144, 176–177ch5n1; *Faulkner: A Biography* 144; *Selected Letters of William Faulkner* 144
Bobbie 62–63
Bobo 53–56
Bookwright, Odum 146–148
The Boy (The Road) 159–172
Brannigan, John 37
British Modernism 38
Brown, Charles Brockden 21
Bruccoli, Matthew J. 118, 123, 176ch4n4
Buchanan, Daisy 118–123, 126, 176ch4n1
Buchanan, Tom 106, 118–124, 126–127, 176ch4n4
Buckley 76
Bunch, Byron 59, 61
Bundren, Addie 81, 94–102
Bundren, Anse 95–101
Bundren, Cash 95–98, 100
Bundren, Dewey Dell 95–96, 98, 101
Bundren, Jewel 95–96, 98
Bundren, Vardaman 96, 98, 100
Burden, Joanna 61, 63–67, 72
Burnham, Michelle 14–15
Burroughs, Edgar Rice 107
Burton, Doc 134, 136–137
Butler, Robert 70, 76–77

California 128, 134, 140, 177ch5n2
California Growers' Association 134–135, 137
Campbell, Mike 110
Canneti, Elias 17, 27–35, 47–48, 55–56, 98–99, 101, 111, 113, 122, 134–136, 139–140, 145–147, 160–162, 167, 169, 173; *Crowds and Power* 27–35, 27–35, 47–48, 55–56, 98–99, 101, 111, 113, 122, 134–136, 139–140, 145–147, 160–162, 167, 169

cannibalism 1–2, 19, 47, 160–165, 170
capitalism 33, 77, 80, 128–129, 132, 140, 143–144, 147–154
captivity narrative 1–21, 23, 25–26, 28, 47
Carraway, Nick 106, 119–120, 122–123
Castiglia, Christopher 16–17, 20–21
Casy, Jim 141
Cather, Willa 140–141
Child of God 158
Christmas, Joe 59–62, 65–69, 75–76, 81, 84, 89
Cities of the Plain 158
Cohn, Robert 108–110, 176*ch*4n7
Cokal, Susann 126
Cole, John Grady 158
Comley, Nancy R. 104, 109–112, 176*ch*4n1
Communism 53, 131, 134, 136–139, 152–154, 177*ch*5n2
Compson, Benjy 85–88, 90, 92–93, 100–101
Compson, Caddy 81, 85–95, 98 101–103, 175–176*ch*3n2
Compson, Caroline Bascomb 87, 175*ch*3n1
Compson, Jason, III 86, 175*ch*3n1
Compson, Jason, IV 85–85, 90–94, 119, 120
Compson, Quentin 85–90, 92–93
Compson, (Miss) Quentin 91–93, 75–176*ch*3n2
Connie 140, 143
Cooper, James Fenimore 21
Cooper, Lydia 169–172
Cooper, Stephen 117–118, 176*ch*4n3
Cowley, Malcolm 114, 144
The Crossing 158
The Crowd: A Study of the Popular Mind 27, 29–32
Crowds and Power 27–35, 27–35, 47–48, 55–56, 98–99, 101, 111, 113, 122, 134–136, 139–140, 145–147, 160–162, 167, 169
Curley 131
Curley's wife 130–131

Dakin 135, 138
Dalton, Henry 71–72, 75, 77
Dalton, Mary 71–74, 78
Dalton, Mrs. 72
Darwin, Charles 132–133
Davis, Margaret H. 3–4, 9, 11, 16
de Certeau, Michel 35–36
democracy 33, 118, 133, 141, 155, 173
Derrida, Jacques 155
de Spain, Manfred 149, 151–152, 154–155
de Vaca, Cabeza 9
Ditsky, John 132
Diver, Dick 106, 123–127, 176*ch*4n10
Diver, Nicole Warren 123–126
Doyle, Don H. 82, 145, 153, 177*ch*5n6
Drake, Temple 101
Dust Bowl 140
Dyer Anti-Lynching Law 43, 49

Eliot, T.S. 88; "The Love Song of J. Alfred Prufrock" 88
Ellis, Jay 177n1
Ely 165–166, 171
Emerson, Ralph Waldo 26, 34, 128; "Self-Reliance" 26, 34
English Renaissance 29
Enlightenment 28

A Fable 156
Faery, Rebecca Blevins 6–7, 14–15, 17, 20
A Farewell to Arms 103, 106, 111–115, 117, 127, 176*ch*4n8
Faulkner, Peter 155n1
Faulkner, William 37, 53, 58–69, 75, 80–103, 128–130, 133, 136, 144–156, 175*ch*2n2, 177*ch*5n4, 177*ch*5n8, 177*ch*5n13; *Absalom, Absalom!* 59, 101, 130; *As I Lay Dying* 59, 83–84, 94–102, 130, 176–177*ch*5n1; *A Fable* 156; *Flags in the Dust* 175*ch*2n2; *Go Down, Moses* 51, 53, 59; *The Hamlet* 101–102, 128, 144–150, 155–156; *Intruder in the Dust* 59; *Light in August* 58–69, 75–76, 81, 176–177*ch*5n1; *The Mansion* 101–102, 128–130, 144–145, 153–156; *Mosquitoes* 175*ch*2n2; *Pylon* 101; *Sanctuary* 59, 84, 101; *Soldier's Pay* 175*ch*2n2; *The Sound and the Fury* 59, 81, 83–95, 98, 101–102, 119, 130, 175*ch*3n1, 175–176*ch*2n2, 176*ch*3n3; *The Town* 101–102, 128–130, 150–152, 156; *The Unvanquished* 59; *The Wild Palms* (*If I Forget Thee Jerusalem*) 101
Faulkner: A Biography 144
Fitzgerald, F. Scott 39–40, 80, 103–106, 118–127; *Flappers and Philosophers* 118; *The Great Gatsby* 103, 106, 118–124, 126–127, 176*ch*4n1, 176*ch*4n4; *Six Tales of the Jazz Age* 118; *Tender Is the Night* 103, 106, 123–127, 176*ch*4n10
Flappers and Philosophers 118
Fleming, Robert E. 42, 44
Foley, Barbara 141, 177*ch*5n2
For Whom the Bell Tolls 103, 106, 115–118, 127, 176*ch*4n9
Foucault, Michel 155, 175*ch*2n3
Fowler, Doreen 85, 88, 91 94–95
Franklin, Benjamin 26
French, Warren 138–139
French Revolution 31
Freud, Sigmund 28, 31, 39, 87, 89, 92

Gajdusek, Robert 103, 109, 123, 176*ch*4n7, 176*ch*4n9
Gallagher, Catherine 37
Gatsby, Jay 106, 118–124, 126–127
Geertz, Clifford 34–36
Gibson, Dilsey 87–88, 91, 93
Go Down, Moses 51, 53, 59
Gold, Mike 80
Goldsby, Jacqueline 38, 43, 48

Index

The Grapes of Wrath 129, 132–133, 140–144, 177ch5n2
Graulund, Rune 171–172
Great Depression 27, 103, 128–156, 177ch5n4
The Great Gatsby 103, 106, 118–124, 126–127, 176ch4n1, 176ch4n4
Great Migration 69, 175ch2n4
Greenblatt, Stephen 3–4, 28–29, 35–37; *Renaissance Self-Fashioning: From More to Shakespeare* 4, 28–29; *Shakespearean Negotiations* 35–36
Grimm, Percy 66–67, 75–76
Groton, Bill 109
Grove, Lena 59
Gwinner, Donovan 165–166

Hakutani, Yoshinobu 56–57
The Hamlet 101–102, 128, 144–150, 155–156
Hannon, Charles 177ch5n13
Hansen, Michael D. 141, 143
Hawthorne, Nathaniel 26
Heidegger, Martin 155
Hemingway, Ernest 33, 176ch4n5; *A Farewell to Arms* 103, 106, 111–115, 117, 127, 176ch4n8; *For Whom the Bell Tolls* 103, 106, 115–118, 127, 176ch4n9; *In Our Time* 105, 176ch4n3; *The Sun Also Rises* 103, 105–113, 127, 176ch4n5, 176ch4n6, 176ch4n7
Henry, Frederic 104, 107, 111–115, 117, 124
Hightower, Reverend Gail 59, 61, 68
Hoffman, Daniel 148–149, 177ch5n5
Holden, Judge 158
Holloway, David 157
Hose, Sam 47
Hoyt, Rosemary 123–126

In Dubious Battle 129, 132–141, 144, 154, 177ch5n3
Incidents in the Life of a Slave Girl 14
Indiana University of Pennsylvania 23–24
Intruder in the Dust 59

Jacksonville, Florida 43
Jacobs, Harriet 14; *Incidents in the Life of a Slave Girl* 14
Japtok, Martin 43
Jefferson, Thomas 128, 140
Jesus Christ 2, 7, 11, 61
Jim Crow 45, 51–53, 175ch1n2
Joad, Rose of Sharon 140, 143–144
Joad, Tom 141
Johnson, James Weldon 24, 41–51, 53, 57, 58–61, 65, 68–69, 77–78, 113, 175ch1n1; *Along This Way* 42–43; *Autobiography of an Ex-Colored Man* 24, 41–51, 53, 77–78, 113, 175ch1n1
Jordan, Robert 104, 106, 115–118, 121, 124, 127
Joseph, Tiffany 106–108, 123, 125, 176ch4n10
Juge, Carol 159

Kestler, Frances Roe 18
The Kid (*Blood Meridian*) 158
King, Rodney 24
King Philip's War 5, 6, 12
Kino 131
Kocela, Chris 155
Kohl, Barton 152
Kohl, Linda Snopes 152–154
Kostelanetz, Richard 41, 43
Ku Klux Klan 24, 27, 119
Kunsa, Ashley 159–160

Labatt, Blair 150
LaCapra, Dominick 36
Lancaster, Massachusetts 5–6 11–12, 17
Le Bon, Gustave 27–35, 38–39, 173; *The Crowd: A Study of the Popular Mind* 27, 29–32; *The Psychology of Revolution* 31
Levy, Eugene 43–45
Lewis, Sinclair 80, 176ch4n5
Light, James F. 103, 123
Light in August 58–69, 75–76, 81, 176–177ch5n1
Logan, Lisa 11, 13
The Long Valley 131; "Flight" 131, 177ch5n3; "The Raid" 131; "The Vigilante" 131
Los Angeles Riots 24
"The Love Song of J. Alfred Prufrock" 88
Luttrull, Daniel 170
lynching 12, 15, 17–19, 24–25, 27, 30, 34, 37–43, 46–60, 63, 65–69, 74–80, 84, 86, 90–95, 99, 103, 105–106, 112, 114–115, 117–120, 123, 130–131, 135, 137, 157, 173, 175ch2n1
Lyotard, Jean-Francois 155

The Man (*The Road*) 159–172
Mann 53
The Mansion 101–102, 128–130, 144–145, 153–156
Maria 104, 116
Mather, Cotton 15
Matthews, John T. 83–84, 86–87, 90–93
Max, Boris 76
McCarthy, Cormac 21, 157–172, 177n1; *All the Pretty Horses* 158; *Blood Meridian* 158; *Child of God* 158; *Cities of the Plain* 158; *The Crossing* 158; *No Country for Old Men* 158, 169, 177n1; *The Orchard Keeper* 158; *Outer Dark* 157; *The Road* 157–172; *Suttree* 158
McClelland, J. S. 32–34
McEachern, Mr. 62–63
McLeod, Mac 134–139, 141, 144
Melville, Herman 26; *Omoo* 26; *Typee* 26
Mencken, H.L. 176ch4n5
Messent, Peter B. 104, 108, 111, 113, 123, 176ch4n6
Mexico 158
Michaels, Walter Benn 45, 85, 87, 119–120
Milton, George 131

Minter, David 60–61, 81–82, 85, 87, 89
Mississippi 66–67, 82, 86, 146, 151, 175ch2n4
Morrison, Toni 39–40, 106; *Playing in the Dark: Whiteness and the Literary Imagination* 39–40, 106
Mortimer, Gail 82, 84
Mosquitoes 175ch2n2

NAACP 42–43, 49, 65
Native Son 50–51, 58, 60–62, 68–79, 175ch2n3, 175ch2n4
New Critics 27, 129
New Deal 128, 141–144
New France 2
New Spain 2
9/11 172–173
Nineteenth Amendment 83
No Country for Old Men 158, 169, 177n1
Nolan, Jim 134–139, 141, 144, 177ch5n3

The Odyssey 94
Of Mice and Men 130–131
Omoo 26
The Orchard Keeper 158
Outer Dark 157
Owens, Louis 130–131, 177ch5n3
Ownby, Arthur 158
Ownby, Ted 153, 155
Oxford, Mississippi 145

Pablo 106, 115–118, 176ch4n9
Parham, Billy 158
Parini, Jay 68, 130, 133, 137–138, 143–144, 149–152, 176–177ch5n1, 177ch5n10
Paris 46, 105, 108–109
Pearce, Roy Harvey 10
The Pearl 131
Pfeiffer, Kathleen 45, 175ch1n1
Pilar 106, 115–117
Plessy v. Ferguson 45
Polk, Noel 58, 68, 81–82, 84, 90–92, 94
Popeye 101
The Portable Faulkner 144
Portuguese Brazil 2
Pound, Ezra 21, 28
The Psychology of Revolution 31
Pulitzer Prize 158
Puritanism 1–21, 26
Pylon 101

Railey, Kevin 100, 102, 145, 149, 177ch5n12
Railsback, Brian E. 132–133
Rambo, Shelly 160–161
Ratliff, V.K. 146–149, 151–152, 154
Reconstruction 27
Renaissance Self-Fashioning: From More to Shakespeare 4, 28–29
Revolutionary War 14–15, 26–27
Rhodes, Chip 59
Rinaldi 112

The Rise of the Coloured Empires 106
Rittenmeyer, Charlotte 101
Roberts, Diane 84, 86–87, 93, 95, 97, 175ch3n1, 176ch3n3
Romanticism 28
Romero, Pedro 110, 176ch4n7
Roosevelt, Franklin D. 128
Rowan Oak 144
Rowlandson, Mary White 1–21, 23, 25–26, 28, 157; *The Sovereignty and Goodness of God, Together, With the Faithfulness of His Promises Displayed; Being a Narrative of the Captivity and Restauration of Mrs. Mary Rowlandson* 2–21, 23, 25–26, 28, 157

Sanctuary 59, 84, 101
Sayre, Gordon M. 2, 5–6, 10, 15
The Scarlet Letter 26
Scheick, William J. 15–16
Scholes, Robert 104, 109–112, 176ch4n1
Schwartz, Lawrence H. 129, 176–177ch5n1
self-fashioning 1, 3–6, 8–10, 19–21, 23, 28–29, 31, 41–49, 51–52, 57–60, 62, 66, 69–70, 73–75, 79–79, 81, 84–85, 90, 98, 102, 111, 122–123, 126, 138, 157, 162, 172–173
"Self-Reliance" 26, 34
Shakespearean Negotiations 35–36
sharecropping 128, 141, 144–148, 150, 152–153
Sheehy, John 45
Shumann, Laverne 101
Silas 53
Sinclair, Upton 80
Singal, Daniel 58–59, 62, 68, 85, 88–89, 93, 95, 102, 129, 146 177ch5n7, 177ch5n11
Six Tales of the Jazz Age 118
slavery 12, 14, 20, 26, 48, 62, 86, 121, 160, 164
Slotkin, Richard 1–3
Small, Lennie 130–131
Smelser, Neil 33–34; *Theory of Collective Behavior* 33–34
Smith, Carol H. 104, 111
Smith, Valerie 44, 48
Snopes, Ab 145, 149
Snopes, Eula Varner 101, 151–153
Snopes, Flem 129, 145–155, 177ch5n6
Snopes, Mink 148, 154, 177ch5n12
Snopes, Montgomery Ward 153
Snopes, Wallstreet Panic 153
Soldier's Pay 175ch2n2
Sorel, George 137–138
Soto, Michael 176ch4n5
The Sound and the Fury 59, 81, 83–95, 98, 101–102, 119, 130, 175ch3n1, 175–176ch2n2, 176ch3n3
The Sovereignty and Goodness of God, Together, With the Faithfulness of His Promises Displayed; Being a Narrative Of the Captivity and Restauration of Mrs. Mary Rowlandson 2–21, 23, 25–26, 28, 157

Spurgeon, Sara 172
Steinbeck, John 30, 33, 37, 39–40, 80, 128–146, 149, 152, 154–156, 177ch5n2, 177ch5n4; *East of Eden* 131, 155; *The Grapes of Wrath* 129, 132–133, 140–144, 177ch5n2; *In Dubious Battle* 129, 132–141, 144, 154, 177ch5n3; *The Long Valley* 131, 177ch5n3; *Of Mice and Men* 130–131; *The Pearl* 131; *Tortilla Flat* 132–133
Stern, Milton R. 124
Stevens, Gavin 147, 149–152, 154
Stoddard, Lothrop 176ch4n4
Stowe, Harriet Beecher 26
Strychacz, Thomas F. 109–110
Su Wang, Maria 37
The Sun Also Rises 103, 105–113, 127, 176ch4n5, 176ch4n6, 176ch4n7
Sutpen, Judith 101
Suttree 158
Szalay, Michael 142

Taylor 53
Tender Is the Night 103, 106, 123–127, 176ch4n10
Tennessee 158
Theory of Collective Behavior 33–34
Thomas, Bigger 60–62, 64, 69–78, 89
Tortilla Flat 132–133
The Town 101–102, 128–130, 150–152, 156
Tratner, Michael 31–32, 34, 38
Tuhkanen, Mikko Juhani 69, 175ch2n3
Tull, Cora 95–96
Tull, Vernon 98
Typee 26

Uncle Tom's Children 41–42, 51–57, 77–78, 175ch1n2; "Big Boy Leaves Home" 42, 53–57; "Bright and Morning Star" 53, 175ch1n2; "Down by the Riverside" 53; "The Ethics of Living Jim Crow" 51–53, 175ch1n2; "Fire and Cloud" 53; "Long Black Song" 53
University of Mississippi 144
The Unvanquished 59
Urgo, Joseph 34, 148, 151–152, 154, 177ch5n8, 177ch5n9

Vanderbeets, Richard 19
Varner, Jody 145
Varner, Will 145, 147, 149
Vernon, Alex 107–108, 113

Waldrep, Christopher 58, 78, 175ch2n1
The Wall Street Journal 159
Warren, Baby 125
Warren, Devereux (Papa) 126
Wartzman, Rick 137, 140
Watson, James Gray 147–148, 151, 153, 177ch5n4, 177ch5n6
Watson, Veronica 23–24
Werlock, H.P. 177ch5n4
Werner, Craig 41
Whitman, Walt 141
Wielenberg, Erik 162–163, 166–167, 169–170
The Wild Palms (*If I Forget Thee Jerusalem*) 101
Williams, David 95, 99
Williamson, Joel 67–68, 83
Wilson, George 123
Wilson, Myrtle 119–120
Winfrey, Oprah 159
Winthrop, John 6, 26
Without Sanctuary 24, 38
Withoutsanctuary.org 24
Wolfsheim, Meyer 106
Wood, Amy Louise 38–39
Woodard, Maureen L. 6, 9, 12–13, 20
World War I 25, 27, 29, 79, 80, 104–110, 118, 128, 132
World War II 104–105
Wright, Richard 41–42, 50–58, 60–62, 68–79, 133, 136, 144; *Native Son* 50–51, 58, 60–62, 68–79, 175ch2n3, 175ch2n4; *Uncle Tom's Children* 41–42, 51–57, 77–78, 175ch1n2

Yoknapatawpha County 144–146, 148–150, 152–153
"Young Goodman Brown" 26

Zender, Karl F. 86, 89

www.ingramcontent.com/pod-product-compliance
Lightning Source LLC
Chambersburg PA
CBHW032102300426
44116CB00007B/851